D0898153

WOMEN
IN ANCIENT
GREECE

WOMEN
IN ANCIENT
GREECE

SECLUSION, EXCLUSION, OR ILLUSION?

PAUL CHRYSTAL

FONTHILL

Chorus: 'The voice of time will change and our glory will ring down the ages.
Women will be honoured. No longer will slander cling to our sex'
Euripides, *Medea* 415-420

Fonthill Media Language Policy

Fonthill Media publishes in the international English language market. One language edition is published worldwide. As there are minor differences in spelling and presentation, especially with regard to American English and British English, a policy is necessary to define which form of English to use. The Fonthill Policy is to use the form of English native to the author. Paul Chrystal was born and educated in Scotland and England; therefore British English has been adopted in this publication.

Fonthill Media Limited
Fonthill Media LLC
www.fonthillmedia.com
office@fonthillmedia.com

First published in the United Kingdom and the United States of America 2017

British Library Cataloguing in Publication Data:
A catalogue record for this book is available from the British Library

Copyright © Paul Chrystal 2017

ISBN 978-1-78155-562-0

The right of Paul Chrystal to be identified as the author of this work has been asserted by him in accordance with the Copyright, Designs and Patents Act 1988.

Typeset in 10.5pt on 13pt MinionPro
Printed and bound in England

Preface

This book is a companion volume to my *Women in Ancient Rome*, first published in 2013. It provides a much-needed analysis of how women behaved in Greek society, how they were regarded and the various restrictions imposed on their freedoms, movements and actions. Naturally, given that ancient Greece in most of its manifestations was very much a man's world, the majority of books on ancient Greek society even now tend to focus almost exclusively on men. This book redresses the balance by shining the spotlight on that other somewhat neglected or dismissed half; women had a significant role to play in many aspects of Greek society and culture and this book illuminates those roles.

Women in Ancient Greece asks the blunt and controversial question: how far is the commonly accepted assumption that women were secluded and excluded just an illusion? It answers the question by extending from the treatment of women in Greek myth, and the role of women in Homer and Hesiod through the playwrights, poets and philosophers to the comparatively liberated and powerful women in Sparta until the end of the Hellenistic era; it covers the lives of women in ancient Athens, Sparta, and in other city states; it examines the role of women in Crete; it describes eminent women writers, philosophers, artists and scientists; it explores love, marriage and divorce, the virtuous and the meretricious, and the key roles women played in Greek death and religion. Crucially, the book is people-based, drawing much of its evidence and many of its conclusions from the lives lived by actual historical Greek women, or types thereof.

In short, *Women in Ancient Greece* provides evidence for the important, and active role women played in ancient Greece, highlighting the contribution they made to one of the most influential and enlightened civilisations in the world. Among many other ground-breaking things, the ancient Greeks developed a form of democracy; however, at the same time, to a large extent, they felt it necessary to keep their women secluded, and excluded from public business. This book acknowledges this seclusion and exclusion as inarguable fact, but contends that it is all very much a question of degree—the presumption through centuries of scholarship has been that women were locked in and at the same time locked out; *Women in Ancient Greece* goes further, to examine just how illusory this generalisation and the scholarly whitewashing that has often gone with it actually were, by spotlighting the manifold areas where women were patently not cloistered or shut out, but were active and obtrusive.

CONTENTS

Introduction

There is no singular place that is ancient Greece. Ancient Greece is, instead, made up of a number of independent political and geographical entities that flourished at different times; it included the Minoan civilisation on Crete, the Mycenaean on the mainland, and the Macedonian. Alongside that, it comprises numerous city states—*poleis*—such as Athens, Sparta, and Thebes, all of which were politically, commercially, militarily, and socially independent to varying degrees; they only really coalesced (if ever) in military, political, or trade alliances, or after conquest by another *polis*. To further complicate matters, these *poleis* established colonies all over the Mediterranean and around the Black Sea, in the Magreb and the Levant, and as far west as Spain.

Ancient Greece was, in some ways, like the Holy Roman Empire; neither was ever a unitary nation-state, for example. However, ancient Greece was never a homogenous world, or a mighty empire in the way that the pagan Roman Empire was. We have, in essence, a very complex picture; the ancient Greeks were never one identifiable people geographically, politically, economically, and socially. It follows then that our study needs to take into account all of these various strands—all the civilisations and locations—if it is to convey as true a picture of women in ancient Greece as we can glean from the evidence.

The history of ancient Greece, such as it is, can be roughly divided into the following periods:

1. Minoan and early Helladic civilization in Crete (3,200–1,200 BCE).
2. The Bronze Age (2,900–2,000 BCE), when early Aegean cultures start to emerge; Mycenaean civilization in mainland Greece (1,600–1,100 BCE); Mycenaeans in control of Crete (1,500–1,100 BCE).
3. The Dark Ages (1,050–800 BCE), when the Dorians and Aeolians destroy the Mycenaean civilisation.
4. The Archaic period (*c.* 800–*c.* 500 BCE) comes to an end with the overthrow of the last tyrant of Athens and the birth of Athenian democracy in 508 BCE; the Greek alphabet is formed from the Phoenician alphabet and western literature begins with Homer and Hesiod in the 800s.

5. The Classical period (*c.* 500–323 BCE) sees the destruction of Athens by the Persians, but ushers in a golden age, epitomized in the arts by the Parthenon. Politically, the period was dominated by Athens and the Delian League in the fifth century BCE, but these were displaced by Sparta in the early fourth century BCE; power then shifted to Thebes and the Boeotian League, and finally to the League of Corinth led by Macedon. This was the age of the Graeco-Persian Wars, and the rise of Alexander the Great.

6. The Hellenistic period (323–146 BCE) dawns with the death of Alexander, and sees Greek culture and power spread into the Near East. Ancient Greece in all its manifestations ends with subjugation by the Romans, at the Battle of Corinth, in 146 BCE.

Generally speaking, the worlds within ancient Greece were run by men for men. Just as significantly, what little we see or hear about women in these masculine worlds is viewed through the eyes of men; women are defined by men and their relationships with men who are in positions of authority and influence, whether powerful citizens or humble peasants. Moreover, the men we hear from are of the elite classes; they are educated, erudite, and influential. We know virtually nothing from men of the lower orders, or about the women in their ordinary lives, everyday marriages, and mundane family affairs. All books on the social history of ancient Greece (and Rome) trot out these caveats as part of the routine; what is important though, is to avoid falling into the trap, as many do, of then treating examples of a narrow masculine vision as actual historical fact. We must modify and temper what we are offered by this intelligent elite, with social and historical context, analysing the agendas each of these men may have, and the axes that are slowly grinding away, almost noiselessly, in the background. Some of this evidence may not be based on historical fact; it is often little more than perception, or personal opinion flavoured by individual experience and prejudice. It is important that we take this into account.

We look at this litany of misogyny from the privileged few, which has echoed down the ages, as supposed evidence for the near-total exclusion, seclusion, trivialization, and undervaluation of women; Aristotle said that 'man is naturally superior to women and so the man should rule and the woman should be ruled'.[1] Demosthenes stated that 'We keep *hetairae* for pleasure, female slaves to look after us and wives to give us legitimate children and to take care of our households'.[2] Menander is often attributed with the remark that 'a man who teaches a woman how to write should know that he is giving poison to an asp'.[3] Euripides armed his women characters with these self-deprecating or misogynistic poisoned arrows:

I am only a woman, a thing which the world hates.[4]

It's a strange thing that whereas there are antidotes, revealed to men by some god, against the venom of fierce serpents, nobody has yet discovered a remedy for a plague worse than fire or any viper—the plague of Woman. Such a curse our sex is to mankind.[5] Sensible men should never let gossiping women visit their wives, for the gossips are up to no good.[6]

Here, Iphigenia urges her father to sacrifice her to Artemis, claiming it is better for one man to live than ten thousand women.

Aristophanes chimed in with Lysistrata, declaring her disappointment with her sisters: 'Calonice, it's more than I can take, I'm boiling over with embarrassment for our sex. Men say we're slippery rogues.' Calonice asks on the subject of staging a coup in Athens: 'How could we pull off such a great and clever deed? We women who live quietly adorning ourselves in a back-room with gowns of lucid gold and gawdy toilets of stately silk and dainty little slippers ...'
Exaggerated as it may be, the men in the audience would have warmed to this condescending portrayal of the woman fussing over her toilette.[7]

Hipponax declared relief first for father, and then husband: 'There are two days on which a woman pleases most: the day when someone marries her [and he carries her into his house], and the day when her husband carries out her dead body'.[8]

Hyperides said that 'a woman who goes outside her house should be old enough for people to ask whose mother she is, not whose wife she is'.[9]

Most famously, or notoriously, Thucydides has Pericles say in his funeral speech:

> Perhaps I should say a word or two on the duties of women to those among you who are now widowed. I can say all I have to say in a short word of advice. Your greater glory is not to be inferior to what God made you, and a woman's reputation is highest when men say little about her, be it good or evil.[10]

Referring to women in general, and alluding to Helen of Troy in particular, seventh century Semonides says bitterly 'this is the worst plague Zeus has made, and he has bound us to them with a fetter that cannot be broken. Because of this some have gone to Hades fighting for a woman'.[11]

As we shall see in the next chapter, there is much worse; Semonides' misogynistic satire on women concedes only one good type out of ten, and that is the bee-type. Other far less complimentary types include the pig woman, squatting in a dung heap, growing obese, her house filthy; another is a yapping bitch of a dog. Such unhealthy leitmotifs emanated from ingrained stereotypes (not least from Hesiod), which went on to paint themselves indelibly on to the male Greek way of thinking about their women. As we shall see, similar sentiments were to be readily expressed in some of the drama—comic and tragic—composed in Athens.

However, we must remember that the dramatists were producing their plays to win a dramatic contest and to beat their rivals, so it is not surprising that they pushed themselves to the limits of convention, and beyond, when it came to attitudes towards women. They were in it to win it, whatever it took, pandering to the prejudices of a largely male audience.

Despite centuries of research and study, the reputation of ancient women began to recover in the 1970s and 1980s, with the spadework done by such scholars as Sarah Pomeroy. It is still not unusual in the twenty-first century to find women in ancient Greece dismissed and stereotyped, existing in a kind of social cocoon or classical version of *purdah*—out of sight and largely out of mind, in much the same way as the Greeks themselves dismissed and repudiated their women centuries before, such as Xenophon here:

> 'How, Socrates', he said, 'could she have known anything when I took her, since she came to me when she was not yet fifteen, and had lived previously under diligent supervision in order that she might see and hear as little as possible and ask the least possible questions? Doesn't it seem to you that we should be happy if she came knowing only how to take up the wool and make clothes, and had seen how the spinning work is distributed among the female attendants.'

Hitherto, the woman in question knew her place; she was unobtrusive, and aware of her responsibility to the loom. Moreover, Xenophon was elsewhere just as concerned that a wife should not just skulk in the shadows, but that she should also control her appetite and figure; obese women, as Semonides also tells us, were repugnant, and expensive: 'for in control of her appetite, Socrates, she had been excellently trained'.[12] The ancient Greeks saw moderation in diet indicative of the axiom that moderation in all things was, generally, a very good thing. If a woman failed to control her diet then she could not possibly control the the *oikos* (the household, the family, and their property), never mind the city, or the army. The stereotype that women cannot be trusted to control their appetites helped to account for their diminished social and political position. Xenophon interrogates the poor girl further, and most patronisingly:

> Well, Socrates, as soon as I found her docile and sufficiently domesticated to carry on conversation, I questioned her to this effect: 'Tell me, dear, have you realized why I took you in and your parents gave you to me? For surely it is obvious to you that we could easily find someone else to share our beds. But I for myself and your parents for you considered who was the best partner to share home and children. I chose you, and your parents, it appears, chose me as the best they could find'.

Xenophon explains where his attitude comes from; it is god-given, ordained by the gods:

> God from the first adapted the woman's nature, I think, to the indoor and man's to the outdoor tasks and cares. For he made the man's body and mind more capable of enduring cold and heat, and journeys and campaigns; and therefore imposed on him the outdoor tasks. To the woman, since he has made her body less capable of such

endurance, I take it that God has assigned the indoor tasks. And knowing that he had created in the woman and had imposed on her the nourishment of the infants, he meted out to her a larger portion of affection for new-born babes than to the man. And since he imposed on the woman the protection of the household stores too, knowing that for protection being frightened is no disadvantage, God gave a larger share of fear to the woman than to the man; and knowing that he who deals with the outdoor tasks will have to be their defender against any criminal he gave him again a larger share of courage.[13]

There is, nevertheless, some common ground, as Xenophon notes; 'but because both must give and take, he granted to both impartially memory and attention; and so you could not distinguish whether the male or the female sex has the larger share of these.' However, in conclusion, division of labour and the necessary separation this entails, still prevails:

Thus, for a woman it is better to stay indoors than to be in the fields, but to the man it is not right to to stay indoors than to attend to the work outside. Thus your duty will be to remain indoors and send out those servants whose work is outside, and superintend those who are to work indoors, and watch over so much as is to be kept in store, and take care that the sum laid by for a year be not spent in a month. And when wool is brought to you, you must see that cloaks are made for those that want them. You must see too that the dry corn is in good condition for making food.[14]

Household (*oikos*) management is indubitably the name of the woman's game. How far, then, have attitudes changed since the days of Xenophon? Of the voluminous standard 'set texts' of not long ago, neither Hammond's 700-page *A History of Greece to 322 BC*, nor Bury and Meiggs' 600-page large format *A History of Greece* cite 'women' or 'wives' in their indexes. All this, despite the inescapable fact that long overdue revisionism had probably begun with Gomme in 1925, then in earnest with Kitto in 1951, and reinforced by Seltman in 1955, all of whom perceptively debunked the scholarly-convenient stereotyping of women in ancient Greece by questioning the mantra that women were absolutely socially excluded, secluded, and confined— in short, taking Xenophon and others at their word.[15, 16, 17] Over sixty years ago, Seltman put it rather well, if a little floridly:

It is essential for us to question our own views and those of our predecessors on the status of women in ancient Athens. With few exceptions these views display a kernel of prejudice and a pulp of misunderstanding, skinned over with the bloom of evasiveness. It is, indeed, odd to observe how inquirers into the social framework of Greek society have been misled, and how few classical scholars have attempted to give the lie to the extravagances spread abroad concerning the alleged attitude of Athenians to their womenfolk.

Things have moved on immeasurably in recent decades, but until recently, scholars took Xenophon at his word, and largely tended to write women out of ancient Greek history. It is undeniably true that ancient Greek women were socially, and often domestically, segregated from their male counterparts; they had no formal place in public or military life, they were politically invisible and could not case a vote, their education was minimal and truncated, and their intellectual development was not encouraged. Most could not own land, which was central to upward mobility and the acquisition of wealth, as the Spartans proved all to clearly.

Prevailing medical science (written by men, although there were female doctors) dictated that women were 'incomplete' versions of men, and prone to womanly hysteria. Prevailing thought had it that women were failed men and men had better watch out; if they did not make the grade as men in this life, they would be reborn, god forbid, as a woman. Most influentially, Aristotle vocalised those sentiments when he taught that women were inferior and called them deformed males; in the *Politics*, he says 'as for the sexes, the male is naturally superior and the female inferior, the male the ruler and the female the subject'.[18]

According to the men like Xenophon, woman's primary role in life was to marry, look after the household, and produce babies—preferably boys. This was similar to Roman women over the sea in Italy, who had to to keep working the wool, and look after the household. In the second century CE, the eminent physician, Soranus of Ephesus, was still telling people all around the Roman world that women marry not for any pleasure but to produce children.[19] Anything that got in the way of this essential, state-ordained, and state-preserving function was actively discouraged, even though it is doubtful that in the discharge of their onerous domestic duties, most women would have had little time for much else anyway. On the face of it, the only consistent relief from this apparent purdah was the undeniable fact that Greek women and girls did, on the other hand, enjoy an active and public community role in religion. They orchestrated funerals, tended tombs, were at the forefront in various festivals, and were priestesses; they enjoyed the privileges those offices brought.

We get an idea of how singular important this religious role was to the Greek woman, from Sophocles' *Antigone*, written around 441 BCE. The heroine was prepared to compromise her reputation and die, in order to ensure that Polyneices (her brother) received proper funeral rites. The absence, or neglect, of such rites condemned the deceased to wander aimlessly around the banks of the infernal Styx for eternity; a fate, quite literally, worse than death. A woman's prominent real-life role at funerals— burying and mourning their dead relatives—gave her a rare chance to do something important and lasting for their families. When Creon forbids the burial of Polyneices, he is denying Antigone the chance to do one of the few valuable things society permitted women to do. Creon is negating her and her role in life; that is why she vehemently opposes him.

The received wisdom has been, and sometimes still is, that ancient Greek women were imprisoned in their own homes, socially ostracised, to be rarely seen and still rarely heard. We have seen how Xenophon meticulously delineated the domestic routine of the Athenian wife, concluding that the better a wife runs the home and raises the children, then the more honour she will attract; a wife's beauty or character, her very self, counts for nothing, whereas her household management and muted subservience to her husband is everything—the ultimate expression of virtue in a Greek woman to a Greek man.[20]

But that is far too simple, unhelpfully black and white; it is one-dimensional. The real picture is much more coloured, complicated, and nuanced. Has Xenophon left us with a reality, or are his dialogues tainted with prejudice and male chauvinism, indicative of a deep male insecurity?

Greek women had a valuable and significant role to play in many aspects of ancient Greek life, the arts, and mythology, albeit limited and restricted. It is the purpose of this book to delineate and adumbrate manifestations of that role, and to reanimate the ancient Greek woman, to rescue her from relative obscurity for the twenty-first century. In so doing, it will show, from the actions, reactions, conduct, and behaviour of women from all corners of ancient Greece—from Crete to Mycenae, from Thebes to Athens, from Sparta to Thessaly—that the ancient, and enduring, notion that women were secluded and excluded, and therefore worthy of little or no comment, was and is something of an illusion.

Before we look at the real world of women, we will begin with women in ancient Greek mythology, and the divine women in the Greek pantheon. In both, they loom large and lifelike, just as actively as their male counterparts; how did this happen, and why?

Goddesses and mythical women

As we have seen, Greek women attracted a bad press amongst the writing classes; women were trouble, even in mythology. According to Hesiod, Greece's first woman (Pandora) was the embodiment of everything to dislike in a human being, as man had made the fatal mistake of learning from Prometheus the secret of producing fire. Pandora was fashioned out of the earth by Hephaestus, by command of Zeus; other gods and goddesses supplied all the other unhealthy physical attributes and characteristics of women traditionally loathed and feared by men: seduction, dishonesty, and manipulation. What you could see before your eyes was beautiful, making her irresistible to men; on the other hand, it was the invisible features donated by the Olympian gods that constituted her true personality—these would bring endless grief, injury, harm, and much trouble to man.

> Prometheus, surpassing all in cunning, you are glad that you have outwitted me and stolen fire—a great plague on you and to all future men. But for the price for fire I will give men an evil thing in which they may all be glad of heart while they embrace their own destruction.

Zeus mocks man's hubris:

> So said the father of men and gods, and laughed aloud. And he told famous Hephaestus to hurry up and mix earth with water and to put in it the voice and strength of human kind, and fashion a sweet, lovely maiden-shape, like an immortal goddesses to look at; and Athena to teach her needlework and weaving; and golden Aphrodite to shed grace upon her head and cruel longing and cares that weary the limbs. And he charged Hermes... to put in her a shameless mind and a deceitful nature...Athena girded and clothed her, and the divine Graces and queenly Persuasion put necklaces of gold upon her, and the rich-haired Hours crowned her head with spring flowers. And Pallas Athena bedecked her form with all manner of finery. Also Hermes gave her lies and crafty words and a deceitful nature...the Herald of the gods put speech in her. And he called this woman Pandora, because all the Olympians gave a gift, a plague to men.

Up until now, all had been well on earth and with man, but when Pandora undid the lid of the jar given to her by Zeus, she was also the undoing of man:

> the tribes of men lived on earth remote and free from ills and hard toil and heavy sicknesses which bring the Fates upon men; for in misery men grow old quickly. But the woman took off the great lid of the jar with her hands and scattered, all these and her thought caused sorrow and mischief to men. Only Hope remained there in an unbreakable home under the rim of the great jar ... But the rest, countless plagues, wander amongst men; for earth is [now] full of evils, and the sea is full. Of themselves diseases come upon men continually by day and by night, bringing stealthy mischief to mortals.[1]

With an air of weary resignation, Hesiod spoke for generations of Greek men when he concluded that 'men could not live with [women] and could not live without them'. Apart from echoing the sentiments of contemporary men, Hesiod influenced successive generations of men against women by injecting prejudice, discrimination, misogyny, fear, and distrust into one half of the population against the other. By opening that fateful jar, Pandora had taken the lid off the bad things in life; she had ended the Golden Age, brought a close to the good old days, and ushered in a world that was now going to be much harder work—it was woman's fault. Before women arrived on the scene, everything was just fine. But the 'grim cares of mankind' were now abroad; all men could do was hope. Lumbered with this poisoned chalice, man had to make the most of it; at lines 699ff, we have Hesiod's prescription for choosing a good wife:

> Marry a virgin, so that you can teach her careful ways, in particular, marry one who lives near you, but have a good look around and ensure that your marriage will not be the laughing stock of the neighbourhood. For a man wins nothing better than a good wife, and nothing worse than a bad one, a greedy soul who roasts her man without fire, as strong as he might be, and brings him an early old age.

At lines 590ff, Hesiod reiterates the doom-laden message in the *Theogeny*, when he asserts that bachelorhood is no escape from misery: a wretched old age awaits the single man as there will be no one around to provide home care. Incidentally, in so doing, the poet inadvertently admits to one of the benefits a good woman can provide: care for a husband in his dotage:

> For from Pandora comes women and female kind: of her is the deadly race and tribe of women who live amongst mortal men to their great trouble, no help meets in hateful poverty, but only in wealth... Zeus... made women to be an evil to mortal men, with a nature to do evil... whoever avoids marriage and the sorrows that women cause, and will not wed, reaches deadly old age without anyone to tend his years.

So much for woman's debut on the world stage. Above all that, the gods reigned supreme. The top gods formed an elite group, known as 'The Twelve Olympians' or the *Dodekatheon* (Δωδεκάθεον). The twelve who qualified for this supreme position are usually given as: Zeus, Hera, Poseidon, Demeter, Athena, Apollo, Artemis, Ares, Aphrodite, Hephaestus, Hermes, and either Hestia or Dionysus. Hades (Pluto) was not always included because his realm was the underworld, and he could never find the time to make it up to Olympus. Female deities, as we can see, are well represented in this higher echelon—an acknowledgement, no doubt, of the fact that women made up half of the population of earth. The Olympians reached their celestial (or chthonic) status in a war of the gods, in which Zeus led his siblings to victory over the Titans. Zeus quickly denied women a role in politics and society and established a patriarchal government on Olympus; despite their numbers in the celestial elite, female deities were nevertheless subordinate to their male counterparts—a situation reflected in the real world. Childbirth was an obvious exception where the female was in charge; although, even this natural function was usurped, when Zeus produced Athena from his own head, and Dionysus from his thigh.

These are the individual portfolios of the goddesses, taking in a wide slice of human life on earth:

Hera—Queen of the gods and the goddess of women, marriage, and family; she was the wife and sister of Zeus. It is possible that Hera was originally the goddess of a matriarchal race who inhabited Greece before the Hellenes. Hera was also worshipped as a virgin; in Stymphalia, Arcadia there was a triple shrine to Hera the Girl (Παις, Pais), the Adult Woman (Τελεια, Teleia), and the Separated (Χήρη, Chḗrē; 'Widowed' or 'Divorced'). The temple of Hera in Hermione was dedicated to Hera the Virgin. Hera renewed her virginity every year, in ineffable rites (arrheton) at the spring of Kanathos, near Nauplia.

Hera was never the ideal mother: having given birth to Hephaestus (without the involvement of Zeus, in an immaculate conception of sorts), she was so disgusted by his ugliness that she threw him off Mount Olympus, hence his limp. Hera produced Hebe, after being impregnated by a head of lettuce. Hera loathed her stepson, Heracles—when he was still a baby, Hera sent two serpents to kill him as he lay in his cot; Heracles was unphased by this, and throttled both. The Milky Way was formed when Zeus tricked Hera into nursing Heracles; when she realised who he was, she tore him from her breast, and a spurt of her milk made the smear across the sky that we now know as the Milky Way.

Demeter—Goddess of fertility, agriculture, nature, and the seasons; she was the middle daughter of Cronus and Rhea.

Athena—Goddess of wisdom, reason, literature, handicrafts and science, defence and strategic warfare, she was the daughter of Zeus and the Oceanid Metis; she rose from her father's head fully grown, and in full battle armour, after he swallowed her mother.

Artemis—Goddess of the hunt, virginity, archery, the moon, and all animals, she was the daughter of Zeus and Leto, and twin sister of Apollo.

Aphrodite—Goddess of love, beauty, pleasure, and procreation, she was the daughter of Zeus and the Oceanid Dione, or, born from the ocean's foam after Uranus' semen dripped into the sea, when he was castrated by his youngest son, Cronus; Cronus then threw his father's genitals into the sea. Her name is the etymological root for 'aphrodisiac'.

Hestia—Goddess of the hearth, domesticity, and the family, she was the first child of Cronus and Rhea, eldest sister of Hades, Demeter, Poseidon, Hera, and Zeus.

All human life is there; women are well represented and, despite their subordination to the male gods, their functions here suggest a balanced share of control in life on earth, and patronage of a reasonable share of what was going on in the real world. Other important female deities who complement the elite include:

Amphitrite—Queen of the Sea; mother of Triton and wife of Poseidon.

Artemis—twin sister of Apollo, she was a hunter of lions, panthers and stags, and the protector of the wilderness and wild animals. When she was three years old, she asked her father Zeus to grant her everlasting virginity, a state which she defended vigorously, visiting terrible punishments on any man who threatened her chastity. This perpetual virgin, ironically, helped women get pregnant, and watched over confinement and childbirth. Girls were initiated into her cult on reaching puberty; when they were about to marry they donated all their toys to her.

Aura—Goddess of breezes and fresh air.

Circe—Goddess of magic.

Eileithyia—Goddess of childbirth; daughter of Hera and Zeus.

Eris—Goddess of discord and strife.

The Three Graces—Goddesses of beauty, and attendants of Aphrodite and Hera.

Hebe—the daughter of Zeus and Hera, and the cupbearer for the deities on Mount Olympus, serving their nectar and ambrosia, until she married Heracles.

Hecate—Goddess of magic, witches and crossroads.

The Moirai—The 'Fates'. Clotho (the spinner), Lachesis (the allotter) and Atropos ('the unturnable').

The Muses—Nine goddesses of science and arts: Calliope, Urania, Clio, Polyhymnia, Melpomene, Terpsichore, Thalia, Euterpe, and Erato.

Nemesis—Goddess of retribution and revenge, daughter of Nyx.

Nike—Goddess of victory.

Persephone—Queen of the Underworld and a daughter of Demeter and Zeus; goddess of spring time. She was the consort of Hades. Demeter was driven mad by her daughter's underground life and, as a result, neglected her duty to the earth, so it became barren. Zeus ordered Hades to allow Persephone to leave the underworld and go back to Demeter. Hades complied, but because Persephone had eaten six of the twelve pomegranate seeds in the underworld, she was still obliged to spend six months in the underworld each year. This created the seasons: for six months everything flourished then, for the rest of the year, everything withered and died. Persephone's marriage to Hades was all arranged by Zeus; her mother, Demeter, had no say in the union; this reflects the situation in Greek society whereby a daughter and her mother had no say in the choice of a husband. In Athens, the dead were called Demetreioi, Demeter's people.

Selene—A Titaness; personification of the moon.

Styx—Goddess of the infernal River Styx, the river on which the gods swear oaths.

Tyche—Goddess of Luck.

Mythology gives us an introduction to real women in ancient Greece—women were represented well in the pantheon; they also had a leading role to play in mortal mythology. The original word, *mythos*, meant word, speech or message but it soon took on connotations of entertainment of dubious veracity. Veracity matters little though; the importance of myths lies in their enduring ability to influence and teach us about our place in the world, and how we might behave and react in certain universal situations. Greek myths, as we have them, are truly ancient; Homer, as we have just seen, introduces a divine genealogy that was anthropomorphic, but mortals such as Achilles, Helen and Hercules, for example, probably have Indo-European or even earlier origins. Many myths are common in one form or another, to different cultures and civilisations, in different historical and prehistoric periods; this is because they deal with basic universals: birth, rebirth, death, gods, fertility, infertility, right and wrong, good and bad, as well as men and women. A major characteristic of Greek myths relating to women (Io, Iphigenia, and Europa, for example) is that they deal with either the potentially volatile period of the transition to womanhood, or with marriage; this is not that surprising when, in the real world, marriage was the goal for all women—it was what the state, and men, required them to do. Fecundity, birth and rebirth, virginity, sexuality, and the family are monopolised by female deities on Olympus and in Hades; fertility and reproduction figure prominently in mythology involving women.

As time went on, myths that had focussed on politics and matters of government were embellished, and new details were added; they became more to do with domestic life and social relationships, and so involved women and family relationships, as we will see in the chapter relating to women in tragedy and comedy. Poets and playwrights developed mythological characters as potent vehicles, to remind their audiences of their own personal situations and cultural realities, and of all the implications that came with them. Poets gave their audience pause for thought. Poetry was held in high esteem; Aristotle himself taught that it was more important than historiography because history dealt in the particular, while poetry expatiated on universals.[2] It showed people how their ancestors conducted themselves, but in so doing, provided a road map for morality and outlined how people should conduct themselves. Given this, the way in which these poets portrayed women had ageless consequences and repercussions for women, for as long as those myths continue to be read or performed.

The telling of myths was an important part of a child's education, fulfiling a similar role to bedtime stories today.[3] The visual arts reflect mythology in abundance; women told myths to each other while working the wool, according to Euripides (*Ion* 196f). Essentially, myth was aetiological—it explained to successive generations of Greeks how the world got to be how it was. It also explained the reason behind the supremacy of males, to restore order after the turmoil created by the chaotic Pandora. Myth explained the origin of various *poleis* such as Thebes and Sparta; it told them how Ionians originated through Io, Aeolians from Aeolus. Stereotypes prevail, in order to convey a specific message about specific types of people—evil women were consigned to bleak mountain tops, maidens to happy valleys; sex with a god often ended in tears, as in the case of Semele reduced to ashes (and tears) by Zeus.

The aetiological function of myth in religion was important too, particularly in view of women's high profile role in many rites and cults; for example, the myth of the Lemnian women explains the segregation of women and men in various rituals. How women were characterised in myth, in popular iconic works like the *Iliad* and the *Odyssey,* and on the tragic stage had a significant impact on how women were considered and treated by subsequent generations. It was essential that girls grew up behaving like Penelope or Nausicaa, not like Clytemnestra or Cassandra.

We owe much to Hesiod for the mythology relating to Greek women. Apart from the *Theogeny* and the *Works and Days*, other works attributed to him include (extant in fragmentary form) the *Catalogue of Women* or *Ehoiai*—a mythological roll-call of mortal women who had slept with gods, and of their offspring; the *Megalai Ehoiai*, a poem similar to the *Catalogue of Women*; Hesiod also gives us a biography of Hecate, the witch goddess; the *Wedding of Ceyx*, Heracles' attendance at the wedding of Ceyx, as the title suggests; *Melampodia*, a genealogical poem which deals with the families of, and myths associated with, the mythical seers of mythology; finally, *a Dirge for Batrachus*, the love of Hesiod's life. The catalogue of women begins as follows:

> *Now do sing of the tribe of women, sweet-voiced*
> *Olympian Muses, daughters of aegis-bearing Zeus,*
> *they who were the best in those days ...*
> *and loosened their girdles ...*
> *mingling with the gods ...* [4]

Notional sex with a god or goddess was an everyday, accepted fact of life. Here is a taste from the fragments that have come down to us featuring intermarriage between gods and mankind:

Zeus saw Europa the daughter of Phoenix gathering flowers in a meadow with some nymphs and fell in love with her. So he came down and changed himself into a bull and breathed out a crocus. In this way he deceived Europa, carried her off and crossed the sea to Crete where he copulated with her. Then in this condition he made her live with Asterion the king of the Cretans. There she conceived and bore three sons, Minos, Sarpedon and Rhadamanthys. The tale is in Hesiod and Bacchylides.[5]

Hesiod says that Endymion was the son of Aethlius the son of Zeus and Calyce, and received the gift from Zeus: '[To be] keeper of death for his own self when he was ready to die.'[6] Concerning the Myrmidons, Hesiod speaks as follows:

> And she conceived and bore Aeacus, delighting in horses. Now when he came to the full measure of desired youth, he chafed at being alone. And the father of men and gods made all the ants that were in the lovely isle into men and wide-girdled women. These were the first who fitted with thwarts ships with curved sides, and the first who used sails, the wings of a sea-going ship.[7]

However, the *Theogeny* tells us a very different story of Hesiod's attitude to women; it is covered in the chapter on invective.[8]

Here is a short catalogue of significant women in Greek mythology; it illustrates the importance of women in the grand scheme of things, and explains, to varying degrees, the social and cultural situation of women in later times.

Aedon became the first nightingale, but it took infanticide to get that distinction. As the wife of Zethus and the mother of Itylus, she killed her son by mistake; Zeus took pity and turned her into the nightingale so that she could lament the murder of her child every night. An alternative version has Aedon as the queen of Thebes, who attempts to murder Niobe's children, but kills her own instead; she is turned into a nightingale for the same reason.

Alcestis is the last word in wifely devotion to a husband. When she came of marriageable age, King Pelias, her father, ordained she would marry the first man who could yoke a lion and a boar (or a bear) to a chariot. Helped by Apollo, King Admetus was the winner, and married Alcestis. After the wedding, Admetus made the error of forgetting to make the required sacrifice to Artemis, for which misdemeanour he found his bed seething with snakes. Apollo rendered the Fates powerless by intoxicating them, so Admetus did not die; instead the god arranged for the Fates to promise that if anyone was happy to die instead of Admetus, they would arrange it. Alcestis stepped forward and died for Admetus. However, all was not lost, as Hercules rescued her from Hades.

Macaria was immortalised in Euripides' *Heracleidae*; she deprecatingly echoes Xenophon's advice that it is best to 'keep your mouth shut' when she states that 'for a woman, silence and self control are best.' She goes one step further, when, like Alcestis, she sacrifices herself; Iolaus and his children (Macaria and her siblings) were hiding from Eurystheus in Athens, which was then ruled by King Demophon, in the hope that Heracles' relationship with the kings will win them sanctuary. As Eurystheus prepares to attack, Demophon is advised by an oracle that he would win, only if a noble woman is sacrificed to Persephone. Macaria selflessly volunteers for this; as a result, she won eternal fame when a spring was named the Macarian spring after her.

Amymone (the 'blameless' one) was the only one of the fifty daughters of Danaus who did not assassinate her Egyptian husband on their wedding night. Poseidon rescued Amymone from a chthonic satyr, who was about to rape her; but then Poseidon had sex with her, and she bore Nauplius, 'the navigator,' who gave his name to that port city of Argos. Her sisters endured eternal punishment in Tartarus for their crimes, by drawing water in leaking pitchers.

Andromeda was the daughter of Cepheus and Cassiopeia, rulers of Aethiopia. Andromeda's mother did her no favours when she boasted that her daughter was fairer than the Nereids. Poseidon was put out by this hubris so he sent a sea monster, Cetus, to devastate the coast of Aethiopia, including the kingdom of the vain queen. A despairing Cepheus consulted the oracle of Apollo, who decreed that nothing would change until the king sacrificed his daughter, Andromeda, to the monster. This he did; stripped naked, Andromeda was chained to a rock on the shore. However, Perseus, fresh from having slain the Gorgon Medusa, found Andromeda, approached Cetus while invisible and killed him. He set Andromeda free, and married her. Pausanias, Strabo, and Josephus all say that the place where Andromeda was chained is modern day Jaffa in Israel.

Arachne, a gifted weaver, demonstrated more hubris when she rashly challenged Athena, goddess of wisdom and craftwork; Athena changed her into a spider for her troubles. Ovid reveals in the *Metamorphoses* that Arachne's weaving showed the ways in which the gods had deceived and abused mortals, particularly Zeus, who seduced many mortal women. [9] Athena took this as an insult to the gods, and was further outraged when she saw that Arachne's work was finer than her own. She ripped Arachne's work into shreds, and showered her with Hecate's occult potion, turning her into a spider and cursing her and her descendants to weave for eternity. The taxonomic name for spider is *arachnida* after Arachne. Another version has Arachne commit suicide after feeling guilty for her hubris, and then being restored as a spider by Athena.

Ariadne, daughter of Minos, king of Crete, helped Theseus defeat the Minotaur and save the sacrificial victims from the monster in its labyrinthine lair with a ball of thread that she supplied. Theseus and Ariadne then fled to Naxos, where Ariadne made the mistake of falling asleep, allowing Theseus to sail away. Some say she then married Dionysus, but was later killed by Perseus at Argos. Others suggest that she hanged herself from a tree. Dionysus then descended into Hades and brought her (and his mother Semele) back, to sit with the gods on Olympus.

Apollodorus gives us an explanation why Lemnos was ruled by women:

Led by Jason, the Argonauts first sailed to Lemnos then totally devoid of men and ruled by Hypsipyle, daughter of Thoas. This state of affairs came about as follows: the women of Lemnos had neglected the cult of Aphrodite. As a punishment, the goddess afflicted them with a foul smell. The men found this repellent and took up with captive women from nearby Thrace. The Lemnian women were outraged at this humiliation and proceeded to murder their fathers and husbands. But not so

Hypsipyle: she hid her father, Thoas, and spared him. The Argonauts slept with the Lemnian women with Hypsipyle sharing Jason's bed.[10]

Somewhat earlier, Apollonius of Rhodes in the third century BCE, told us this is in his *The Voyage of the Argo*:

The Lemnian women found it easier to look after cattle, put on a suit of bronze, and plough the earth for corn rather than to devote themselves, as they had done before, to the tasks of which Athene is the patroness [handicraft]. Nevertheless, they lived in dire dread of the Thracians... so when they saw the Argo rowing up to the island, they immediately got ready for war... Hypsipyle joined them, dressed in her father Thoas' armour. [11]

She advised conciliation and provisioning them on their ships to keep them at bay. Apollonius goes on to have Polyxo speak, with the wisdom and foresight that only comes from age and experience:

...The next to get up was her dear nurse Polyxo, an aged woman tottering on withered feet and leaning on a staff, but nonetheless determined to be heard... 'Hypsipyle is right. We must accommodate these strangers... there are many troubles worse than war that you will have to meet as time goes on. When the older ones among us have died off, how are you younger women, without children, going to face the miseries of age? Will the oxen yoke themselves? Will they go out into the fields and drag the plowshare through the stubborn fallow? Will they watch the changing seasons and reap at the right time?'

In the *Libation Bearers*, the second play in the *Oresteia*, Aeschylus puts the actions of the Lemnians into some sort of literary context, a benchmark for female atrocity against men:

But who can tell of man's over-proud spirit, and of the reckless passions of women hardened of soul, partners of the woes of mortals? Inordinate passion, overmastering the female, gains a fatal victory ... Indeed the Lemnian holds first place among evils as stories go: it has long been told with groans as an abominable calamity. Men compare each new horror to Lemnian troubles; and because of a woeful deed abhorred by the gods a race has disappeared, cast out in infamy from among mortals.[12]

St. Augustine, in *On the City of God*, naturally critical of the heathen gods, narrates the myths relating to the naming of Athens, and the reason why women lost the right to vote in ancient Greece:

Now this is the reason Varro gives for the city's being called Athens, a name that is certainly derived from Minerva, who is called Athene in Greek. When an olive tree suddenly sprouted there, and on another spot water gushed forth, these portents alarmed the king, so he sent to Delphic Apollo to ask what the meaning of this was and what was to be done. Apollo answered that the olive signified [female] Minerva and the spring [male] Neptune, and that it was up to the citizens to decide from which of the two gods, whose symbols these were, they preferred for the city to be named after. When Cecrops received this oracle he called together all the citizens of both sexes—for at that time it was customary in that area that the women should have a part in public deliberations—to take a vote…the men voted for Neptune and the women for Minerva, and because there was more women than men, Minerva was victorious.

Then Neptune in his rage devastated the lands of the Athenians with great floods of sea-water… To appease his wrath, Varro tells us, the women were subjected by the Athenians to a triple punishment: namely that they should never vote from then on, that none of their children should bear their mother's name, and that no one should call them Athenian women… Minerva, though victorious, was also defeated. Nor did she defend the women who had voted for her; when they lost the right of suffrage for the future, and their sons were cut off from their mothers' names, she might at least have seen to it that they had the privilege of being called Athenians and of bearing the name of the goddess, since they had given her the victory over the male god by their votes.[13]

Despite winning the vote by democratic means for their female deity, women lost the vote in the long term by undemocratic means, dictated by a male god.

Cassiopeia, as we have seen, landed her daughter, Andromeda, in a difficult situation. The story continues, with Poseidon believing that Cassiopeia should not escape punishment, so he exiled her to the heavens, tied to a chair in such a position that she is upside-down half the time. The chair represented an instrument of torture; it still does today, in the form of the electric chair. Cassiopeia is sometimes shown holding a mirror, indicative of her vanity. The constellation Cassiopeia can be easily seen the whole year from the northern hemisphere, although sometimes it is visibly upside down. It has its distinctive 'M' shape when at its high point, but in higher northern locations, when near its lower points in spring and summer, it has a 'W' shape, formed by its five bright stars.

Danaë was the daughter, and only child, of King Acrisius of Argos and his wife Queen Eurydice. She was also indirectly involved in the accidental killing of her father by her son, Perseus. Acrisius was troubled by his inability to father a male heir, so he asked the oracle at Delphi if things were likely to change. The bad news was that he would never have a son, yet his daughter would; what was worse was that this son would eventually kill him. In an attempt to prevent the inevitable, King Acrisius imprisoned Danae in a bronze chamber under his palace (other versions say in a tall brass tower with a single richly adorned chamber, but with no doors or windows, just a sky-light for light and air). However, Zeus took a fancy to her and impregnated her in the form of golden rain that poured in through the roof of the subterranean chamber and into her womb. Perseus was then born.

Acrisius prevailed in vain on the Furies for permission to kill his grandchild, and so cast Danaë and Perseus into the sea in a wooden chest. However, Poseidon calmed the sea, and at the request of Zeus, the pair survived to land on the island of Seriphos, where they were taken in by Dictys—the brother of King Polydectes—who raised Perseus to manhood. The king took a shine to Danaë, but she was not interested; he agreed not to force her into marriage, if Perseus could bring him the head of the Gorgon, Medusa. Perseus cleverly avoided Medusa's gaze and decapitated her, presenting the head to Acrisius. Unfortunately, the oracle came true when Perseus set out for Argos, but learning of the prophecy, diverted to Larissa, where athletic games were being held attended by Acrisius: Perseus accidentally struck him on the head with his javelin and killed him.

The Fates are usually depicted as a group of three mythological goddesses—white-robed weavers of a tapestry on a loom, with the tapestry dictating the unalterable life span from birth to death, and destinies, of all men and women. Known as the Moirae, they were Clotho (spinner), Lachesis (allotter), and Atropos (unturnable). Gods and mortals alike bowed to them, according to Hesiod in the *Theogeny*.[14] In his *Republic*, Plato says the Three Fates are daughters of Ananke (necessity), and that they sing in harmony with the Sirens; Lachesis sings the things that were, Clotho the things that are, and Atropos the things that are to be.[15]

Clotho spun the thread of life from her distaff onto her spindle. Lachesis, the drawer of lots, measured out the thread of life allotted to each person with her measuring rod. Atropos ('inexorable' or 'inevitable'), sometimes called Aisa, was the cutter of the thread of life. She chose how each person died; when their time was come, she cut their life-thread with what Milton called her 'abhorred shears', confusing her somewhat with that other fearsome cabal, the Furies: *Comes the blind Fury with th'abhorred shears, / And slits the thin spun life.*[16]

In his *Hymn to the Fates*, Pindar calls them to send their sisters Horae (Hours—goddesses of law and order who safeguarded the stability of society, Eunomia (Lawfulness), Dike (Right), and Eirene (Peace), to stop the internal civil strife:

> Listen Fates, who sit nearest of gods to the throne of Zeus, and weave with shuttles of adamant, inescapable devices for councils of every kind beyond counting, Aisa, Clotho and Lachesis, fine-armed daughters of Night, listen to our prayers, all-terrible goddesses, of sky and earth. Send us rose-bossomed Lawfulness, and her sisters on glittering thrones,
>
> Right and crowned Peace, and make this city forget the misfortunes which lie heavily on her heart.[17]

The association of the Moirai with newborns may explain how they can be associated with the fairy tale. In Greek folklore, fairies bring gifts to the newborn child, at the side of the cradle. Pausanias explains how 'The Lycian Olen, an earlier poet, who composed for the Delians, among other hymns, one to Eileithyia, styles her 'the clever spinner', clearly identifying her with Fate, and makes her older than Cronus.'[18] Eileithyia was the goddess of childbirth.

The Moirai were typically ugly old women, sometimes deformed and lame; they were uncompromising, unbending, and stern. Clotho is identified by a spindle or a roll (the book of fate), Lachesis a staff with which she points to the horoscope on a globe, and Atropos (Aisa) carries a scroll, a wax tablet, a sundial, a pair of scales, or a cutting instrument. At the birth of each baby, they appeared spinning, measuring, and cutting the thread of life. The Moirai turned up three nights after a child's birth to map out the course of its life, according to the story of Meleager by Apollodorus; based on the lexicon of Hesychius, others posit seven days to correspond with the custom of waiting seven days to decide whether to accept the infant into the *oikos* and give it a name.[19] At Sparta, Pausanias noted that the temple dedicated to the Moirai was located near the communal hearth of the *polis*.

The old women who routinely took services at the temples were often deformed, and considered by some to be representations of the Moirai—native to the underworld. It is only a short step from there to an association with witches and witchcraft. The Moirae too had links with the avenging Furies. At the birth of Hercules, the Moirae used magic art to free him from any 'bonds' and 'knots'.

The Moirae caught the imagination of various composers in the late 1960s and early 1970s. 'The Three Fates' is a three-part 'pseudo suite' written and performed by Keith Emerson. It comprises three movements, one for each of the three Fates. Roger Chapman caught the essence of the Moirae in *The Weaver's Answer*:

> *Weaver of life, let me look and see*
> *The pattern of my life gone by,*
> *Shown on your tapestry.*
> *Just for one second, one glance upon your loom*
> *The flower of my childhood could appear within this room...*
> *After days of wondering I see the reason why.*
> *You kept it to this minute, for I'm about to die.*[20]

The Three Graces are at the other end of the popularity spectrum from the Moirae. The Graces were daughters of Zeus and the Oceanid Eurynome. They are Aglaia, symbolizing Beauty, Euphrosyne, the Grace of Delight and Thalia, the Grace of Blossom. According to Pindar, these goddesses were created to fill the world with pleasantness and bonhomie. Usually, the Graces attended on Aphrodite and Eros, dancing around in a circle to Apollo's divine music, together with the Nymphs and the Muses.

The Erinyes were decidedly unpleasant, and utterly devoid of bonhomie; also known as Furies, they were female chthonic deities of retribution and vengeance, sometimes referred to as 'infernal goddesses' (χθόνιαι θεαί). In the *Iliad*, they are invoked as 'those who beneath the earth punish whosoever has sworn a false oath.'[21] The Furies have a particularly repulsive origin; according to Hesiod's *Theogony*, when Kronus castrated Uranus, and threw his genitals into the sea, the Erinyes—as well as the Meliae (nymphs of the ash tree)—emerged from the blood when it spattered the earth.

> Then the son [Kronos] from his ambush stretched out his left hand and in his right took the great long sickle with jagged teeth, and swiftly lopped off his own father's [Ouranos'] genitals and threw them away... Gaia got the bloody drops that gushed out and as the seasons moved round she gave birth to the mighty Erinyes.[22]

Aeschylus, Lycophron, Ovid, and Virgil all attest them to being the daughter of Nox, or Night.[23]

The Erinyes live in Erebus in the Underworld; as they are older than any of the Olympians, they are not under the jurisdiction of Zeus. Their job is to hear complaints brought by mortals for various transgressions, including the disrespect by the young to the elderly, by children to parents, of hosts to guests, perjury, and of householders or city authorities to suppliants. Crimes of murder were a speciality, particularly the murder of a family member. They punish such crimes by stalking and hounding culprits relentlessly. The curse of the Erinyes could be called down on a perpetrator by the victim; the most powerful of these was the curse of parent on the child—something the Erinyes knew all about because they were born of just such a crime. The Erinyes were typically old ugly crones and variously sport snakes for hair, dog's heads, coal black skin, bat's wings, and blood-shot bleeding eyes.[24] Orestes cries in terror when he sees the Erinyes: 'Ah, ah! You handmaidens, look at them there: like Gorgones, wrapped in black cloaks, entwined with swarming snakes!'

They were armed with brass-studded whips, or cups of poison, and their victims would die in eye-watering agony; they could even crowd in as storm clouds or swarms of insects. Unbearably painful madness was inflicted on patricides or matricides; illness or disease awaiting murderers, while any state harbouring such a criminal, would find itself plagued by hunger and disease. Once incurred, the wrath of the Erinyes could only be assuaged through ritual purification, and the satisfactory completion of tasks assigned for atonement.

Plato tells us about their chthonic work in the underworld. When the dead first arrive in Hades, they go before the three Judges—if good, they are then handed over to the Erinyes, who purify them of their sins and let them pass; those judged to be wicked are dragged off to the Tartarean dungeon of the damned, where the Erinyes are the jailers, overseeing the tortures inflicted up the criminals.[25]

The names of the Furies appear in Bacchylides' *Orphic Hymn to Apollo* and Apollodorus—later taken up by Virgil in the *Aeneid*: he names them as Alecto ('unremitting'), Megaera ('grudging'), and Tisiphone ('jealous destruction').[26] In Aeschylus' *Libation Bearers*, it makes no difference to the Erinyes that Orestes was divinely sanctioned, ordered by Apollo to kill Clytemnestra and Aegisthus; to them, murder is murder and matricide is matricide, so they pursue him with a vengeance. In the *Eumenides*, the final play in the *Oresteia* trilogy, Orestes finds himself in an Athenian court, to be tried by a jury of Athenian citizens; the Erinyes are council for the prosecution, while Athena represents Orestes. Athena acquits Orestes, but the angry Erinyes threaten to torment everyone in Athens, and poison the surrounding countryside. Athena diplomatically offers the Erinyes the new role of protectors of justice, a complete reversal of their preoccupation with vengeance; at the same time, the goddess ominously reminds them that she still has the key to the storehouse where Zeus keeps his thunderbolts. The Erinyes are placated and are now called Semnai (Venerable Ones), honored by the citizens of Athens.

In his *Orestes*, Euripides is the first to call the Erinyes the Eumenides—the gracious ones, or kindly ones. It was deemed unwise to call the Erinyes by name in case it attracted their attention so a euphemistic name was used, in much the same way as Hades, god of the dead, is called Pluton, or Pluto (the rich one). The safest bet was not to name them at all: 'As for the sacred rituals for the Fates and the Nameless Goddesses, all these would not be holy if performed by men, but prosper in women's hands.'[27]

Other hideous, monstrous women took the shape of the Harpies—the spirits of sudden, sharp gusts of wind. They were the hounds of Zeus, and used by him to snatch away (*harpazô*) people and things from the earth; sudden, unaccountable disappearances were often attributed to the Harpies. An example is the daughters of King Pandareus, who were given as servants to the Erinyes.[28, 29]

The Harpies were depicted as winged women, usually with ugly faces, or with the lower bodies of birds.[30] One of their victims was blind King Phineus of Thrace, whom they punished for revealing the secrets of the gods. Whenever he sat down to a plate of food, the Harpies would swoop down and snatch it away, fouling anything left behind. Virgil described them:

> No viler monstrosity than they, no pest more atrocious did ever the wrath of god conjure up out of hell's swamp. Bird-bodied, girl-faced things they [the Harpies] are; abominable their droppings, their hands are talons, their faces haggard with hunger insatiable... we are most richly feasting. But, the next moment, we hear a hoarse vibration of wing-beats—the Harpyiae (Harpies) are on us, horribly swooping down from the mountains. They tear the banquet to pieces, filthying all with their bestial touch. Hideous the sounds, nauseous the stench about us.[31]

The Sirens (Σειρῆνες) were deadly, but beautiful creatures, who enticed sailors with their enchanting music and voices, so they would crash their ships on the rocks around their island. Some have contended that the Sirens were cannibals, based on Circe's description of them, 'lolling there in their meadow, round them heaps of corpses rotting away, rags of skin shriveling on their bones.'[32]

In early Greek art, Sirens were depicted as birds with large heads of women, bird feathers and scaly feet. Later, they were represented as females with the legs of birds, with or without wings, playing musical instruments, especially harps. The *Suda* says that, from their chests up, Sirens were sparrows, and below were women. Later Sirens were depicted as beautiful women, whose bodies as well as their voices, were seductive. Pliny the Elder said 'Dinon, the father of Clearchus, a celebrated writer, asserts that they exist in India, and that they charm men by their song, and, having first lulled them to sleep, tear them to pieces.'[33] Odysseus was one of the only—if not the only—man to hear the siren song, and live to tell the tale. He wanted to hear them, and so, on the advice of Circe, he had all of his sailors plug their ears with beeswax, and tie him to the mast.

Other mythological characters reinforce the ubiquity of women in the nebulous world of the divine. Sparta was the daughter of Eurotas by Clete. She was wife of Lacedaemon, who was also her uncle, by whom she became the mother of Amyclas and Eurydice of Argos (no relation to Orpheus' Eurydice). The city of Sparta was named after her, although it was often called Lacedaemon as well. Armies would shout her name when going into battle.

Gorgophone was a daughter of Perseus and Andromeda. Her name means 'Gorgon Slayer', a tribute to her father who killed Medusa, the mortal Gorgon. Gorgophone figures prominently in Spartan mythology: she was married to two kings, Oebalus of Laconia and Perieres of Messenia, and was the first woman in the world to have married twice.[34]

Illicit sex has its risks, as Leimone was to discover to her cost. She was the daughter of Hippomenes, a descendant of King Codrus, but her noble lineage was of no use when her father caught her having sex; he killed her lover, and locked Leimone in an empty house with only a horse for company. When the horse got hungry, it devoured Leimone. The remains of the house were still there in the times of Aeschines (389–314 BCE), the Greek statesman and one of the ten Attic orators. It was known imaginatively as 'At the Horse and the Maiden'.[35]

Other mythical women of note include:

Amymone—an Argive princess seduced by Poseidon when she came to Lerna, looking for water during a drought.

Antiope—a Boiotian princess seduced by Zeus, when in the guise of a satyr. She bore him twin sons, Amphion and Zethos.

Atalanta—an Arcadian huntress, brought up in the wilderness by a bear. She hunted the Calydonian boar, slew Centaurs, defeated Peleus in wrestling, and was married by Melanion who defeated her in a race.

Callisto—an Arcadian princess and hunting companion of Artemis. She was loved by Zeus, but when it was reveaed that she was pregnant, she was turned into a bear.

Coronis—a Thesallian princess loved by Apollo. When she committed adultery, Artemis shot her with an arrow.

Cyrene—another Thessalian princess and huntress loved by Apollo, who first spied her as she was wrestling a lion.

Europa—a Phoenician princess abducted to Crete by Zeus, who carried her across the sea, disguised as a bull.

Evadne—an Arcadian princess loved by Apollo, who abandoned their son Iamus in a bed of violets where he was nursed by bees.

Io—an Argive princess beloved of Zeus, who turned her into a heifer to hide her from the jealous gaze of Hera. The goddess sent a gadfly to torment her, so she walked all the way to Egypt, where she gave birth to her son.

Leda—a queen of Sparta, who was seduced by Zeus in the guise of swan. She laid an egg, from which was hatched Helen and the Dioscuri twins.

Minyades—three princesses of Orchomenus, who scorned the worship of Dionysus. They were consequently driven mad, and dismembered one of their sons, before being transformed into owls and bats.

Otrera—a bride of the war-god Ares and the mother of the Amazon nation.

Pasiphae—a queen of Crete, the wife of King Minos. She fell in love with a bull, and by ingenious and imaginative use of a wooden cow, had sex with it and gave birth to the Minotaur.

Penthesilea—an Amazon queen, who led her troops to the Trojan War, only to be slain by Achilles.

Psyche—a princess loved by Eros. He abandoned her when she tried to discover his true identity, but they were reconciled after performing hard labours for Aphrodite.

Tyro—a Thessalian princess who was seduced by Poseidon in the guise of the river Enipeus. She bore him the sons Neleus and Pelias.

While this short catalogue reveals some good in the women here (wifely devotion and the like), what we are left with are women whose characteristics feature horror, turpitude, ugliness, terror, death, and destruction. There is no suggestion, of course, that the men who these male writers might describe are all innocent of such traits, but it is significant that, like Pandora before them, they seem to share a monopoly on all the bad things in life.

2

Epic, tragic, and comedic women

There is, in fact, no literature, no art of any country, in which women are more prominent, more imortant, more carefully studied and with more interest, than in the tragedy, sculpture and painting of fifth century Athens.[1]

Greek mythology, of course, elides neatly in to Greek epic poetry, tragedy, and comedy; the one sustains the others. Seltman makes the point that grown-up Greek men created epic heroines, and a host of tragic women, to mirror what they considered to be the women they consorted with in everyday life, and as a vehicle for their attitudes to women in general.[2] Gomme is absolutely correct in his statement, quoted above, about the prominence of women in Greek tragedy; however, we must also take heed of Cartledge's caveat, as paraphrased by Syropoulos:

No matter how 'aggressively female' appears the speech of a female character of Athenian tragedy, we must not forget that these words were composed by a male dramatist and that this female character came to life in front of an audience consisting at great parts or wholly of men. In a society where sex segregation and division is dominant, up to what extent can a man experience and re-enact convincingly the life of women, especially when the recipients of this process are also men? To put it simply, the voice of woman is male voice. At best, it is no more than an inspired male view of female voice.

However, as Syropoulos points out:

it is also a fact that dramatic convention allows theatrical women more freedom than what women enjoy in reality... it seems that female characters often have the chance to oppose counter-arguments against all that men charge them with and even blame men for their misfortunes.[3]

This is what is important; this is what tells us that there was a school of thought among some men that women after all had their advantages, that their views were worth considering, and that they deserved a voice.

It remains a fact that the preponderance of women in the public forum of the Athenian theatre is something of a paradox. Of the surviving thirty-two tragedies, only one has no female characters: Sophocles' *Philoctetes*. Tragic choruses made up of women also outnumber male choruses twenty-one to ten. If women were that secluded, marginalised, and unappreciated, would they really have been the centre of so much attention, spotlighted to this extent by tragedians, comedians and their audiences? A fascination for, and mystery surrounding women intentionally closeted away cannot explain the Greek woman's starring role on the stage, nor her elevation there by Greek men; nor can it explain how and why woman made good crowd-pleasing material, as the audiences continued to file into the theatres year on year. Clearly, there was a body of opinion amongst influential men— not just playwrights—that believed it important to showcase the whole range of universal human experience including fear, sorrow, and rejection, and to do that, they needed to cast women, give them a platform, and lend them a powerful voice.

Moreover, some of the most dramatic and tragic roles are triggered by women picking up the pieces after a male character has been shown to have made a mess, selfishly or dictatorially wreaking havoc with their lives; for example, Sophocles' Antigone reacts after her uncle, Creon, refuses to bury her brother, Polynices. In Aeschylus' *Oresteia*, Clytemnestra takes over in Argos because her husband (Agamemnon) has been absent fighting at Troy for long ten years and has been unfaithful to her; Medea takes it badly when her husband Jason duplicitously deserts her for a new, politically advantageous marriage.

In Homer's *Odyssey*, ever-patient Penelope (wife of the peripatetic, philandering Odysseus) represented the ideal wife and woman. Circe, Calypso, and Charybdis, on the other hand, were anathema to Greek men—exhibiting everything a woman should not exhibit; they were seductive, sexy, witchy, and dangerous. Likewise Clytemnestra, Electra, Antigone, Ismene, Deianeira, Iocasta, Medea, Alcestis, Phaedra, Iphigenia, Creusa, Hecabe, Andromache, and Helen were all types of 'living Athenian women', good, bad and worse than bad. The way that they are drawn and the parts they play, tell us unequivocally that misogyny, male insecurity, and paranoia were very much alive and well on the storyboards and stages of the Greek theatres. The important thing, however was that despite being played by men in the theatre, female characters were very much present in the scripts of any surviving plays, taking essential roles in Greek epic, comedy, and tragedy. Moreover, storyboards are not historical documents; they are a vehicle for a plot that is intended to enthral, intrigue, and hopefully win a dramatic contest for its author as well as the fame that accompanies such a victory. If the playwrights needed women to achieve that end, then they would need to be drawn as strong characters, displaying the whole gamut of human emotion from infanticide to incest, from human sacrifice to self-sacrifice. No one went to see a boring play with a dull cast more than once; no one listened to a humdrum epic more than once. John Sheppard wrote of *Lysistrata* that it is 'a living refutation of the doctrine that Athenian women were reduced by their secluded lives to blank stupidity'.

Penelope is not the only embodiment of the paragon of feminine virtue. The (stereo)type persisted and four hundred or so years years later, Euripides extolled the best of women in his *The True-Hearted Wife*, stating that innate 'goodness' is the key to a wife's love:

Beauty wins not love for woman from the yokemate of her life: Many a one by goodness wins it; for to each true-hearted wife, tied up in love to her husband, is Discretion's secret told. These her gifts are: though her husband be all uncomely to behold, To her heart and eyes shall he be handsome, so her wit be sound; ('Tis not eyes that judge the man; within is true discernment found): Whensoe'er he speaks, or holds his peace, shall she his sense commend, Prompt with sweet suggestion when with speech he would rather please a friend.

Glad she is, if anything untoward happens, to show she feels his care: Joy and sorrow of the husband the loyal wife will share: Yes, if you are ill, in spirit will your wife be ill with you. Bear half of all your burdens ' naught unsweet accounteth she: For with those we love our duty bids us taste the cup of bliss Not alone, the cup of sorrow also—what is love if this is not?

The onus, though, is largely on the woman to make the marriage work, by ever pleasing her husband. There is little suggestion that the man has any responsibility in the relationship; if things fail to work out, then the implication is that the woman is wholly to blame. Penelope, perfect as she was, was of course trapped in a one-sided marriage: while Odysseus was gadding about for ten years, trying to reach home via the beds of Circe and Calypso, she was working the wool, running the house, raising Telemachus, and discouraging a stream of obnoxious suitors with rival claims to her bed and body.[4]

The gods started the Trojan War. The favoured date for the legendary fall of Troy at the hands of the Mycenaean Greek armies is 1183 BCE, under the command of Agamemnon, and with the tragic deployment of the duplicitous Trojan horse. This calamity for the Trojans was ten years after the start of the war on Troy; excavations have revealed that it was full of bins and pits dug for the emergency storage of grain and other staples, dragged in by country folk seeking refuge and making preparations for a long siege. The numerous shanties discovered were the other defining characteristic, and just as indicative of a city preparing to sit out a protracted blockade.

It all began when Athena, Hera, and Aphrodite squabbled, after Eris, the goddess of all things disputatious and discordant, mischievously gave them a golden apple, the Apple of Discord, inscribed 'for the fairest'. Eris had not been allowed to go to the wedding of Peleus and Thetis, and was somewhat insulted as a result. Zeus sent the three quarrelling goddesses to the Trojan, Paris, for judgement; Paris was working humbly as a shepherd, in a bid to thwart a prophecy that would see him bring about the end of Troy. After bathing in the spring of Ida, the three goddesses appeared before him naked, either in the hope that the sight of them with no clothes on would help them win, or because this was what Paris wanted. Paris, though, could not decide between them, so the goddesses resorted to yet more bribery: Athena offered Paris wisdom, skill in battle, and the ability to compete with the greatest warriors; Hera offered him political power and control over all of Asia; and Aphrodite offered him the love of the most beautiful woman in the world, Helen of Sparta. We have no way of knowing how long he deliberated on this, but Paris gave the fateful apple to Aphrodite, and eventually returned to Troy with Helen. This caused the Trojan War.

Agamemnon, king of Mycenae and the brother of Helen's husband Menelaus, led an expedition of Achaean (Greek) troops to Troy and besieged the city for ten years, to avenge Paris' impudence. Heroes fell, including Greek Achilles and Ajax, and the Trojans Hector and Paris, before Troy itself fell. The Greeks massacred the Trojans, sparing a few women and children who were enslaved, but made the mistake of hubristically desecrating the Trojans temples, incurring the wrath of the gods. As a result of their iconoclasm, few of the Greeks ever reached home.

The siege of Troy is, of course, described in Homer's epic *Iliad*, with aspects appearing in the fragmentary *Epic Cycle*, in Greek and Roman tragedy, and in the work of Virgil and Ovid. In the *Odyssey*, we learn all about Odysseus' long, tortuous, and circuitous journey home to Ithaca; the equally eventful journey made by Trojan Aeneas to Italy, to found the city and empire that was Rome, and establish the Roman race, is narrated in Virgil's *Aeneid*. The Trojan horse and Aeneas' flight from the burning ruin of Troy is described in vivid detail in Book II.

Helen is an ambivalent figure, thanks to the contradictory sources. She had previously run away with strange men, in her elopement with Theseus when just twelve years old. The Oath of Tyndareus acted as insurance indemnifying against further indiscretions; it was required to be sworn by all suitors to provide military assistance in case of her abduction. Whether she was abducted by Paris, or seduced by him, remains unclear. Homer is sympathetic to Helen, portraying her as sad, and regretting her precipitate actions. What has never been in doubt, though, is her manifest beauty, so well described in Christopher Marlowe's lines in his tragedy *Doctor Faustus* (scene XIII, lines 88–89): 'Was this the face that launch'd a thousand ships/And burnt the topless towers of Ilium?'

As a result of her renowned beauty, Helen was nothing less than a catalyst for the war, but Homer's *Iliad* and *Odyssey* feature a number of other prominent mortal women. The pathos in Andromache's lament as she prepares to part with her husband Hector is palpable in Pope's translation, and clearly delineates the family values she holds so dear:

> Yet while my Hector still survives, I see my father, mother, brethren, all, in thee. Alas! my parents, brothers, kindred, all, once more will perish if my Hector falls. Your wife, your child, in thy danger share; Oh prove a husband's and a father's care! (Scene II, lines 25-30)

If Helen is the *casus belli* of the Trojan War—responsible for dragging all those men from their homes for ten dangerous years—then Penelope is one of the many female victims of the war, all either waiting patiently like her or widowed; she is destined to wait patiently at home, besieged herself by unsuitable suitors and working her wifely wool, while Odysseus enjoyed ten years of tourism with some of the less human epic females. These were usually nymphs with one thing in common: they were capable of inflicting real consternation, harm, and damage to any man they met, be it through sorcery, lust, or destruction. The nymph Charybdis was now a whirlpool, sucking in water and spewing it back out, wrecking any passing ship. The nymph Scylla, exulting in her six heads and eighteen rows of teeth, swallowed six of Odysseus' crew, while the singing Sirens seduced susceptible sailors onto their razor sharp rocks. Circe was a witchy kind of woman; she drugged Odysseus' men, turning them into swine, but not before Hermes had prescribed Odysseus an antidote to avoid similar emasculation; sex with Circe was, it would seem, the only way out for the homebound hero. Further long-term tarrying was caused by the nymph Calypso who detained Odysseus on her island for seven long years in the hope of eventually hooking him as husband; it took the intervention of the gods to free Odysseus from his long detention. Petrifying Medusa is another female monstrosity. Some Homeric women were dangerous, destructive, and duplicitous, in that they diverted men from their proper duty and responsibilities; they were licentious and, unlike Penelope, Andromache, and Nausicaa, they were anti-family.

There is, however, a rare expression of love from a male Homeric hero that comes when Achilles opens his heart, and speaks of how much he loves Briseis in Book 9 of the *Iliad*; he talks about her as if she were his wife. His love was reciprocated, even though it originated at the wrong end of a spear. To Achilles, to love your woman was the right and decent thing to do. Attitudes, of course, were somewhat different among the vocal elite in civilised Athens a few centuries later. Being at the centre of a damaging spat between Achilles and Agamemnon, Briseis is clearly central to the very plot of the *Iliad*, and her destiny has massive implications for the Greek army in the Trojan War. She reputedly had long golden hair, blue eyes, and fair skin; she was very beautiful and clever. Achilles took her as war booty, and killed her father, mother, three brothers, and husband.

Briseis had lost her country, her family, and her freedom (like Andromache); she was comforted, though, by Patroclus, who promised to have Achilles marry her and to throw a wedding feast for them when they returned to Phthia after the war; marriage was the proper thing to do. Things went badly wrong, when Apollo forced Agamemnon to give up his concubine, Chryseis, and he selfishly and tactlessly demanded Briseis as compensation. Achilles compares his relationship with Briseis with that between Menelaus and Helen, the breaching of which sparked the major war in which they were all now engaged. If that could start a war then what how else should Achilles react to Agamemnon for taking Briseis from him? In the event, Agamemnon swore that he never laid a hand on Briseis.[5]

The love between Achilles and Briseis brings us closer to Penelope and her family values. Penelope was a paragon of patience, tolerance, and what the Romans called *pudicitia*—sexual propriety. She championed family values, the proper raising of children, and fidelity towards her husband—all in a dignified and unobtrusive manner, everything a Greek man sought in a Greek woman. She is grief-stricken by Odysseus' long absence during the Trojan War, and his subsequent long and winding journey home; she cries herself to sleep at night.[6] Compliant and dignified, Penelope was in some ways the forerunner of those three Roman paragons of feminine virtue: Lucretia, Verginia, and Cornelia who lived for, and in two cases, died for, their virtue. Beseiged by self-interested suitors, and with her marriage vulnerable, Penelope holds out and remains faithful to her husband and to their family. When her son, Telemachus, tells her to get on with the wool working and leave the real work of negotiating to him as head of the house, Penelope recedes with docility:

No, go to your room, and busy yourself with your own work, the loom and the distaff, and tell your maids to get on with their tasks; the men will do the talking, for all, but most of all for me; since I am the boss in this house. Penelope thought this awesome and wonderful; she went back to her room having taken to heart the wise words of her son.[7]

Women, and slaves, traditionally fetched water from the well, baked bread, and did the spinning and weaving, all of which are abundantly portrayed on Greek vases and on terracotta statuettes. So that Odysseus will feel himself in familiar surroundings when he reaches Ithaca, the goddess Pallas Athena reveals herself, in the guise of a young girl carrying a water pitcher, when she comes down to offer him advice. As if there was any doubt about the domestic role played by Homeric women, Nausicaa, who does have the freedom to come and go wherever she wants, had already described, not without humour, the domestic scenario Odysseus would encounter:

> But when you get to the house and courtyard, pass quickly through the great hall till you reach my mother, who sits at the hearth by the light of the fire, spinning the purple yarn, a wonder to see, leaning against a pillar; her maids sit behind her... my father sits on his throne and drinks his wine, like a god. Ignore him, and clasp your hands around my mother's knees.[8]

The women are busy working the wool, but significantly, it is astute Queen Arete, not bibulous King Alcinous, who holds the key to Odysseus' homecoming and rehabilitation. Domesticity reigns too in the Nestor household; his queen made the royal bed, and his daughter bathed his guests. Nausicaa, Penelope, Helen, Andromache, Briseis, Chryseis, Queen Arete and Queen Eurydice are all free to come and go as they please; they are certainly not secluded or segregated from their men. Their domestic roles are clearly delineated but they are active and integral to their respective households.

When Odysseus finally gets home, he wastes no time in getting Penelope into bed. Here, the pillow talk reveals her constancy and fidelity, in stark contrast to his confessed serial adultery, which is accepted and tolerated, expected even, by Penelope, the model wife. Interestingly, the dalliance wih Nausicaa is never mentioned. The double standard is hardly surprising coming from a man who advises 'never be too kind to your wife or tell her all of your plans, however well you know them; tell her only a bit and conceal the rest'—duplicitous and dishonest by our standards, and insensitive to the doubt relating to paternity that such permissiveness might engender. Telemachus asserts that 'my mother says that I am the son of Odysseus, but I don't know. No one can know his own seed by himself'. The suggestion is that such doubts were commonplace, and not of the consequence they can be today. In the *Iliad*, Agamemnon too advises secrecy: 'bring your ships back to your homeland in secret and not openly: you can never trust a woman'. He was right to be cautious.

Illegitimacy and mixed birth between woman and god were also of little consequence in Homer's world, as the catalogue of Achilles' army in the *Iliad* reveals;

Menesthius was the love child of the river god Spercheus and Polydora, daughter of Peleus. Eudorus was born of the union of Hermes and Polymele, unmarried daughter of Phylas; Polymele was a beautiful dancer.

If Penelope was the role model for the good and virtuous Greek wife, then Clytemnestra was the polar opposite. Agamemnon bitterly and graphically describes to Odysseus during the necromancy how his welcome home was to be butchered:

> Aegisthus and my wicked wife were the death of me between them. He asked me to his house, feasted me, and then butchered me most miserably as though I were a fat beast in a slaughter house, while all around me my comrades were slain like sheep or pigs for the wedding breakfast, or picnic, or gorgeous banquet of some great nobleman. You must have seen numbers of men killed either in a general engagement, or in single combat, but you never saw anything so truly pitiable as the way in which we fell in that cloister, with the mixing-bowl and the loaded tables lying all about, and the ground reeking with our blood. I heard Priam's daughter Cassandra scream as Clytemnestra slew her close beside me. I lay dying upon the earth with the sword in my body, and raised my hands to kill the slag of a murderess, but she slipped away from me; she would not even close my lips nor my eyes when I was dying, for there is nothing in this world so cruel and so sluttish as a woman when she has fallen into such guilt as hers was. Fancy murdering her own husband! I thought I was going to be welcomed home by my children and my servants, but her abominable crime has brought disgrace on herself and all women who shall come after—even on the good ones. (Homer, *Odyssey* 11, 386ff)

Indeed, as far as Agamemnon is concerned, Clytemnestra has written the script for the male reception of women forever. All women are blemished from now on; the eternal hostility, fear, and suspicion begin here. In fact, Agamemnon is so bitter that he ironically warns Odysseus to beware Penelope when he arrives home, fearing a similar bloody reception from her. From a distance, we can see with the example of Penelope that all women were not bad; however, Agamemnon sees it very differently, and bad reputations stick.

It could be argued that there were some mitigating circumstances for Clytemnestra's odious behaviour, such as a life lived in a dysfunctional family torn apart with traumatic slaughter, fear and loathing. Her father, king Tyndareus of Sparta, betrothed her to Tantalus as a young girl; Tantalus was the son of Thyestes and king of Mycenae. Clytemnestra, therefore, on marriage, became queen; she gave Tantalus a son. Agamemnon murdered Tantalus because he was the son of Thyestes, who had violated his mother. He also killed the son, and acquired Clytemnestra, the property of the man he had slain. Clytemnestra was queen of Mycenae, so Agamemnon became king. The couple had four children: Chrysothemis, Iphigenia, Electra and Orestes. Agamemnon sacrificed Iphigenia to Artemis, in order to fight at Troy. During the war, Clytemnestra was seduced by Aegisthus to reject Agamemnon, ending in the murder of Agamemnon and Cassandra, his consort, as described above. Clytemnestra was easily persuaded because she was a bereft widow and mother looking for revenge, destroyed by the loss of first husband and son, as revealed in Euripides' *Iphigenia in Aulis*: 'I never loved you! Tantalus you slew, my first dear husband; and my little son. You tore him from my breast.' [lines 1146-51] Aegisthus and Clytemnestra lived together as king and queen of Mycenae until Orestes took vengeance on them and killed them both.

Cassandra was wronged by men and by gods, both of whom regarded her as something of a liability. She was a daughter of Priam and Hecabe, and was beautiful, if a little mad (on account of her gift of prophecy). When she was a girl, she was left with her brother, Helenus, in the temple of Thymbraean Apollo overnight; the next morning, the children were found entwined with serpents, which flicked their tongues into the children's ears, thus enabling Cassandra and Helenus to divine the future. Cassandra repeated this some years later, only to be assaulted by Apollo. She resisted, and so was punished for her chaste behaviour, by having her prophecies always disbelieved, even though they were true.

When the Trojan War began, Cassandra predicted the disasters lying in store for the Trojans. Nobody believed her, of course; however, Priam, deciding she was bad for morale, had locked her away, incarcerated like a lunatic. The highpoint came when she declared that there were men in the wooden horse, dismissed as more ravings of a madwoman. When Troy fell, she took sanctuary in the temple of Athena, where she embraced the statue of the goddess as a suppliant. Ajax found her there and dragged her from the temple, after having raped her in the sanctuary. This hubristic act on consecrated ground violated not only Cassandra, but also the powerful and inviolable rules of Greek religion; Cassandra was later awarded to Agamemnon who took her with him back to Mycenae; she became pregnant and bore twins—Teledamus and Pelops.

Ajax, it must be said, did not get away with his sacrilege, iconoclasm, and arrogance. He himself was drowned by Poseidon for more hubris. His native Locrians were forced to send two maidens to Troy every year for a thousand years, to serve as slaves in Athena's temple.

Being damned by the gods, raped by a war hero in a sacred temple, and considered crazy by her own father and by everyone else cannot have done much good for any issues Cassandra had with her mental health. The frustration of being damned to being disbelieved when you know you are right must have been devastating, particularly when the safety of your country and its citizens were at stake, and their terrible fate could have been avoided. As Homer well knew, the truth is often unpopular and sometimes hurts; it was up to subsequent generations to decide whether to place confidence in intelligent, slightly eccentric women like her, or dismiss them as mad women.

Circe features more prominently later, in the chapter on witches. Calypso, like Circe, detains Odysseus, and maintains their intimacy with her hypnotic singing—a kind of *eros* spell to seduce Odysseus, grieving for Penelope back home. Nevertheless, according to Homer, it takes Odysseus seven years to tear himself away from Calypso and Ogygia, although Pseudo-Apollodorus says five years, and Hyginus a more charitable one year. Zeus and Hermes had to intervene to get him on his way again, and Calypso provisions him for his journey—she was looking for a wedding, with the promise to Odysseus of immortality. In the Roman era, Lucian extends and embellishes the story, claiming that Odysseus wrote to Calypso after his death, from the island of the Blessed, saying how sorry he was to have left, and that he would come back one day.[9] Hyginus is less optimistic; he has her commit suicide, pining for Odysseus' love.[10]

Nausicaa, whom we have already met, is the daughter of King Alcinous and Queen Arete of Phaeacia. Ominously for Odysseus, her name means 'burner of ships' in Greek. However, he need not have worried, since it is Alcinous who provides him with ships, to enable him to continue his journey home to Ithaca.

Nausicaa and Odysseus meet in Book Six of the *Odyssey*, when Odysseus is shipwrecked on the coast of Scheria, or Phaeacia in some translations. Nausicaa, prompted by a dream inspired by Athena, and her servants go down to the beach, to wash clothes and play ball. Odysseus is woken by their games, and emerges from the forest almost naked, scaring the servants away; Nausicaa would probably have fled too, were she not emboldened by Athena. Odysseus implores Nausicaa to help him; she gives Odysseus sustinence and clothes, and takes him to the edge of the town. Not wanting to be seen with him on account of the scandalous rumours it would cause, she goes ahead into town, after telling Odysseus to go straight to Alcinous' palace and see her mother, Arete, who was known to be even wiser than Alcinous. Odysseus does as advised, and wins Arete over; he is received as a guest by Alcinous. Interestingly, it is the woman who is the wiser of the royal couple.

Odysseus then recounts his adventures so far to Alcinous and his court, telling a tale which covers most of the *Odyssey*. Alcinous then provides Odysseus with the ships he needs to take him home to Ithaca.

It goes without saying that Nausicaa is young and attractive; Odysseus likens her to Artemis. She later married Telemachus, son of Odysseus, and had a son named Perseptolis. The relationship between Nausicaa and Odysseus, such as it was, may be the earliest example of unrequited love we have in literature. There is no romance between the two, even though she confides in a friend that she would love her husband to be just like him, and Alcinous tells Odysseus that he would let Odysseus marry her. Nausicaa says to him 'Never forget me, for I gave you life,' referring to the help she has given him in starting a new life, when he reaches home; Odysseus grants that she has saved his life, and that he will never forget her.[11] Interestingly, as already noted, Odysseus never tells Penelope about Nausicaa, even though he does admit to affairs with Circe and Calypso— perhaps because, with Nausicaa, it was never physical. On a more mundane level, we have Nausicaa to thank for all games involving a ball, if the second-century BCE grammarian Agallis is to be believed—he attributed the invention of ball games to Nausicaä, because she was the first person to be described as playing with a ball.

Arete is not the only woman in the family to be ascribed great intelligence. In his 1892 lecture, *The Humour of Homer*, Samuel Butler decides that Nausicaa herself was the real author of the *Odyssey*, since the laundry scene is more realistic and plausible than most other scenes in the epic; his theory that the *Odyssey* was written by a woman is developed in his 1897 book, *The Authoress of the Odyssey*. Robert Graves' 1955 novel *Homer's Daughter*, which draws on experiences and influences from her own life, also gives Nausicaa as the author of the *Odyssey*.

Andromache is one of mythology's great tragic heroines. Her name, ironically, means 'man fighter', 'fighter of men' (like the famous Amazon warrior called Andromache), 'man's battle' or 'manly virtue'—an early example of outstanding women being defemininised with the attribution of masculine qualities. Her misfortunes began when Thebes, her home city, was sacked by Achilles, and her father and seven brothers died in the carnage. Her mother then succumbed to an illness, and she became one of the many spoils of war after the destruction of Troy; she was later rescued by Hector, who wooed her with opulent wedding-gifts. Hector was doing the right thing by Greek standards, providing his intended with material support and security, in contrast to Paris in his abduction of Helen. This becomes more tragic, as Andromache's life is torn apart when Achilles kills Hector, leaving her bereft, rootless, and alone in the world—a displaced person reduced to the margins of society, and the epitome of the fate that awaits conquered women in ancient warfare; Hector bewails the fact that Andromache will be forced into slavery—weaving at another's command and fetching the water:

> Some one will say: 'There goes the wife of Hector, of all the horse-taming Trojans pre-eminent in war, in the days when men fought over Troy.' And to you will come fresh grief, without a man like me to ward off the day of bondage. But let me die, and let the heap of earth cover me before I hear you cry out loud as they haul you off into captivity.[12]

By contrast, domestic harmony prevails, as Hector describes a typical scenario with women weaving and men warring.[13]

> [He] laid his child in his dear wife's arms, and she took him to her fragrant bosom, smiling through her tears; and her husband was touched with pity at the sight of her, and he caressed her with his hand, and said: 'My dear wife, do not grieve too much … go home and busy yourself with your own tasks, the loom and the distaff, and tell your maids to get on with their work: war is for men.

Significantly and unusually, this conversation takes place on the exposed and dangerous war setting of the ramparts of Troy. Even more unconventional and surprising to the audience is the gender role-reversal implicit when Andromache gives Hector military advice.[14] Desperate remedies for desperate situations, as women too had a civic responsibility to provide civil defence when their homeland, their *oikoi*, were threatened. Moreover, by detaining Hector with a lesson in military strategy, she keeps her husband in relative safety, away from the much more dangerous open fighting taking place down below:

> Come on, take pity, and stay here on the wall, in case you orphan your child and make your wife a widow. Post your army by that wild fig-tree, where the wall is most vulnerable to a scaled assault, and the city is exposed. Three times already…[the Greeks] have tried to get in there.

Andromache, like Penelope, is the perfect wife. She weaves a cloak for Hector in the seclusion and safety of the interior rooms of the house, as instructed by him (above); she runs a bath for him, for when he returns from battle.[15] Andromache's role as a mother, a fundamental element of her position in marriage, is emphasized within this same conversation. We have seen that their infant son, Astyanax, is also present at the ramparts as a maid tends to him. Hector takes his son from the maid, yet returns him to his wife, a small action that provides great insight into the importance Homer placed on Andromache's duties as mother.[16] A vivid bonding moment between mother and father occurs in this scene, when Hector's helmet scares Astyanax, providing a moment of light relief in the story. After Hector's death in *Iliad* 22, Andromache's foremost concern is Astyanax's fate as a mistreated orphan.[17] Andromache is never named in *Iliad* 22, referred to only as the wife of Hector (*alokhos*), in harmony with the Greek practice of maintaining the anonymity of respectable Greek women, underlining the importance of her status as Hector's wife, and of the marriage state itself.

Things got worse before they got better for Andromache; Astyanax was slain by Neoptolemus, who then took Andromache as a concubine, and Hector's brother, Helenus, as a slave. When Neoptolemus died, Andromache married Helenus, becoming queen of Epirus.

The story of the good wife Andromache, and the pathos she aroused, was very popular in antiquity and, like Penelope's plight, highlighted the best in women and wives, juxtaposed as it was against the iniquitous Helens and Clytemnestras of the world. She makes numerous appearances in Homer's *Iliad*.[18] She also appears in Sappho's Fragment 44: 'Hector and his men are bringing a dancing girl from holy Thebes and from onflowing Plakia—delicate Andromache on ships over the salt sea.'[19] There are also references in Apollodorus' *Bibliotheca* 3,12,6, and *Epitome* 5, 23; 6 12; Euripides' *Andromache* of course, and *The Trojan Women*; Roman Virgil's *Aeneid* 3, 294–355; Ovid's *Ars Amatoria* 3, 777–778 and, in 54 CE, in Seneca's *The Trojan Women*.

In Euripides' eponymous play, Andromache has to admit that her virtue and credentials as a good wife have done her no good at all; in fact, they have helped to make her a trophy prisoner for Achilles' son, Neoptolemus, and have been her ruin.[20] Andromache was later celebrated by French tragedian Jean Racine (1639–1699), in his *Andromaque*, in Shakespeare's *Troilus and Cressida*, and in Baudelaire's poem, *Le Cygne*, in *Les Fleurs du Mal* in 1857.

Odysseus' philandering—and attitudes towards it—permeated real ancient Greek life, where men could stray, but women had to remain faithful not just to their husbands, but even to the husband's memory, as Penelope was obliged to do for twenty long years. Diogenes Laërtius tells us of an Athenian law that permits men to marry a woman and have children by another.[21] Callias, Socrates, and Euripides each had two wives.

Women loom large in Greek tragedy, for good or ill. Speaking generally, Sophocles (reminiscent of Thucydides)in the *Ajax* (293), asserts thas 'silence is a woman's glory', and then goes on, with Aeschylus and Euripides, to endow them with some of the greatest parts in the history of western drama.

Euripides' Alcestis is, like Penelope, a good wife; she is strong-minded, dutiful, and religious. She loves and looks after her children, and honours her gods; her marriage bed is sacred and she is prepared to die for her man.[22] To Phaedra in the *Hippolytus*, preserving her reputation is paramount, while her love for the eponymous hero ends in her suicide: 'I cannot bear that I be found a traitor to my husband and children'.[23] Clytemnestra was the antithesis of Alcestis and Phaedra—unconventional, frightening, rather like a man according to the Chorus, a *domaton cyna*, a house-bitch, shameless and brazen. Clytemnestra sees herself as a redoubtable enemy, fiercely loyal and implacable, but as the Chorus says, she is a masculine bitch of a woman.[24] If Clytemnestra is bad, then Medea is worse still, and must rank as one of literature's most repugnant and reprehensible mothers. She unequivocally declares her hatred for her children early on in the play that bears her name: 'You accursed sons of a mother who know nothing but hate, damn you, your father and your whole house'.[25] Her rejection by Jason has sown an unnatural hatred in her heart, which results ultimately in the infanticide of her children.

Interestingly, Euripides shows us a woman's perspective on life in the same play:

> What they say is that we women have a quiet time, staying at home, while they are off fighting in war. They couldn't be more wrong. I would rather stand three times in a battle line than give birth to one child.[26]

This comes at the end of a speech that perfectly encapsulates all that is suffocating and tedious for a woman in a loveless marriage to a hypocritical, insensitive husband:

> Of all things that are living and can form a judgment
> We women are the most unfortunate creatures.
> Firstly, with an excess of wealth [dowry] it is required
> For us to buy a husband and take one for our bodies
> A master; for not to take one is even worse.
> And now the question is serious whether we take
> A good one or bad one; for there is no easy escape
> For a woman, nor can she say no to her marriage.
> She arrives among new ways of behaving and manners,
> And needs prophetic power, unless she has learned at home,
> How best to manage him who shares the bed with her.
> And if this works out well and carefully,
> And the husband lives with us and lightly bears his yoke,
> Then life is enviable. If not, I'd rather die.
> A man, when he's tired of the company in his home,
> Goes out of the house and puts an end to his boredom
> And turns to a friend or companion of his own age.
> But we are forced to keep our eyes on one alone.

Euripides, Medea 218-248

Euripides may have been a lone voice; in articulating such sentiments, he at least seems to understand and sympathise with the drudgery and marital iniquity tolerated by women—whether he actually agreed with them, of course, is a different matter. Medea's perceptive analysis of the imbalance between man and woman must be seen in the context of the play, and a contributory factor to later tragic developments. Fragment 499 from *Melannipe Captive* has a more positive, but equally contentious, message: 'Men's criticism of women is worthless twanging of bowstring and evil talk. Women are better than men, as I will show ... women run households ... without a woman no home is clean or prosperous.'

Euripides also appreciates that women are capable of decisive dynamic action when, in the *Ion*, the old slave urges Creusa to 'do something womanly; take to the sword; poison him!'[27] Most of his contemporaries would have described 'taking the sword' not as a womanly action, but instead, masculine in its nature.

This fragment by Aristophon in Callonides quoted in *The Deipnosophistae* of Athenaeus of Naucratis Book XIII: Concerning Women encapsulates what was probably closer to the prevailing, clichéd view:

> O Zeus why do we need to talk about the evil of women in detail? It would be enough just to say 'woman'. I wish a terrible death on the second man ever who took a wife. I don't blame the first man: he had no idea of the evil involved. The second man knew exactly what evil he was taking on.

Sophocles has the last word, however, in a fragment from his lost *Tereus*, in which Procne echoes Euripides by deprecatingly bewailing the miserable lot of women: 'But now I am nothing on my own. But I have often regarded the nature of women in this way, seeing that we amount to nothing.' Procne concedes that, as children living with their father, girls 'live the happiest life.' But then they are 'pushed out and sold, away from our paternal gods and from our parents, some to foreign husbands, some to barbarians, some to joyless homes, and some to homes that are hostile.' Indeed, pushed into unhappy marriages: 'And all this: once the first night has yoked us to our husbands we are forced to praise and say that all is well.'[28]

The variation from the normal societal values and attitudes in these few examples is refreshing. Despite it all, though, we must remember that the words put into the mouths of Antigone, Clytemnestra, Medea, and all the others were put there by a male playwright, and the parts of these female protagonists were all played by men masquerading as women. The sentiments expressed were, to a large extent, due to the exigencies of the plot and the genre, but at the same time, do suggest a latent sympathy towards a woman's lot, at least by the educated elite.

Antigone's tragedy (known principally to us through Sophocles' *Antigone*) lies in her struggle to secure funeral rites for her brother Polynices—one of the two brothers she lost in an internecine feud, when Eteocles reneged on his agreement to share rule with Polynices. While Eteocles expelled his brother, Polynices recruited an army, and attacked the city of Thebes in a conflict celebrated by Aeschylus in the Seven Against

Thebes. Both brothers died in the ensuing battle. King Creon acceded to the throne, and prohibited Polynices to be buried or mourned, on pain of death by stoning. Antigone defied the order and was caught. In Sophocles' tragedies *Oedipus at Colonus* and *Antigone*, this occurs after the banishment and death of Oedipus.

She is brought before Creon, bravely admitting that she was aware of Creon's law, but chose to break it, resting her case on the precedence of divine law over secular law. However, it all goes wrong for Antigone, as the play careers towards its tragic conclusion. Creon locks Antigone in a tomb, then relents, only to find it is too late; he finds that his son Hæmon, who was engaged to Antigone, has stabbed himself in despair, on seeing that Antigone had hanged herself in the tomb. Queen Eurydice, Creon's wife, also kills herself in reaction to her son's suicide. Eurydice was compelled to weave an allusion to the power of the Fates throughout the entire tragedy.

Euripides also wrote an *Antigone*, now largely lost, except for some references in later writings and in his *Phoenissae*. A famous painting by Philostratus depicts Antigone placing the body of Polynices on the funeral pyre; this is also featured on a sarcophagus in the Villa Doria Pamphili in Rome.[29] Antigone also features in numerous other works, including *Antigone*, a play by Jean Cocteau (1889–1963); *Antigone*, an opera by Carl Orff (1895–1982) and *Antigone*, another play, by Jean Anouilh (1910–1987).

Iphigenia demonstrates the utter dispensibility of women in the headlong pursuit of conflict and conquest. Iphigenia was the daughter of Agamemnon and Clytemnestra. While the Greek army was preparing to set sail for Troy, Agamemnon annoyed Artemis by killing a sacred deer. Artemis then resolved to make life difficult for Agamemnon by calming all winds, thus stalling the entire Greek fleet. The only way out, according to the seer Calchas, was to appease the goddess, by sacrificing Iphigenia to her. Although initially reluctant, Agamemnon was forced to comply. He lied to his daughter and Clytemnestra, saying that Iphigenia was to marry Achilles before leaving for Troy. Mother and daughter duly went to the port of Aulis, where they discovered the horrible truth. Achilles was unaware that his name was being used in such a deception, and tried to prevent the sacrifice, but Iphigenia heroically and bravely sacrificed herself anyway, for the sake of Greece.

Our main source is Euripides' *Iphigenia in Aulis*, in which Iphigenia is surreptitiously replaced with a deer by the gods and escapes to Tauris (in modern Crimea), where she is priestess in charge of sacrificing errant Athenians to Artemis, one of which is her brother, Orestes, whom Iphigenia had assumed was dead. The story of how they eventually recognise each other and escape Tauris is told in Euripides' *Iphigenia in Tauris*. There are many other versions of what happened to Iphigenia in Aulis; according to Hyginus' *Fabulae*, Iphigenia was not sacrificed. Some sources, like Euripides above, claim that Iphigenia was taken by Artemis to Tauris just before the sacrifice, and that the goddess substituted a deer or a goat (Pan in disguise) in her place.[30] The *Hesiodic Catalogue of Women* called her Iphimede (Ἰφιμέδη)—as confirmed by Pausanias— and told that Artemis transformed her into the goddess Hecate.[31] The grammarian Antoninus Liberalis said that Iphigenia went to the island of Leuke, where she married the immortalized Achilles under the name of Orsilochia.

Just as it was incumbent upon a tragedian to leave his audience with a distinct feeling of catharsis as they leave the theatre, it was equally important for a comic playwright to make his audience laugh. If Greek comedy—Old, Middle, and New—reflected aspects of Greek (especially Athenian) life, then the very fact that Aristophanes wrote three surviving plays in which women feature prominently—*Ecclesiazusae, Lysistrata* and *Thesmophoriazusae,* plus the lost *Lemnians, Phoenician Women* and *Women in Tents* (Σκηνάς Καταλαμβάνουσαι *Skenas Katalambanousai*)—is significant. As soon as elite Greeks stop writing exclusively about elite men and women, and focus on the man and woman in the agora, then women obviously become more prominent.

Aristophanes, Menander, and their contemporaries produced a host of comedies in which women are integral to plot. However, just as with the tragedians, the comedians were governed by the exigencies of their genre. The material first and foremost had to be funny; everything else was subordinate to that, including reality and verisimilitude. The plot and script had to amuse the men in the audience. This explains to a large extent the fantastic situations presented in some of Aristophanes' plots; *Ecclesiazusae, Women in the Assembly,* is a prime example—he has women assume political control in Athens, in a bid to rescue the city from the shambles brought about by the menfolk. The notion is absurd; *Lysistrata,* in which women withdraw their sexual favours, is equally surreal.

At first sight, it might seem like Aristophanes is making an attempt to champion the cause of women, with the suggestion that women can do a better job at running Athens than the men dictating government policy on war. Not so, as Aristophanes lets social equality, woman power and female emancipation run riot in this female Utopia, especially when it extends to matters sexual: in the *Ecclesiazusae,* we learn that before a man or woman can have intercourse with a beautiful woman or a handsome man, they each have to sleep with an old man or woman whom beauty has passed by:

> The women have decreed that if a young man desires a young girl, he can only lay her after having satisfied an old woman; and if he refuses and goes to seek the maiden, the old women are authorized to grab him and drag him in.[32]

Then, the same old clichés and stereotypes eventually come through, to the delight, no doubt, of the largely male audience:

> Women kneel to bake their bread, tote their laundry on the head,—just like Mother always did. They always follow the recipe, Keep Demeter's yearly spree—just like Mother. Nag their husbands till they're dead, hide their lovers under the bed—just like Mother. Pad the grocery bill with snacks, take a drink or three to relax, prefer their pleasure on their backs, happy nymphomaniacs—just like Mother.[33]

Ultimately for the women, and for real world women, Aristophanes has the women fail in their attempt at political control and civic management, but not without some benefit; desperate times demanded desperate remedies, and the political elevation and empowerment of women, absurd as it may have sounded to most men in the audience, was one way of vocalising and addressing the serious straits Athens faced, and which may have given less dogmatic, conservative men pause for thought.

Aristophanes, as with any comic playwright, had to play to his audience, and do his best to make them laugh; that audience was almost totally male so, sensibly, he pandered to their sexist, male exclusive, chauvinistic tastes. This goes some way to explaining why the hackneyed views of women relating to seclusion and exclusion in Greek society are trotted out with some regularity in the surviving plays and fragments and encapsulated in the quotation above. This is what the paying audience, the men, wanted. Aristophanes remains, nevertheless, a valuable source for our knowledge of women in ancient Greek, especially Athenian, society.

We have noted at the beginning of the book how women are portrayed by Euripides and Aristophanes as self-deprecating. That is only one perspective, a negative side of the picture: here is what the Chorus, when addressing the audience in the *Thesmophoriazusae,* has to say about the good things inherent in a woman:

> Let us address ourselves to the audience to sing our praises, despite the fact that each one says lots of bad things about women. If the men are to be believed, we are a plague to them; through us come all their troubles, quarrels, disputes, sedition, griefs and wars. But if we are really such a pest, why marry us? Why forbid us to go out or show ourselves at the window? You want to keep this pest, and take a thousand cares to do it. If your wife goes out and you meet her away from the house, you fly into a fury. Ought you not rather rejoice and give thanks to the gods? for if the pest is nowhere to be seen, you will no longer find it at home. If we fall asleep at friends' houses tired from playing and sporting, each of you comes prowling round the bed to contemplate the features of this pest. If we seat ourselves at the window, each one wants to see the pest, and if we withdraw through modesty, each wants all the more to see the pest perch herself there again. It is thus clear that we are better than you, and the proof of this is easy. Let us find out which is the worse of the two sexes. We say, 'It's you,' while you swear 'it's we.'[34]

After the praise for the oratorical skills of Mnesilochus, disguised as a woman, the Chorus insinuates that women are capable of such oratory.

> where did all that come from? What does such a bold woman come from? Oh! you wretch! I should not have thought ever any one of us could have spoken in public with such satire. It's clear, however, that we must rule nothing out and, as the old proverb goes, must leave no stone unturned, lest it conceal some orator ready to sting us.[35]

Aristophanes articulates the popular male suspicious estimation of women through Euripides in the same play, with some powerful female retorts.

> I have long been pained to see us women insulted by this Euripides, this son of the green-stuff woman, who loads us with every kind of indignity. Has he not hit

us enough … Does he not style us adulterous, lecherous, bibulous, treacherous, and garrulous? Does he not repeat that we are all vice, that we are the curse of our husbands? So that, as soon as they come back from the theatre, they look at us doubtfully and go searching in every corner, fearing there may be some hidden lover. We can do none of the things we used to, so many are the false ideas which he has instilled into our husbands. If a woman weaving a garland for herself, it's because she is in love. Does she drop a vase while going or returning to the house? her husband asks her in whose honour she has broken it: 'It can only be for that Corinthian stranger.' … 'A woman is the tyrant of the old man who marries her.' Again, it is because of Euripides that we are incessantly watched, that we are shut up behind bolts and bars, and that dogs frighten off the adulterers. Once it was we who looked after the food, who fetched the flour from the storeroom, the oil and the wine; we can't do that any more. … this pestilent Euripides … we should rid ourselves of this enemy of ours by poison or by any other means, so long as he dies.[36]

Aristophanes himself pedalled the stereotype, saying that women were bibulous, unreliable, and neglected their most important wifely duties as a result—a cliché, with its associated suggestion that the drink led to permissive sexual behaviour, and a stereotype that persisted right through the Classical era and beyond.

Oh! you hot women, you tippling women, who think of nothing but wine; you are a gold mine to the drinking-shops and are our ruin; for the sake of drink, you neglect both your household and your shuttle![37]

If a woman had the temerity to ask about current affairs or political matters, she was abruptly invited to shut up, with the threat of physical violence. As shocking as it is to us today, the very presence of the notion would suggest that domestic abuse in classical Athens was quite acceptable behaviour.

Lysistrata: Before now, and for quite a long time, we kept our cool and suffered, whatever you men did, because you wouldn't let us make a sound. But you weren't exactly everything a woman could ask for. No, we knew your game and often we'd hear about a bad decision you'd made on some great matter of state. Then, hiding the pain in our hearts, we'd smirk and ask, 'How did it go in the Assembly today...?' And my husband would retort: 'What's that got to do with you? Shut up!' So I'd shut up.
Old Woman: I wouldn't have shut up!
Magistrate: If you hadn't have shut up you'd have got a thrashing.
Lysistrata: Well, that's why I did shut up—then. But later on we began to hear about even worse decisions you'd made, and then we would ask, 'Husband, how come you're handling this so ineptly?' And he'd immediately glare at me and tell me to get back to my sewing if I didn't want my head smashed in.[38]

The threat of divorce was used cynically, as a weapon to instil obedience in a woman. Marriages were not always weighted towards the man though. In *Clouds*, we hear of an elite aristocratic woman and her dull, rustic husband, reflecting on their squabbling over the naming of their baby.

> Alas! Would that the match-maker had perished miserably, he who induced me to marry your mother. For a country life used to be most agreeable to me, dirty, unshaven, reclining when I wanted, abounding in bees, and sheep, and oil-cake. Then I, a rustic, married a niece of Megacles, the son of Megacles, from the city, haughty, luxurious.[39]

Love and affection are decidedly rare, and may reflect the business-like, pragmatic nature of most marriages, in which women were to a large degree sidelined, except in their reproductive role and as providers of sexual gratification. Indeed, in *Peace*, it is 'kissing the pretty Thracian' slave girl who excites desire when the wife is out of the way in the bath; when she gets out of the bath, then she can make a meal: 'Come on wife, cook three measures of beans, adding a little wheat to them, and give us some figs.'[40] Aristophanes confirms how leaving the house had its difficulties for Athenian women, what with all those chores.

> It's hard for women, you know, To get away. There's so much to do; husbands to be patted and put in a good mood: servants to be wheedled out: children washed or soothed with lullabies or fed with mouthfuls of mush.

He also comments on the insecure jealousy of those husbands, as quoted above. In the *Ecclesiazusae*, Blepyrus is beside himself, and typically suspicious when his wife goes absent:

> What does this mean? My wife has vanished! it is nearly daybreak and she's not back! ... Ah! what a damned fool I was to take a wife at my age, and how I could beat myself up for having acted so stupidly! She's not gone out for any honest purpose, that's for sure.[41]

Indeed, the only way for a woman to get out was by stealth.[42] However, the women of *Lysistrata* have turned the tables, according to these disgruntled men:

> How upside-down and wrong-way-round a long life sees things grow. Ah, Strymodorus, who'd have thought affairs could tangle so? The women whom at home we fed, like witless fools, with fostering bread, have impiously come to this—They've stolen the Acropolis, with bolts and bars our orders flout and shut us out.[43]

No man ever visits the *gynaekonitis* in Aristophanes, be it in his own house or in another's.

We know of about 100 comic playwrights who were active between 404 and 323 BCE, with a combined output of 700 plays, including a good number of burlesques of mythology. Sadly, what precisely happened during the eighty-one year transition between Aristophanes and Menander, from Old to New comedy—Middle comedy—is largely lost to us. However, we can safely deduce from what has survived in the Old and the New that Middle comedy was quite phenomenal; it is reasonable to assume, again, given what survives from Old and New and the uptake later of the New by Titinius, Plautus, and Terence in Rome, that one of those phenomena was character development; this must have developed apace and included the stock female characters we are familiar with. Another was the drift away from fantasies, including visits to the underworld and women taking charge of the *polis*, to productions about everyday people in domestic settings, not that dissimilar from some of today's soaps.

The exploration of personal relationships, love lost and refound, children lost and found was central to plays in which slaves, heart of gold prostitutes, old women and violated virgins, mercenaries, and parasites—all liminal souls from the edge of society—were the stars. These were a far cry from the incestuous, mother and child murdering heroes and villains, and the funny, incongruous fantasies of Aristophanes. The recognisable characters now have real names like Chrysis, Chremes, and Demeas; they also speak more in a vernacular that would have been spoken in the local agora. Much of the Aristophanic bawdiness has gone, and the characters wear the same clothes as the audience. The themes explored are less focussed on the problems of Athens; they are universal—domestic and mundane—and of interest and relevance to a much wider audience than just metropolitan Athens. Menandrian comedy, where it showcased wronged daughters or long lost children, for example, had family appeal because most of the men in the theatre would themselves be the fathers of children, and half of these children would have been girls.

There is evidence that Aristophanes began this shift toward realism, but it is later dramatists like the prolific Alexis of Thurii (with his one hundred and forty plays which survive in over three hundred fragments) who would have been a leading architect of this change. He was joined by Menander, the playwright whose many works have survived best and in greatest abundance.

If Menander was to raise a laugh (after all, that was his job, and exactly what his audience paid for), then he would surely have imbued his characters and plots with traits and mannerisms that were immediately recognisable to his audiences from their own everyday experience; the plots would reflect Greek life to some degree and his characters identifiable as real life Greeks. His comedies are particularly important to us because they shine a rare light on aspects of non-elite Greek family life; unlike much of the rest of the literary evidence we have, they describe commonplace domestic situations and the experiences of the average person.

Although played by men, women characters obviously feature in these reflections of real world situations. The courtesan, old woman, scheming wife, and love stricken young girl are among the stock characters who populate Greek New Comedy. As noted, they were now dressed in conventional contemporary clothes, representing the men and women, free and slave, who could be encountered in a Greek street or home. Masks were still worn; those of young men and women were good looking, those of the elderly and slaves were often grotesque.

Prominent amongst the playwrights are Philemon (*c.* 368–267 BCE), Diphilus (*c.* 360–290 BCE), and Menander (*c.* 342–291 BCE), writing around 100 plays each. Philemon actually won more festival victories than Menander at the Lenaea and the City Dionysia, although Menander, , has come down to us as the acknowledged leading light of the genre because much more of his work has survived. *The Dyskolos* (*The Old Moaner*), which premiered in 316 BCE, is the most complete surviving play; significant portions of six other plays also still exist. Over 900 quotations from Menander's work are preserved in secondary sources; romance is never very far away in his domestic dramas, so women feature in these new, character-driven productions. Of the fragments from eighty-two plays, there are twenty-seven in which women appear in the title, suggesting some prominence in the plot. They include:

Empimpramene ('Woman On Fire'); *Kanephoros* ('The Ritual-Basket Bearer'); *Pallake* ('The Concubine'); *Didymai* ('Twin Sisters'); *Auton Penthon* ('Grieving For Him'); *Chera* ('The Widow'); *Progamoi* ('People About to Get Married'); *Rhapizomene* ('Woman Getting Her Face Slapped'); *Synaristosai* ('Women Who Eat Together At Noon' or 'The Ladies Who Lunch'); *Arrhephoros, or Auletris* ('The Female Flute-Player'); *Synepheboi* ('Fellow Adolescents'); *Epikleros* ('The Heiress'); *Hiereia* ('The Priestess'); *Synerosa* ('Woman In Love'); *Koneiazomenai* ('Women Drinking Hemlock'); *Thais* ('Thaïs'); *Theophoroumene* ('The Girl Possessed by a God') and *Titthe* ('The Wet-Nurse') as well as nine plays bearing the title *The Woman from ... Andros, Boeotia* and other specific geographical locations.

We know that Posidippus (316–*c.* 250 BCE) wrote forty plays; of the eighteen we know, the following celebrate women in the title: *Apokleiomene* ('The Barred Woman'); *Ephesia* ('The Ephesian Girl'); *Locrides* ('The Locrian Women'); *Choreuousai* ('Dancing Girls').

In addition, we can add the following five titles from twenty-one plays we know about from Apollodorus of Carystus, who flourished in Athens between 300 and 260 BCE: *Apoleipousa* ('The Woman Who Leaves'); *Hiereia* ('The Priestess'); *Proikizomene* ('The Woman with a Dowry') or *Himatiopolis* ('The Female Clothes-Seller'); *Lakaina* ('The Laconian Woman') and the melodramatically, onomatopoeically titled *Sphattomene* ('The Woman Being Slaughtered').

From Diphilus, we can add *Diamartanousa* ('The Woman Who Is Failing Utterly') and *Aleiptria* ('Masseuse')—just two examples out of the eleven with women in the titles from the fifty-four plays we have titles for; Philemon adds *Ananeoumene* ('The Born Again Woman') and *Ptoche* ('The Poor Woman'); and Rhinthon (*c.* 323–285 BCE), bucking the trend, wrote a *Medea*.

All life is here, with woman performing in a vast range of everyday scenarios; this is just the fragmentary output we know about, from a few of the many prolific New Comedy writers.

We can sum up the new types of *dramatis personae* and the new kinds of plots with:

> Long-lost children end up living next-door to their grieving parents, young men compromise women who seem to be prostitutes but fortuitously turn out to be marriageable maidens in love with their attacker, and gentle courtesans welcome home nubile virgin sisters to the lusty arms of well-meaning and well-endowed Athenian bachelors.[44]

The Olympians barely get a look in here; more abstract but personalised deities are in control, for example, when a goddess personified as *Ignorance* delivers the prologue of Menander's *Perikeiromene*, 'The Cropped Girl' or 'The Rape of the Locks' (translated after George Bernard Shaw, after Pope's *The Rape of the Lock*). Significant in this play is the independence and assertiveness of Glykera, the poor girl who has been assaulted; the perpetrator was a Corinthian soldier (Polemon) who always treated the girl as his wife, but violently and angrily assaulted her when he discovered she had kissed another man. The domestic violence (the forced haircut) is typical of the uncivilised behaviour of mercenaries at the time; what redeems him is that Agnoia (Ignorance personified) explicitly claims responsibility for his violent act at 163–66 so his actions are not seen as typical of the man. A friendly neighbour reveals the truth for Polemon—Glykera has left him because he is not treating her right. Pataikos, the good neighbour, turns out to be Glykera's long lost father who had abandoned his children when his wife died in childbirth, and he himself was shipwrecked. The man who had been caught kissing Glykera was in fact her twin brother; all is well, as reconciliation and marriage ensue. A typical scenario (full of coincidence and improbability, in which the girl plays a central part), it reflects not only the fact that life is just as strange as fiction, but also that a woman's place in the family, personal relationships, and society at large was now being acknowledged. Women had a role to play in the course of human relationships. It emerges in the avaricious prostitute who turns out to be a canny but caring madam, concealing her generosity behind a mask of greed and grasping; or in the bombastic soldier who not only boasts of the countless enemies he has slain, but also how well he treats the woman he loves. Madams will always be meretricious and greedy, soldiers will always brag; the point is that there is also a good side to these larger than life characters.

Significantly, we know of no play of Menander's which does not deal with *eros* (love) in some form or another. Love can often assume marriage, another recurring theme in the new comedy; marriage was always arranged between the father and his intended son-in-law, with the bride ever consensual, and sidelined until the wedding night. What Menander, and presumably his New Comedy play-writing colleagues, show us is that it was possible by now for a woman to have some say in the marriage arrangements—not least the choice of husband—and to influence the courtship through her own desires and actions. Menander, and his audience, were pioneering the view that this was the right thing to do, and that the wishes of the daughter and future wife could, and should, be taken into account.

These lines from *Misoumenos*, sums up what goes wrong when the wife is richer than the husband; Menander's audience would have recognised this conundrum from their own lives:

> Manners, not money, makes a woman's charm.
> When you fair woman see, marvel not; great beauty's often to countless faults allied.
> Where women are, there every ill is found.
> Marriage, if truth be told (of this be sure), an evil is—but one we must endure.
> A good woman is the rudder of her household.
> A sympathetic wife is man's chiefest treasure.
> A rich wife is a burden. She doesn't allow her
> husband to live as he pleases. Nevertheless, there is
> one good thing to be gained from her: and that is children.
> She watches over his couch, if he's sick,
> With tender care; she's always by his side
> When fortune frowns; and should he happen to die,
> The last sad rites with honour due she pays.
>
> Menander, Misoumenos 1-13

The problem with the rich wife is that her wealth gives her power over and above the social norms dictated by her gender, power that can drastically curtail a man's freedom to behave as he likes. However, there are two sides to every coin, even to a rich wife. No matter how rich the wife, their primary purpose was always to provide a man with much-wanted children.

The speaker in a fragment from a comedy by Anaxandrides would agree; he asserts that where a woman is the breadwinner in a marriage, it transforms that marriage into slavery—the wife is a tyrant, and the husband a slave.[45]

There is, of course, no suggestion that the plays of the New Comedy, or the relatively little we know about them, reflect actual life. The unreal scenarios, unlikely situations, and farcical coincidences were all comic devices, deployed to drive the plots and to make the audience laugh. However, it is reasonable to argue that the prominent role of girls and women in these plays did reflect a growing acknowledgement of the active, positive, and decisive role of women in the family, not simply about working the wool and household management. Women now had an increasing say in who they married and how they behaved, where they went and when.

Misogyny and invective

We have seen how Hesiod set the tone for centuries of invective and satire, relentlessly vilifying women in his *Works and Days* and *Theogony*, composed in about 700 BCE.

> Pernicious is the race; the woman tribe
> Dwells upon earth, a mighty bane to men.[1]

Semonides of Amorgos, quoted at length in Chapter One, maintains the *Theogeny* misogyny around the same time, or soon after, with his iambic, satirical *Types of Women*; the premise within these 118 lines is that Zeus created men and women differently, specifically forging ten distinctive types of woman, based on the world of nature. Semonides is probably not being entirely serious; his tongue may well have been firmly in his cheek. We have Stobaeus to thank for its survival.

Here are the ten types, nine of which are less than complimentary and paint a picture of a world full of awful women: the dirty woman derives from a pig; the cunning woman originates from a fox; the endlessly curious and high-maintenance woman comes from a dog; the lazy or apathetic woman is formed from earth or soil; the capricious woman of mood swings comes from sea water; the stubborn woman derives from a donkey; the unreliable and uncontrollable woman comes from a weasel or skunk; the proud woman comes from a mare; and the worst and ugliest type of woman comes from an ape or monkey. The opening stanza gives a taste of the invective:

> In different ways god made the mind of woman in the beginning. He made one from the bristly sow through whose sty everything, caked in mud, lies in dishevelment and rolls on the ground. Filthy and in dirty clothes herself, she sits among the dunghills and grows obese.[2]

The obligatory sexual slur, highlighting woman's insatiable sexual appetite is, of course, there:

Another was made from a skunk, wretched and baneful. Nothing beautiful, nothing nice about her, nothing pleasant, and nothing sexy, either. But she's mad for the bed and sex, and when he's around, she makes her husband feel sick. She steals from the neighbours and commits every possible evil. She even eats sacrifices that are waiting to be offered.[3]

Only the bee woman is virtuous and has anything to commend her, according to Semonides, but she is, unfortunately, discounted as an impossible ideal. The bee reference echoes Hesiod in the *Theogony*. What a contrast to the other nine—as with Pandora, there is a glimmer of hope:

Another from a bee. Anyone getting her is lucky. She alone attracts no blame, but life flourishes with her and blossoms. She loves her husband, and he loves her. She bears him noble and famous sons. They grow old together. Conspicuous among all women is she, she is imbued with divine grace. She takes no pleasure in sitting among women when all they talk about is sex. Women like her Zeus gives to men. They are the best and most accomplished of women.[4]

Types of Women could well have been written for performance at *symposia* which would explain its essentially misogynist and stereotypical tone and import. As Robin Osborne states, it was clearly written to emphasise male domination in society that 'depended on, and [was] constantly reinforced by, [the] abuse of women'[5]. At the same time, though, it should be pointed out that, despite this literary flexing of male muscle, men in the poem come out of it looking somewhat impotent, when they present their wives behaving in the ways attributed to them in the poem.The tradition continues with Phokylides of Miletus, around 440 BCE, obviously influenced by Semonides:

The tribe of women is of these four kinds—that of a dog, that of a bee, that of a burly sow, and that of a long-maned mare. This last is manageable, quick, fond of gadding about, fine of figure; the sow kind is neither good nor bad; that of the dog is difficult and snarling; but the bee-like woman is a good housekeeper, and knows how to work. This desirable marriage, pray to obtain, dear friend.[6]

Euripides's Hippolytus, faced with the prospect of an amorous stepmother, Phaedra, criticises Zeus for creating women. Men might then live in 'liberated homes, without women...it is clear that woman is a major evil'. This would help for economic reasons: father has to come up with a dowry, husband has to finance her spending on clothes and jewellery. Hipploytus moans that a man is best off with a nothing of a woman: 'a woman who sits in the house, useless in her stupidity. I hate clever women. I don't want a woman in my house thinking more than a woman should think'.[7]

Slaves are complicit in this conspiracy of clever women (women are thus implicitly on a level with slaves), and should stay away from free women instead of delivering their evil plans. Slaves should be replaced with mute, biting beasts to avoid any communication. Once he has got this off his chest, Hipploytus vilifies the prospect of sex with Phaedra. Aristarchus, a friend of Socrates, echoes the sentiment when he finds his house full of refugees after the revolt against the Thirty in 403 BCE; the fourteen displaced, educated people were relatives of his who, unfortunately, were ruining him financially, because his land was occupied and ravaged, and he now had no income. Socrates' tactful advice to him is to set them, educated or not, weaving and spinning like slaves, so that they can sell their wares and pay for their upkeep.

Carcinus II, the fourth-century tragic poet, in a fragment from his *Semele*, questions why anyone needs to enumerate the evils of women, when just uttering the word 'woman' says it all.[8] Alexis, the fourth century BCE comic playwright, piles on the invective:

Poor men! We sold away our freedom of speech and our comfort and lead the life of slaves with our wives. We're not free. We can't say we don't pay a price for their dowries: bitterness and women's anger. compared to that, a man's is honey, for men forgive when someone does them wrong, but women do you wrong and keep on recriminating. They control what doesn't belong to them and neglect what they should control. They break their promises. When there's nothing wrong, they say they're sick every time.[9]

According to Amphis, another comic dramatist active around the same time, a *hetaira* is better than a wife; the latter sits at home sulking while the *hetaira* has to work at being good company.[10]

In a fragment, Menander describes a husband who married a woman called Crobyle for her money, and then complains when she insists he gets rid of his pretty young slave girl. He calls Crobyle a 'jackass among apes', domineering, with a nose one cubit long.[11]

With the wise words of Theognis in *On Marriage*, from around 550 BCE, man and woman are perceived as bad as each other; though things can only get worse:

Rams and asses, Cyrnus, and horses, we choose of good breed, and wish them to have good pedigrees; but a noble man does not hesitate to marry a low born girl if she brings him lots of money; nor does a noble woman refuse to be the wife of a base but wealthy man, but she chooses the rich instead of the noble. For they honour money; and the noble weds the low born, and the base the highborn; wealth has mixed the race. So, do not wonder, Polypaides, that the race of the citizens deteriorates, for the bad is mixed with the good.

Antiphanes, writing on *Women* in about 300 BCE, has a decidedly brief catalogue of good women to call on:

What! when you have a secret, will you tell it to a woman? You might as well tell all the criers in the public squares! It's hard to say which of them blares loudest. Great Zeus, may I perish, if I ever spoke against woman, the most precious of all acquisitions. For if Medea was an objectionable person, surely Penelope was an excellent creature. Does anyone abuse Clytemnestra? I oppose the admirable Alcestis. But perhaps someone may abuse Phaedra; then I say, by Zeus! what a capital person was... Oh, dear! the catalogue of good women is already exhausted...[12]

These misogynistic rantings encapsulate the general feeling among certain men of intellect. Women are seen as the root of all evil with little to redeem them; they exist on a level with beasts and are treated as such. The derogatory insults reflect Hesiod and are themselves reflected, as we have seen, in later literature, tempered only slowly (but surely for all that) by a more nuanced and considered attitude hinted at, indirectly at least, by Aeschylus, Euripedes, and the comic dramatists.

Women and
the (re-) writing of history

Herodotus, the father of history (*c.* 484–425 BCE), refers to women in his *Histories* 375 times; Thucydides, his successor (*c.* 460–*c.* 400 BCE) bothers himself with women on significantly fewer occasions. We should qualify the comparative frequency of Herodotus' references by stating that women are never at centre stage; they are bystanders, supporting figures in much bigger events than they could be responsible for on their own. Nevertheless, Herodotus paints a wider canvas than Thucydides when he describes Medea, Io, and Helen, albeit in the context of their roles in various Mediterreanean conflicts; he features Egyptian and Babylonian queens, Babylonian marriage customs, and the role of women in Egypt, among other woman-related events, as we shall see below. Thucydides seems to have taken his own advice when he has Pericles state that the widows of the Peloponnesian War should be grateful if men refrain from talking about them, in whatever context. Thucydides clearly subscribed to the view that women should not be discussed or named in public, not necessarily because he believed that they should be seen and not heard, but to respect their reputation and dignity. He was, of course, focussed on writing a history of the Peloponnesian Wars, so it is not surprising that women rarely figure, the few exceptions being those widows in Pericles' Funeral Oration, and an episode of defensive tile-slinging.

Women feature prominently as evidence in Herodotus' entertaining ethnographical excursions around the Mediterranean; Herodotus found the wider world a very strange and wondrous place. Apart from monstrous ants the size of foxes and incredible hippopotamuses, Libyan dog-headed men and headless men with eyes in their breasts, the historian found even the civilised Egyptians quite amazing, not least because 'the women go to market and men stay at home and weave [the exact opposite to Greek practice]. Women even urinate standing up and men sitting down.'

The Egyptians had stood the world on its head. Urine, or the wrong sort of urine, also played a big part in the cautionary tale of the adulterous wife of King Pheros:

Pheros was a king of Egypt who went blind. After 10 years, the oracle at Buto said he had served his punishment and would be cured if he washed his eyes out with the urine of a woman who had never slept with any man except her husband. So, he tried his wife's urine … it didn't work, then many other women until one worked and he could see again. All those women whose urine failed were collected together and burned. He then married the lady whose urine worked.[1]

Herodotus' aim in such observations was to prove that the Greek way is the right and proper way; all barbarians, even clever barbarians like the Egyptians, were wrong. Some of his episodes are undoubtedly fictitious, but that matters little: his objective is to establish the contrariness of the non-Greek, the barbarian world in relation to the normative behaviour and customs of his fellow Greeks. And that, of course, applies to women. As an example, when Herodotus tells us about the Lycians in Anatolia, who were unique in two ways:

> In one of their customs, that of taking the mother's name instead of the father's, they are unique. Ask a Lycian who he is, and he will tell you his own name and his mother's, then his grandmother's and great grandmother's and so on. And if a free woman has a child by a slave, the child is considered legitimate, whereas the children of a free man, however distinguished he may be, and a foreign wife or mistress have no citizen rights at all...[2]

Herodotus is wrong on the first count, as the Lycians did not use matronymics; we have no way of gauging the historicity of the second.

To Herodotus, the Libyans were particularly barbaric, especially the nomadic Ausoi, and the desert-living Garamantes; Herodotus describes them as bestial, not because they copulate with their beasts, but because they 'copulate promiscuously with their women', just as animals do, 'in the manner of flocks and herds'. Sex in public was presumably beyond the pale for most ancient Greeks.[3] Furthermore, when a Libyan child reached adolescence, it was subjected to a kind of quarterly beauty contest in which it becomes the property of the man whom he or she most closely resembles. The girls of the Ausoi and Machlyes play an ancient game in which they fight each other with sticks and stones; if any girl dies in the fighting, then this is proof that she had lost her virginity.[4] Libyan Gindanes women were avid trophy hunters, indicating the number of lovers they had enjoyed, with leather anklets donated by those lovers.[5] Old-style Greek monogamy and adultery were of little consequence to the Massagetai, or the Nasamontes in the south of Libya. If a man was having sex with a married women and he did not want to be disturbed, he simply left his calling card at the door of her wagon; the phallic spear or quiver indicated quite clearly that she was busy, and so he could take her 'without fear' of being interrupted by another chancer, or by her husband who was quite relaxed about it all. By contrast, if that husband were an Athenian, he might legally kill him.[6] There was no such unpleasantness amongst the free-loving Massagetai. The Massegetai occupied land in Scythia covering parts of modern day Turkmenistan, Afghanistan, Uzbekistan, and Kazakhstan.

Fragment 40A from Hesiod's *Catalogue of Women* gives us more information on the decidedly strange Massagetai, and their even stranger neighbours:

> [The Sons of Boreas pursued the Harpies] to the lands of the Massagetae and of the proud Half-Dog men, of the Underground-folk and of the feeble Pygmies; and to the tribes of the boundless Black-skins and the Libyans. Huge Earth bare these to Epaphus—soothsaying people, knowing seercraft by the will of Zeus the lord of oracles, but deceivers, to the end that men whose thought passes their utterance might be subject to the gods and suffer harm—Aethiopians and Libyans and mare-milking Scythians.[7]

The Nasamontes certainly enjoyed their weddings: all the male guests were permitted to have sex with the bride. Herodotus nonchalantly adds that in return for this multiple pleasuring, the bride receives a present from each of her wedding night partners, 'something or other they have brought with them from home'. The Adyrmachidae were no less permissive: 'They are also the only tribe with whom the custom obtains of bringing all women about to become brides before the king, that he may choose such as are agreeable to him'.[8] Few, if any, would have left the king's bed a virgin on their wedding night.

Another cautionary tale involved Pheretima (d. 515 BCE), wife of the Greek Cyrenaean King Battus III, and the last queen of the Battiad dynasty. Herodotus tells us that when Battus (the father of Pheretima and grandfather of Pheretima's son Arcesilaus), died in 530 BCE, Arcesilaus III became king. He was defeated in a civil war after 518 BCE, and exiled to Samos while Pheretima went to the court of King Euelthon in Salamis, Cyprus. Arcesilaus, however, recruited an army in Samos, returned with it to Cyrenaica, and regained his position by murdering and exiling his political opponents, urged on no doubt by Pheretima. When Arcesilaus left Cyrene for Barca, Pheretima ruled the city. Arcesilaus was murdered by the exiled Cyrenaeans, intent on revenge. Pheretima went to Arysandes, the Persian governor of Egypt, to get help in avenging the death of her son; Arysandes loaned her Egypt's army and navy. She marched to Barca, and demanded the surrender of those responsible for the murder of Arcesilaus; when the Barcaeans refused, Pheretima laid siege to Barca for nine months. Amasis, her Persian commander, played a trick on the Barcaeans, in which he ordered his soldiers to dig a large trench in front of the city that was to be camouflaged with wooden planks and earth. He then lured the Barcaeans out of the city with a promise of a well-rewarded armistice; they fell into the trap. Pheretima ordered the Barcaean wives' breasts to be cut off, and enslaved the rest of the Barcaeans to the Persians.

Having avenged her son, Pheretima returned to Egypt, and gave the army and navy back to the governor. However, while in Egypt, Pheretima contracted a contagious parasitic skin disease, and died in late 515 BCE. Herodotus tells us that she was eaten alive by the worms, as punishment by the gods for her butchery of the women of Barca.[9] She lives on in the name of the worm that infested her—*Pheretima* is a genus of earthworm found in New Guinea and other parts of Southeast Asia; the worms are used as a medicine in China and carry biological agents efficacious in the treatment of epilepsy. The *Pheretima aspergillum* worm contains hypoxanthine, a herb used as an antipyretic, sedative, and anticonvulsant; it lowers blood pressure and contains a platelet-activating factor.

Another cruel, unusually militaristic woman was Queen Tomyris of the Scythian-like Massagetai. She is famous for slaying King Cyrus the Great, the founder of the Achaemenid Empire, when he invaded her country. Strabo, Polyaenus, Cassiodorus, and Jordanes, as well as Herodotus, all mention her.[10] Cyrus fooled Tomyris' army, then under the command of her son, Spargapises, into drinking copious amounts of wine that Cyrus had left behind. Scythians were not used to drinking wine, being much more partial to hashish and fermented mare's milk; accordingly, they drank themselves stupid—and were successfully attacked by the Persians while under the influence. Spargapises was captured; he persuaded Cyrus to remove his bonds and, once free to move, committed suicide. A vengeful Tomyris challenged Cyrus to a second battle, promising him his fill of blood. She won, and Cyrus was killed. Tomyris ordered his head be cut off, and his corpse crucified; she then shoved his head into a wineskin full of human blood.

> 'Search was made among the slain by order of the queen for the body of Cyrus, and when it was found she took a skin, and, filling it full of human blood, she dipped the head of Cyrus in the gore, saying, as she thus insulted the corpse, 'I live and have conquered you in fight, and yet by you am I ruined, for you took my son with guile; but thus I make good my threat, and give you your fill of blood.'[11]

To the Greeks, women and war simply did not mix. Herodotus' rather sensational telling of these escapades was designed not just to illuminate what he saw as the perverse and blood-thirsty behaviour of barbarian women (compared with the so-called civilised women of Greece), but to demonstrate just how far removed from Greek women they were. The preceding fanciful and slightly prurient descriptions of the permissive sexual mores of barbarian women are manifestations of Greek men attacking the soft underbelly of their enemy, by denigrating and slurring the sexual behaviour of their women. This insidious, and demoralizing tactic continued to be deployed to good effect well into the Roman period and beyond. It surfaces at the beginning of Herodotus' general description of the Massagetai, along with routine human sacrifice.

> Each man has only one wife, but all these wives are held in common…Human life does not end normally with these people; but when a man grows very old, all his kinsfolk collect together and offer him up in sacrifice; offering at the same time some cattle too. After the sacrifice they boil the flesh and eat it; they who end their days like that are reckoned the happiest. If a man dies of disease they do not eat him, but bury

him in the ground, bewailing his bad luck that he did not get to be sacrificed. They sow no grain, but live on their herds, and on fish, of which there is great plenty in the Araxes River. Milk is what they drink most. The only god they worship is the sun, and to him they offer the horse in sacrifice; believing they are giving to the swiftest of the gods the swiftest of all mortal creatures.[12]

In Herodotus' birthplace of Halicarnassus (modern Bodrum, in Turkey), King Mausolos (r. 387–353) ruled in consort with his wife Queen Artemisia, a woman whom Herodotus described as 'wondrous'. Decrees and laws were issued in joint names and honours were heaped on them, as an egalitarian regal couple. When Mausolos died, Artemisia ruled on her own from 353 to 351 BCE. Her expressions of grief for her husband were legendary; she is even reputed to have concocted and drunk a potion comprising her husband's bones and ashes. She organised poetry and oratory competitions to honour her husband, and completed the building of his mausoleum, which became one of the Seven Wonders of the World, known as the Mausoleum of Halicarnassus. She embarrassed the people of Rhodes when she beat off their attack; the Rhodians found it hard to accept that they had been repelled by a woman.

Similar female belligerence comes from Plutarch when he describes the brave military action of soldier-poet Telesilla at Argos, and Pausanias leaves us an account of Marpessa in the defence of Tegea in the seventh century.[13]

Artemesia also gives us an example of the pen being mightier than the sword, in the words of Polyaenus:

> Artemisia planted soldiers in ambush near Latmus; and herself, with a large train of women, eunuchs and musicians, celebrated a sacrifice at the grove of the Mother of the Gods, which was about seven stades distant from the city. When the inhabitants of Latmus came out to see the magnificent procession, the soldiers entered the city and took possession of it. Thus did Artemisia, by flutes and cymbals, possess herself of what she had in vain endeavoured to obtain by force of arms.[14]

She was not the first powerful Artemisia; her namesake, Queen of Halicarnassus and commander of the Carian navy, acquitted herself very well, with bravery, *andreia*, at the Battle of Salamis in 480 BCE—an epithet that Herodotus only uses for a woman here when she and her navy supported the Persians against the Greeks. Indeed, Artemisia had won a hard-earned seat on Xerxes' councils of war, dispensing the best advice and winning the epithet *androboulos*—advising like a man.[15] Before Salamis, Xerxes summoned together all his naval commanders, and sent Mardonios to ask whether or not they thought he should fight the battle. All advised him to fight, except Artemisia:

> Tell the king to spare his ships and not do a naval battle because our enemies are much stronger than us in the sea, as men are to women. And why does he need to risk a naval battle? Athens for which he did undertake this expedition is his and the

rest of Greece too… If Xerxes chose not to rush into a naval encounter, but instead kept his ships close to the shore and either stayed there or moved them towards the Peloponnese, victory would be his. The Greeks can't hold out against him for very long. They will leave for their cities, because they don't have food in store on this island… But if he hurries to engage I am afraid that the navy will be defeated and the land-forces will be weakened as well. In addition, he should also consider that he has certain untrustworthy allies, like the Egyptians, the Cyprians, the Kilikians and the Pamphylians, who are completely useless.[16]

Xerxes, though impressed, fought the battle anyway. He observed Artemisia being pursued by the ship of Ameinias of Pallene. To shake him off, she attacked and rammed another Persian vessel fighting on her side, and so convinced the Athenian captain that her ship was an ally; quite reasonably, Ameinias gave up the chase. The friendly victim was manned by the people of Persian ally Calyndos, and went down with all hands. Xerxes, looking on, thought that she had successfully attacked an enemy Greek ship, and seeing the indifferent performance of his other commanders, commented 'My men have become women, and my women men'. The baffled Xerxes summed it all up with:

And even in the heat of the action, observing the manner in which she distinguished herself, he exclaimed: 'O Zeus, surely you have formed women out of man's materials, and men out of woman's.[17]

Xerxes was not the only one that day who had his eyes opened by a woman; Herodotus says:

'Now if [Ameinias] had known that Artemisia was sailing in this ship, he would not have given up until either he had captured her or had been taken himself; for orders had been given to the Athenian captains, and moreover a reward was offered of 10,000 drachmas for the man who should take her alive; since they thought it intolerable that a woman should make an expedition against Athens'.[18]

Artemisia made inspired use of the Persian and Greek flags she kept on board:

Artemisia always … carried on board with her Greek, as well as barbarian, colours. When she chased a Greek ship, she hoisted the barbarian colours; but when she was chased by a Greek ship, she hoisted the Greek colours; so that the enemy might mistake her for a Greek, and give up the pursuit.

More tactical wizardry followed, in the words of Polyaenus:

Artemisia…found that the Persians were defeated, and she herself was near to falling into the hands of the Greeks. She ordered the Persian colours to be taken down, and the master of the ship to bear down upon, and attack a Persian vessel, that was passing by her. The Greeks, seeing this, supposed her to be one of their allies; they drew off and left her alone, directing their forces against other parts of the Persian fleet. Artemisia in the meantime sheered off, and escaped safely to Caria.[19]

After the battle, Xerxes rewarded her sterling performance—the best of all his commanders—with a complete suit of Greek armour, rubbing salt in male wounds and exemplifying hurt pride, he simultaneously awarded the captain of her ship a distaff and spindle. Xerxes and Artemisia, like Herodotus' Egyptians before him, were turning the world on its head.

More sound Artemisian advice followed when Xerxes asked her whether he should now lead his troops to the Peloponnese himself, or he would withdraw from Greece and leave his general Mardonius to do it. Artemisia replied that he should retreat back to Asia Minor and advocated the plan suggested by Mardonius, who requested 300,000 Persian soldiers with which he would defeat the Greeks.

According to Herodotus, her response was well-considered:

I think that you should retire and leave Mardonius behind with those whom he desires to have. If he succeeds, the honour will be yours because your slaves performed it. If on the other hand, he fails, it would be no great matter as you would be safe … In addition, if Mardonius were to suffer a disaster who would care? He is just your slave and the Greeks will have but a poor triumph. As for yourself, you will be going home with the object for your campaign accomplished, for you have burnt Athens.[20]

Xerxes took her advice this time, leaving Mardonius to pursue the war in Greece. He sent Artemesia to Ephesus, to take care of his illegitimate sons, a task considerably less challenging (and somewhat demeaning) than fighting in the battle of Salamis and being chief military advisor to Xerxes.

According to Plutarch, an anonymous woman was personally responsible for ending the occupation of Thebes by the Spartans, and subsequently driving them out of the city. The Thebans in exile in Athens had planned a coup, but those in occupied Thebes had second thoughts at the last minute, and called off the attack. A messenger was sent to Athens to apprise them of this plan but when said messenger went home to prepare his horse, he found, to his consternation, that his wife had loaned his only bridle to a friend. Borrowing another, or demanding his own back, would have aroused suspicion, so he did nothing and stayed at home in Thebes. Consequently, the exiles in Athens, none the wiser, launched the attack as planned and regained their city from the Spartans. The subsequent rise in power enjoyed by the Thebans was all due to the neighbourliness of one exiled Theban woman in Athens.

Thebe, the wife of the Thessalian tyrant, Alexander of Pherae (r. 369–357 BCE), exerted her power when she stabbed him to death; she then invited her sons to stick the knife in too. Plutarch tells us how, on the fateful night, the usual guards were not posted at Alexander's bedchamber, which was at the top of a ladder; a ferocious dog guarded the door. Thebe had concealed her three brothers in the house and removed the dog. When Alexander had gone to bed as usual, she cleverly draped the steps of the ladder with sound-muffling wool, and called her brothers to her husband's chamber. Plutarch says that it was the brothers alone who stabbed him, after Thebe had removed Alexander's sword and threatened to wake him if they refused. The tyrant's body was dumped in the street where it suffered every indignity.

What was Thebe's motive? Plutarch says she was driven by fear of her husband and his brutal behaviour; Cicero says the deed was caused by jealousy. Others say that Alexander had taken Thebe's youngest brother as his *eromenos* and imprisoned him. Angered by his wife's pleas to release the boy, he murdered him; his assassination was her revenge.[21]

Candaules, also known as Myrsilos, was a king of the ancient Kingdom of Lydia from 735 to 718 BCE. Herodotus says his name means 'dog throttler'; in telling his story, he provides another tale of caution in which a vengeful woman is involved.[22] Candaules is betrayed and murdered by his wife, Nyssia, due to his pride and possessiveness; he was in the habit of bragging about his wife's prodigious beauty to his bodyguard, Gyges of Lydia. 'If you don't believe me when I tell you how lovely my wife is,' said Candaules, 'A man always believes his eyes more than his ears; so do as I tell you—get to see her getting undressed.' At first Gyges refused, aware of the taboos surrounding nudity in Persian society, and fearful of how unpredictably Candaules might actually react.[23] Candaules eventually prevailed, and revealed a plan in which Gyges would hide behind a door in the royal bedroom to watch Nyssia undressing; Gyges would then steal away while the queen's back was turned. That night, Gyges took up his position and ogled as planned, but the queen caught sight of Gyges, and saw immediately that she had been betrayed and humiliated by her own husband. She swore revenge, and formulated her plan. Next day, Nyssia summoned Gyges and confronted him: 'One of you must die. Either my husband, or you, who have outraged protocol by seeing me naked.' Eventually, Gyges sensibly chose to betray the king, and save his own skin. Nyssia's scheme involved an element of *déjà vu*; Gyges hid behind the door of the bedroom, armed with a knife furnished by the queen, and slew Candaules in his sleep. Gyges married the queen, and became king.

Candaules did not just pay with his life. He has the dubious privilege of giving his name to candaulism, a sexual practice in which a man exposes his (usually) female partner, or images of her, to other people for their voyeuristic pleasure. The term is also applied to the practice of undressing or exposing a female partner's body to others, or forcing her into having sex with a third person, into prostitution or pornography. Today, the term is increasingly applied to the posting of revealing images of a female partner on the internet, or forcing her to wear sexually suggestive clothing for perverted public consumption.

Nyssia was obviously shrewd, a fact that makes Herodotus' story all the more disturbing for the average Greek, and all the more careful to keep his women under wraps, and shielded from the prying eyes of strangers.

Xerxes made the mistake of falling in love with his brother's wife; she, however, was obdurately chaste, so Xerxes attempted to resolve his dilemma by arranging a marriage between one of his sons and her daughter.[24] Herodotus names her as Artaynte, but he does not name her chaste and respectable mother, who remains anonymous. Things get yet more Byzantine when Xerxes then falls in love with Artaynte, his daughter-in-law—another woman of guile and intelligence. She puts Xerxes on the spot by demanding he gives her the 'coat of many colours', woven especially for him by his principle wife, Amestris. Appropriately, Artaynte's name means 'strong woman'. Displeased, Amestris ordered Artaynte's mother to be mutilated. Thus, Amestris exacts her vengeance, while Herodotus succeeded in showing the Persian Xerxes as weak, not in control of his wife or mistresses, and the victim of yet another avenging woman. Amestris was acting in character—she was notoriously cruel and even implicated in child sacrifice if Herodotus is to be believed; 'I am informed that Amestris, the wife of Xerxes, when she had grown old, insured her own life with Hades by burying seven children of famous Persians on two occasions'.[25]

With Xenophon (*c.* 430–354 BCE), things are much simpler; men are men and women are women, both co-existing at their respective polarities. In his *Oeconomicus* (a Socratic dialogue on household management and agriculture), Xenophon toes the male party line, for the most part; the gods determined the gender differences, instilled maternal instinct, and determined the activities and roles of men and women, with women married only to procreate. He is comfortable with the belief that women should be married off early, so that her husband, somewhat older and apparently wiser, might mould her in the way he wanted her to be. However, Socrates in the *Oeconomicus* does concede that Ischomachos' wife displays an intellect worthy of a man (*dianoia*). Out of respect, the wife, Chrysilla, is never named.

Chrysilla is not the only woman in Xenophon's good books. In the *Anabasis*, he tells us that while in Pergamum, he is advised by Hellas, wife of the Persian sympathizer Gongylus of Eretria, to launch a night attack with 300 men. She tells him that he will capture a wealthy Persian called Asidates, complete with booty, horses, and family. Despite good omens, the attack fails, but does succeed at a second attempt.[26]

He describes Mania in the *Hellenica*. She was the wife of Zenis, the satrap of ancient Dardanus under Pharnabazus II; she herself took over as satrap in about 399 BCE, after her husband's death.[27] Xenophon tells us how she shrewdly won over Pharnabazus:

> Pharnabazus was preparing to give the satrapy to another man [but] Mania, the wife of Zenis, who was also a Dardanian, fitted out a great retinue, took presents with her to give to Pharnabazus himself and to use for winning the favour of his concubines and the men who had the greatest influence at the court of Pharnabazus, and set forth to visit him. And when she had gained an audience with him, she said: 'Pharnabazus, my husband was not only a friend to you in all other ways, but he also paid over the tributes which were your due, so that you commended and honoured him. Now, therefore, if I serve you no less faithfully than he, why should you appoint another as satrap? And if I fail to please you in any point, surely it will be within your power to deprive me of my office and give it to another.' When Pharnabazus heard this, he decided that the woman should be satrap. And when she had become mistress of the

province, she not only paid over the tributes no less faithfully than had her husband, but besides this, whenever she went to the court of Pharnabazus she always carried him gifts, and whenever he came down to her province she received him with far more magnificence and courtesy than any of his other governors'.[28]

When Mania got the job, she executed it with due deference and respect. Xenophon goes on to describe how she not only secured the cities inherited from her husband for Pharnabazus, but also additional cities on the coast, such as Larisa, Hamaxitus, and Colonae; when attacking their walls with a well-equipped Greek mercenary force, she was on the spot, observing proceedings from a chariot. She also accompanied Pharnabazus in the field, in return for which Pharnabazus heaped magnificent honours on her, and sometimes asked her to help him as a counsellor. Polyaenus too describes her in glowing terms; her glory, however, incurred the jealousy of less well-rewarded men.[29]

> She always went to battle, drawn in a chariot; she gave her orders at the time of action, formed her lines, and rewarded every man who fought well, as she saw he deserved. And—what has scarcely happened to any general, except herself—she never suffered a defeat. But Meidias, who had married her daughter, and might from that close relationship have been supposed to be faithful to her, secretly entered her apartments, and murdered her.

Mania was a victim of her own success as a military commander. As Polyaenus said, she was never defeated in the field, with the unfortunate result that the men around her moaned that it was 'a disgraceful thing for a woman to be the ruler'; they were so unnerved by (and suspicious of) her success that she was strangled by her seventeen year old son-in-law, Meidias.

Pantheia was a third woman whom Xenophon celebrates, this time at some length in his partly fictional biography of Cyrus the Great, the Cyropaedia. Abradatas (*fl.* sixth century BCE) was a king of Susa, and an ally of the Assyrians against Cyrus the Great. When Cyrus captured the Assyrian camp, he also took Abradatas' wife, Pantheia, when Abradatas was away on a mission to the Bactrians. As a result of the good treatment that Pantheia received from Cyrus, Abradatas was persuaded to ally with Cyrus. Unfortunately, he died in battle, while fighting against Croesus, during the conquest of Lydia in 547 BCE. Pantheia was inconsolable and committed suicide.[30] Pantheia wins Xenophon's admiration for her devotion to her husband and her suicide, which she committed with a sword, a masculine way of killing herself, rather than in the usual womanly way by hanging. Her dignified death would surely have been seemly for any Greek woman, and was on a par with the many Roman women who took their lives on the death of a husband.[31]

Elpinice (*fl. c.* 450 BCE) was a women of noble birth from Athens, the daughter of Miltiades, tyrant of the Greek colonies on the Thracian Chersonese, and half-sister of Cimon. Most of our information comes from Plutarch's *Life of Pericles* where she appears twice in political spats with the Athenian statesman. Elpinice was first married to her brother, but was later wed to Callias, one of the richest men in Athens; Greek law permitted marriage between a brother and sister, so long as they had different mothers. This marriage with Callias was the condition for paying, on Cimon's behalf, the fine that had been imposed upon their father, for which Cimon had taken on responsibility. Elpinice represents an early example of a woman being used as a pawn in the political machinations of menfolk. Later, Cimon was charged with treason for taking bribes from Alexander I, king of Macedonia; Elpinice negotiated his acquittal with Pericles.[32]

Pericles admonished Elpinice for being an outspoken woman. Nevertheless, she would not lie down, and when the people of Samos revolted against Athens, Pericles inflicted savage reprisals in 440 BCE, by demolishing their city walls, confiscating their navy, and forcing them to pay a hefty fine. Elpinice was not impressed by the jingoism surrounding this victory, which found voice at the state funeral Pericles organised; as a lone voice in the obsequious crowd, she boldly remarked that a costly victory was won over the Athenians and their allies, rather than against the city's real enemies, the Phoenicians or Medes. Pericles dismissed her argument out of hand, and rebuked her again with ridicule: 'As an old woman you should not anoint yourself with perfumes.' Apart from belittling Elpinice, the insult cast a sexual slur on her, and implied that women's only power lay solely in their sexuality.[33]

The episode highlights a number of key issues in the ancient Greek attitude towards obtrusive women and to women in general. Firstly, it is another example of the tendency to vilify what were seen as difficult women by their alleged sexual behaviour; secondly, it exemplifies a habit of denigrating older women, by inviting prejudicial and humiliating attitudes to them as a group; thirdly, it implies desperation on the part of some women, to enhance their attraction to men by splashing on perfume and, by extension perhaps, layering on make-up—such decoration only led them to denigration and disrespect by men. Just as crucially though, the episode gives us a rare example of a woman speaking out in public, finding a voice in the public arena. Elpinice's radical stand not only goes against the proper and accepted norms of a woman's behaviour in a man's political and military world, but it was also made at a time when public expression, particularly joking in public, had become an offence. Elpinice's bravery is all the more notable for this—she was audibly and visibly crossing a number of well-established boundaries—social, political, military, and personal.

Elpinice was also a mistress of the artist Polygnotus of Thasos, who used her as a model in his painting of the Trojan Laodice. She was buried in the family tomb and not in her husband's, suggesting either an enduring affinity with her birth family, or a disaffection towards her husband's.

Women in the Family

There should have been some way for men to give birth to their children, dispensing with the help of women.

So said Jason, somewhat revealingly, in Euripides' *Medea*, chiming with Hippoytus' sentiments. 'Seclusion' is a word that frequently springs to mind when we consider the place and role of women in the Greek family. Obviously, wives were a biological necessity if the family, tribe, or race was to have any future; pragmatically, wives were assigned a utilitarian role, and were taken specifically to produce (ideally male) offspring. The marital bed—indeed any bed—was a dangerous place for the ancient Greek woman and her offspring: if Athens is taken as typical, on average, women had six confinements during their lives, while infant mortality ran between twenty and forty per cent. Mortality in childbirth no doubt accounted for some of the difference in life expectancy between men and women; girls could, and did, marry from the age of twelve and, in some cases, may have been subjected to regular sexual activity before menarche, which would typically occur around age fourteen—'too soon to marry, too soon to carry'. The serial childbirth that often followed would, over time, have had a damaging impact on a woman's physical and mental health. Add to that the risk of dystocia (difficult labour), hemorrhage, infection, puerperal sepsis, eclampsia, obstructed labour, thromboembolism, and the fact that precocious sex might eventually lead to cervical cancer, there is little wonder that a woman's life expectancy was generally shorter than a man's.

Athenian law required an Athenian woman to be under the control and protection of a *kyrios* or guardian; he was responsible for her safety and well-being, and acted for her in all financial transactions and litigation. This obviously included the control of any money or property that she might possess. As a child, her father would fulfil this role; on becoming a wife, her father would automatically pass the responsibility to her husband. The guardian was free to dispose of anything and everything his ward possessed; the *quid pro quo* was that he had to ensure she was provisioned with food, clothing, shelter, and a dowry when she was of a marriageable age. If he failed in any of these obligations, the archon would intervene and enforce it.

Despite these social limitations, women were an integral part of the ancient Greek family, or *oikos*. This word is socially significant, embracing much more than our word, 'family'. In effect, it included the extended family living in the household as well as the house itself, any farm, and the slaves. *Oikos* was 'the household' in its broadest sense.

To illustrate how financially restricted women were, a woman could not make a contract or enter a financial transaction worth more than a *medimnos* of barley, a pittance enough only to feed a family for a few days.[1] She could sell vegetables and crafts, and purchase household shopping on a day to day basis, but for anything else, theoretically at least, she required the permission of her *kyrios*. Prostitution was one of the few ways out of this constriction: a number of *hetairae*, both freed and citizen-born, amassed considerable wealth, with no sign of a *kyrios* with his fingers in their money pouches. No doubt, more than just a handful of barley would have frequently changed hands between women and men in the marketplace, but only in the sure knowledge that such black market transactions were not enforceable in a court of law.

On the credit side, a woman could possess and use all kinds of property, with no upper limit on its value. She might also have her own personal slave, jewellery, or furniture. There was, however, a caveat: a woman might own the use of a personal slave or jewellery, but not own the slave or the actual jewels herself.

Her all-important dowry was also significant; it supplemented any personal wealth, and brought bargaining power. As we shall see in the chapter on marriage, depending on its size, the dowry attracted the right kind of husband, and provided the bride's allocation of the family's wealth. It was usually pecuniary, though some poorer families paid in kind, in household goods, all of which were meticulously recorded for repayment and witnessed in the event of a divorce. The death of one of the partners required various different resolutions: if the marriage had produced a son, a widower could retain his dead wife's dowry until her son was old enough to inherit; if it was the husband who died the widow could either return to her family with her dowry, or she and her dowry could remain with her husband's family. In the event of the husband or his heirs reneging on repayment of the dowry after a divorce, whatever the grounds, interest was payable at the rate of 18 per cent per annum.[2]

The dowry then represented a quasi-inheritance for the daughter or daughters in the family; the girls got their inheritance up front while her brothers had to wait until the death of the father. If it became clear that a father was never going to have a son, he would often adopt the man (not a baby, but a grown man, such as a brother-in-law) he was planning to pick as his daughter's husband, so the estate went to the couple in the normal way—a virtual dowry, assuring the legal existence of the family. Things got complicated when a man died with a surviving daughter but no son, adopted or otherwise. The daughter was the logical heir, but such a succession meant the end of the father's line, and the eventual passing of his estate into another family. The demise of the *oikos* was nothing less than a domestic and social disaster, and was to be avoided at all costs.

Boys, we know, were the babies of choice; they secured the male line and the *oikos*. However, the family was happy if they had a daughter when the survival of the *oikos* was in peril. Women were pivotal in one of the ways in which the death of an *oikos* could be averted, in legislation attributed to Solon. In her role as an heiress, an *epikleros* (literally 'attached to the family property'), was a brotherless daughter. She was obliged to marry her nearest male relative on the paternal side of their family, starting with their father's brother; she then held the family estate in a kind of trust. In Attic law, it was permissible for uncle to marry niece and half-brother to marry half-sister. In Sparta and Gortyn, they were sole heiresses—*patrouchoi* (πατροῦχοι). The hope was to produce a son who would, in time, inherit his grandfather's estate and, in so doing, preserve the *oikos*. Marrying this relative was no different from the arranged marriage a girl could typically expect; the only potential problem was that if she was already married, then her husband had to be divorced, in order to make way for father's next of kin.[3] The new husband who married the *epikleros* managed and lived off the estate, but had to surrender these rights when any resulting son came of age. The son would then inherit the property, allowing his grandfather's *oikos* to continue.

The odds of an Athenian woman becoming an *epikleros* are based on the fact that roughly one out of seven fathers died without biological sons; because Athenian law allowed for a man to adopt another male as a son in his will, not all daughters without brothers would have become *epikleroi*. It is estimated that 20 per cent of families would have had only daughters, and another 20 per cent would have been childless so, in any event, the *epikleros* was by no means rare.[4]

Famous *epikleroi* include Agariste (*fl.* sixth century BCE, to around 560 BCE), the daughter of the tyrant of Sicyon, Cleisthenes, and Agiatis, widow of Agis IV (*c.* 265–241 BCE), the twenty-fifth king of the Eurypontid dynasty of Sparta. Agis was betrayed by friends, and executed by Leonidas' men by strangulation; his mother Agesistrate and his grandmother were strangled over his body. Agiatis was forced to marry Cleomenes III by his father, Leonidas, but they eventually developed a mutual affection for each other.[5]

Agariste's father had high hopes for her; he wanted to marry her to the 'best of the Hellenes', and so arranged a competition in which the prize was Agariste's hand in marriage. Twelve hopeful contestants turned up at the banquet held to decide the contest. If Cleisthenes had a preference, it was for the former archon Hippocleides, who was 'the handsomest and wealthiest of the Athenians', according to Herodotus; however, Hipplocleides ruined his chances when he got drunk and started acting ridiculously; he stood on his head and kicked his legs in the air, in time to the flute music. Hippocleides was duly informed that he had 'danced away his bride,' to which he replied: οὐ φροντίς Ἱπποκλείδη—'Hippocleides doesn't care'. The Greek phrase 'danced the bride away' can also be translated as 'showed your balls', referring to Hippocleides' impromptu handstand when, doing his hand-stand, his tunic would have fallen up, exposing his genitals to the guests. In the end, the more sober Megacles of the Alcmaeonids was chosen to marry Agariste, who gave birth to two sons, Hippocrates and Cleisthenes, the architect of the reform of Athenian democracy.[6]

Love and marriage, dowries and divorce

In elite families, marriage in ancient Greece was, on the surface, little more than a pragmatic business transaction. Love was an incidental ingredient and, where it did arise, it would probably be due to the kindling of mutual respect and companionship over years of being together. It was the father's responsibility to get his daughters successfully married; a dowry had to be provided and a suitable groom found, so the stakes were high. Motivating factors in this may have included an element of concern to provide his daughter with a good husband; the driving force would be the social, financial, and political opportunities a son-in-law might provide through his own family, and commercial or military aspirations. After all, the father had to compensate for the immediate loss of a portion of his estate in dowry payments. The selection of a son-in-law was, to a large extent, an investment decision of some importance; the long term view, apart from getting a male heir to prolong the *oikos,* was to recoup the dowry and capitalise on it. A girl's feelings and trepidation in meeting her husband close to (or even on) the wedding day would have held little importance in many families.

The father was all powerful in the triangle he formed with his daughter and her intended. To complicate things, the father could always change his mind, presumably if he got a better offer for the girl. This is what supposedly happened to Neobule (the name means 'New Decision') and the seventh century BCE poet Archilochus. Archilochus was engaged to the girl before her father Lycambes reneged and married her off to someone else. Archilochus retaliated in verse so bitterly that her father and her sisters all hanged themselves in despair. In telling the calamitous tale, Archilocus incidentally laid the foundations of satire in western literature, and provided a foretaste of what was to come in the form of twenty-first century hate mail.

Dioscorides piles on the anguish, in an elegy in which the victims speak from the grave:

We here, the daughters of Lycambes who earned a hateful reputation, swear by the reverence in which this tomb of the dead is held that we did not shame our virginity or our parents or Paros, pre-eminent among holy islands, but Archilochus spewed out a frightful reproach and a hateful report against our family. We swear by the gods and spirits that we did not set eyes on Archilochus either in the streets or in Hera's great precinct. If we had been lustful and wicked, he would have not wanted to beget legitimate children from us.[1]

Love, then, was a nebulous, elusive, and incidental thing; Athenaeus even tells of people who have fallen in love with someone they know only in a dream—such must have been the yearning for real love. This concerns Odatis and Zariadres:

> And we must not wonder at people having on some occasions fallen in love with others from the mere report of their beauty, when Chares of Mytilene, in the tenth book of his History of Alexander, says that some people have even seen in dreams those whom they have never beheld before, and fallen in love with them in this way... it is written in the Histories, that she in her sleep beheld Zariadres, and fell in love with him; and that the very same thing happened to him with respect to her. And so for a long time they were in love with one another, simply on account of the visions which they had seen in their dreams. And Odatis was the most beautiful of all the women in Asia; and Zariadres also was very handsome. Accordingly, when Zariadres sent to Omartes and expressed a desire to marry the girl, Omartes would not agree to it, because he did not have any male offspring; for he wished to give her to one of his own people about his court.[2]

The besotted couple contrived to meet at a wedding ceremony given by Omartes' father:

> But he had not said beforehand to whom he was going to give his daughter. And as the wine went round, her father summoned Odatis to the banquet, and said... 'We, my daughter Odatis, are now celebrating your marriage feast; so now do you look around, and survey all those who are present, and then take a golden goblet and fill it, and give it to the man to whom you like to be married; for you shall be called his wife.[3]

After this, they eloped. However, love was certainly not always absent; we see it on the emotional and loving inscriptions found on gravestones and in epitaphs. Indeed, one of the tombs of Ceramicus depicts: Damasistrate and her husband clasp hands at parting. A child and a kinsman stand beside the chair, but husband and wife have no eyes save for each other, and the calm intensity of their parting gaze answers all questionings as to the position of the wife and mother in Attic society.[4]

Archedice, from fifth-century Athens, is praised:

> The dust hides Archedice, daughter of Hippias, the most important man in Greece in his day. But though her father, husband, brothers and children were tyrants, her mind was never overwhelmed by arrogance.[5]

As is Aspasia: 'Of a worthy wife this is the tomb—here by the road that is busy with people—of Aspasia, who has passed away; in recognition of her noble disposition

Euopides set up this monument for her; she was his consort.' Dionysia (fourth-century Athens) belies the stereotype that all women were wastrels and extravagant: 'It was not clothes, it was not gold that this woman admired during her lifetime; it was her husband and the good sense that she showed in her behaviour ... your tomb is adorned by your husband, Antiphilus.' A bereaved husband acknowledges Melite, his wife, as good and loving: 'You were the best, and so he laments your death, for you were a good woman.' The picture shows her holding out her hand to him as she says 'and to you farewell, dearest of men; love my children.'[6]

In first-century BCE Sardis, Menophila is officially honoured, although the eulogy in this case is not inscribed by a husband—the significance here lies in the fact that she was honoured in the first place, and earned the praise not by being locked away in her quarters; indeed the suggestion is that she had some public responsibility and authority:

> This stone marks a woman of accomplishment and beauty. Who she is the Muses' inscriptions reveal: Menophila. Why she is honoured is shown by a carved lily and an alpha, a book and a basket, and with these a wreath. The book shows that you were wise, the wreath that you wore on your head shows that you were a leader; the letter alpha that you were an only child; the basket is a sign of your orderly excellence; the flower shows the prime of your life, which Fate stole away. May the dust lie light on you in death. Alas; your parents are childless; to them you have left tears. (Peek, 1881)

Parental love is also represented in the moving epitaphs of sons and daughters indicating real emotion and devotion for lost daughters and sisters. Phrasicleia died in Athens around 540 BCE, before she was married; we can sense the feeling of failure felt in not attaining the status of 'wife'—'I shall be called a maiden always. This is the name the gods gave me in place of 'wife'.'[6]

Bitte poignantly announces to the world that 'I lie here, a marble statue instead of a woman, a memorial to Bitte, and of her mother's sad grief.'[7] Xenoclea, mother of two girls, died of grief after the death of her eight year old son, Phoenix, drowned out at sea.[8]

Love is clearly a factor in Menander's *Men at Arbitration*, two men squabble over who owns some trinkets, a crisis that had driven a newly married couple asunder, despite still being very much in love. Prior to their meeting, and before they married, the man had raped the girl one night in another town, although neither now recognized the other. When he learned about the resulting baby she had given away, the man concluded that he had married a woman of dubious morals whom Athenian law and *mores* required him to divorce. However, his love for her meant he could not bear to do this, while the bride's father urged her to divorce her husband because they wrongly believed he was seeing a mistress. Love prevailed. Given that the plot of the play may have reflected aspects of real life (despite some highly unlikely elements), the play shows that love was an ingredient in some marriages in or around Menander's time (*c.* 342–*c.* 290 BCE).

Love shines through in a Menandrian fragment which describes a distraught, faithful husband of five months bewailing the fact that his wife is unfaithful and that he loved her and (thought that) she loved him. She was dignified and unassuming. The passage is doubly significant in that it is the only example in ancient Greek where the three distinct words for human love – *erao, phileo* and *agapeo* occur in close textual proximity[9].

Plato and Xenophon give us a rare glimpse into an Athenian domestic situation. Xanthippe was Socrates's first wife and mother of their three sons: Lamprocles, Sophroniscus, and Menexenus . Her name means 'yellow horse', with the horse part indicating her aristocratic lineage—*hippeis* (knights) were one of the higher socio-economic groups in Athens. She was forty years or so younger than Socrates. From Plato's *Phaedo* and Xenophon's *Memorabilia*, we learn that she was a devoted wife and mother, although she did had a reputation for being 'difficult'.[10] It is her son, Lamprocles, who says this, although it must be acknowledged that such criticism was not uncharacteristic of an adolescent son's view of his mother. In Xenophon's *Symposium*, however, Socrates tells us why he chose her of all women, 'the hardest to get along with of all the women there are', in a classic back-handed compliment:

'Because,' he replied, 'I observe that men who wish to become expert horsemen do not go for the most docile horses but rather those that are highly strung, believing that if they can master this kind, they will easily cope with any other. My course is similar. Mankind at large is what I wish to deal and associate with; and so I have got her, in the knowledge that if I can put up with her, I shall have no difficulty in my relations with all the rest of human kind.'[11]

Anger management, however, really was an issue. Once, Xanthippe tipped over the dinner table in a rage; further to that, she was so angry with her husband on one occasion that she poured a brimming chamber pot over Socrates' head, to which the philosopher reacted philosophically by saying, 'After thunder comes the rain.' Aelian describes her as a jealous shrew when she tramples on a large, beautiful cake sent to Socrates by Alcibiades [12]. Diogenes says that Alcibiades and others urged him to fight back against her. Creon had had a similar problem in *Medea* (line 316), which forces him to say 'the hot-tempered woman, like the tempered man, is easier guarded against than the cunning and silent.'

Without doubt, Xanthippe was notoriously difficult, and not an easy woman to live with, but we ought to resist drawing any conclusions about typical wifely behaviour in Greece based on her intemperate actions.[13] For Socrates, she is a means to an end, providing a living exemplum for a point he was at pains to prove. The anger may not be totally unrelated to the fact that Xanthippe had to share Socrates with another woman. Myrto was the alleged interloper, as featured in Aristotle's *On Being Well-Born*.

Over the centuries, Xanthippe has found it hard to shake off her reputation, and has since come to symbolize a nagging, shrewish wife; in Shakespeare's *The Taming of the Shrew*,

Petruchio compares Katherina to Xanthippe or worse in Act 1 Scene 2: 'Be she as foul as was Florentius' love, As old as Sibyl, and as curst and shrewd As Socrates' Xanthippe or a worse.'

Although Diogenes Laërtius describes Myrto as Socrates' second wife, living alongside Xanthippe in a thinking family's *ménage a trois*, Myrto was presumably a common-law wife; Plutarch describes Myrto as merely living 'together with the sage Socrates, who had another woman but took up this one as she remained a widow due to her poverty and lacked the necessities of life.'[14] Was this Socrates taking advantage of a law permitting bigamy, or just being charitable to a woman in need?

> For they say that the Athenians were short of men and, wishing to increase the population, passed a decree permitting a citizen to marry one Athenian woman and have children by another; and that Socrates accordingly did so.[15]

Socrates' mother was Phaenarete, wife of Sophroniscus. The name Phaenarete means 'she who brings virtue to light', so perhaps she introduced an element of calm to the tempestuous household. In Plato's *Theaetetus*, Socrates compares his own work as a philosopher with hers as a *maia* midwife.[16]

Other glimpses of married life show how Xenophon's Ischomachus is looking for a clean slate, a woman with nothing on her mind or in her brain, the type of woman who crops up later in the jurist Gaius' *Institutiones* (*fl.* 130–180 CE) when he confirmed that, on reaching puberty, Roman boys relinquished their guardians, but not girls—the reason being *propter animi levitatem*—as they were considered to be what today some would disparagingly call 'airheads'. Ischomachus is happy for her to be completely ignorant, so that he can mould and shape her as he sees fit, impressing on her only the characteristics and knowledge he wants. This was marriage by numbers. This is but one of Ischomachus' many rules for training and moulding the good wife—the secret of which is having her run the household effectively and efficiently—to his specific requirements, because that is what the gods, and he decrees. Here is an example:

> 'It will be your job', I [Ischomachus] said, 'to remain indoors and to send out those of members of the household who must work outdoors, and to supervise those who must work indoors, and to receive what is brought in and to allocate what each must spend, and you must decide what surplus needs to remain, and watch that the expenditure set aside for a year is not used up in a month. When fleeces are brought to you, you must take care that they become cloaks for those who need them. And you must take care that the grain that is stored remains edible. One of your duties, however', I said, 'you may find unwelcome, which is, if one of the household slaves is ill, you must see to it that he is looked after'. (Xenophon, *Oeconomicus* 7, 36)

No peace, then, for the wife of Ischomacus.

At what age did the ancient Greeks marry? Men left it to their late twenties or early thirties, while girls were married off when only fourteen or fifteen as soon as they were deemed capable of bearing children. The men were obviously anxious to establish or complete a military career before settling down, as well as to maximise the pleasures and opportunities offered by a single life for as long as possible. A shortage of women may also have been a factor, made worse by the exposure of baby girls or the lack of dowries permitting marriage. On the other hand, in the fullness of time, the man would usually die first, either from natural causes or as a casualty of war, thus creating a pool of widows looking for second and third husbands. Moreover, the age gap of the typical married couple made it all the more inevitable that the more mature man would be in control of the relationship.

Betrothals and the actual marriage were decidedly low key affairs that couples more or less grew into over time; a betrothal took place in front of witnesses, the value of the dowry was agreed and duly transferred to the groom. The dowry was crucial and consequential. It was the woman's contribution to running the house, as well as her living costs. It had to be paid in advance out of family savings, savings that might otherwise have formed the parents' retirement 'pension' and, unlike a deathbed legacy, represented a real diminution of wealth to be endured in lifetime. However, a generous dowry was prestigious, and a useful lever in acquiring a good son-in-law with commercial and social potential. The payment of dowries explains why families were reluctant to have daughters in the first place, and were prepared to abandon or expose superfluous baby girls. A wife's dowry might account for around 20 per cent of her new husband's wealth, but was usually much less, often under 10 per cent, a meagre contribution to the living costs of the wife in the new home.

Girls were short term, transitory members of their *oikos* of birth; as they depleted the *oikos'* resources, they were a liability. A woman's function was to give birth to sons who would continue the family line, sons who would contribute to the family business and sustain the *oikos*. These sons married, and their wives brought a dowry that enriched the household; other people's daughters were fine. A father would only raise as many girls as he could provide a decent dowry for. The rest were deemed superfluous to needs.

The dowry was repayable on the husband's death, or if he divorced her, and so afforded a woman a degree of insurance and security; depending on her age, it offered a chance to remarry if young enough, or an incentive for a relative to take her in. It also gave her a bargaining counter in the relationship; Plato proposed the abolition of the dowry on the grounds that it would reduce a woman's control and make men less servile. Moreover, if married life became unbearable, the woman could always leave, obliging her husband to sell off sufficient assets to raise the cash needed to repay the dowry.

A woman could divorce her husband, but the proceedings had to be sanctioned by and initiated through her guardian. It came at a heavy price; the woman surrendered custody of her children to the husband, and had to return her dowry to her father to pay for her upkeep back at home. Men were naturally hesitant about divorcing because the repayment of the dowry (no doubt part or all spent) could lead to financial ruin and the calamitous end of the *oikos*.

This is what Aristotle prescribed, if she were to be a good wife, in his *Oikonomikos* from about 330 BCE:

> A good wife should be the mistress of her home, having under her care all that is within it, according to the rules we have laid down. She should allow none to enter without her husband's knowledge, dreading above all things the gossip of gadding women, which tends to poison the soul. (Aristotle, *Oiconomicos*, 3, 1)

She should budget and control the money spent on entertainment, as approved by her husband, thus restricting spending on her wardrobe and jewellery; men were too busy for such detail.

> Let it be her aim to obey her husband; ignoring public affairs and having no part in arranging the marriages of her children… let her at these times always listen to her husband… If, through sickness or misjudgement, his good fortune fails, then she must show her quality, encouraging him with cheerful words of cheer and obeying him, doing nothing bad or unworthy. No complaining or blaming, she will serve him better than if she had been a slave…indeed, he has bought her at a great price—what with sharing his life with her and giving her children. (*Ibid.*)

The husband, though, still has responsibilities to his wife, to their marriage and to their children. Fidelity is key; he must lead by example for the optimum result.

> Now a virtuous wife is best honoured when she sees that her husband is faithful to her, and has no preference for another woman; but before all others loves and trusts her and holds her as his own. And so much the more will the woman seek to be what he accounts her. If she perceives that her husband's affection for her is faithful and righteous, she too will be faithful and righteous towards him.[17]

The Athenian wife might consider herself fortunate compared to barbarian women in Aristotle's *Politics*, who he says are no better than slaves.[18] Philemon has it in a nutshell in his *The Good Wife*, written about 350 BCE: 'A good wife's duty 'tis, Nicostratus, not to command, but to obey her spouse; most mischievous a wife who rules her husband.' Before that, Susarion's *On Marriage* from 440 BCE saw little choice as 'women are an evil; and yet, my countrymen, one cannot set up house without evil; for to be married or not to be married is just as bad.'

As severe and punitive as much of this sounds, we must remember that Aristotle was expressing an ideal, and not necessarily anything that was gleaned from actuality; an impression of women and of social conventions were used to illustrate what was essentially a personal philosophy.

January was the most popular month for weddings as this was Hera's month. The ceremony itself would have included a sacrifice performed by the bride's father, a snip of the bride's hair, and a ritual bath in sacred water, followed later by the wedding feast with friends and family at the bride's home to celebrate the union. At nightfall, the guests marched in procession to the accompaniment of music and singing to the couple's new home, while the bride, groom, and the groom's best man were conveyed there in a chariot drawn by donkeys or horses. The Greeks showered the couple with nuts and dried fruit, as these were symbols of fertility and prosperity. The bride would be welcomed by her mother-in-law and taken to the hearth, the focal point of life in every ancient Greek home.

We have already quoted from Sappho's poem on the joyful wedding between Hector and Andromache; here it is in full:

> ... Hector and his comrades are bringing a girl with dark eyes in from holy Thebes and
> ... Plakia, gentle Andromache in their ships across the salt sea; many curved bands of
> gold and purple robes and intricate playthings, countless silver cups and ivory.' ...
> Then the Trojan women led mules to wheeled carts and a crowd of women came out
> ... ankled maidens, and separately the daughters of Priam and men brought horses
> with chariots ... and the sweet-sounding aulos was mixed with the clack of castanets,
> and the maidens sang a sacred song and the holy sound reached heaven ... bowls
> and goblets ... perfume and cassia and incense were mixed and all the older women
> shouted out, and all the men sang a loud song, calling on Paean, the far-shooter, the
> lyre player, to sing of Hector and Andromache, who were like gods ...[19]

A number of wedding hymns survive, for example, Aristophanes' *Wedding Song to Hymenaios*, from about 400 BCE; Anacreon's *The Morning Nuptial Chant*, from around the same time, says: 'Behold, young man, behold your wife! Arise, O Straticlus, favoured of Aphrodite, Husband of Myrilla, admire your bride! Her freshness, her grace, her charms, Make her shine among all women.' and Theocritus', *The Bridal Hymn*, from about 250 BCE.

On the day of the wedding, the bride would be washed and dressed by female relatives in a white dress as befitting a religious ceremony. The girl would also wear a crown, and carry a pomegranate, or another fruit with many seeds, because seeds symbolized fertility. The bride's father sacrificed offerings at the family altar, announcing that he was giving his daughter away – the *engue* was when the father of the bride and the groom, with two male witnesses present (but not the bride) pledged the bride, and transferred the dowry. The girl's toys would be offered to Artemis, as attested by the following text:

> 'Timareta, being about to be married, has consecrated to thee, O Artemis of the
> Marshes, her tambourines, and the ball she was so fond of, and her hairnet, her dolls,
> too, she has dedicated in a befitting manner, with her clothes -a virgin's offering to
> thee, O Goddess.'[20]

At the wedding itself which often took place in the evening with bride veiled, celebrations or *'gamos'* marked the transition of a girl from her father to her husband.

The bride would not be named. The new bride and groom would be escorted to the groom's home, where he would pretend to abduct her, and then carry her across the threshold. The couple and close family would then kneel before the hearth, where the bride would be formally introduced to the divinity of her new home. After this *sunoikein* started, the consummation, and cohabitation of the marriage. On the next day, a feast was held for both families. However, the bride only really arrived at her new home when she gave birth to her first child. The bride, then, was something of a spectator or bystander at her own wedding; apart from being there, she had no real role to play, as the men did all the important things, further underlining the woman's subordinate role in society and culture. The mother of the bride had a similarly restricted role.

On the one hand, the bride brought a welcome injection of income to the family budget and the probability of extending the *oikos* through male offspring; on the other hand, she may be a threat to that *oikos* if her behaviour or conduct was in any way deemed compromising or questionable.

Once settled in, the new wife got on with her new life. Her tasks included: cooking; managing the house; organising the slaves; working the wool (*lanem fecit* as the Romans prescribed it for their *matronae*); baking bread (in rural and rustic families) dispensing first aid and folk medicine as required; looking after the household gods; raising a family; working the fields or helping on a stall in the poorer families.

Wool and other textile work was crucial, as in other societies before and after. Not only did it provide essential clothing, it was a powerful emblem of the respectable, compliant wife. Aristophanes describes the process in some detail, in *Lysistrata*, as a metaphor for the political issues the revolutionary women are grappling with:

LYSISTRATA

Well, first as we wash the dirty wool to cleanse it, so with a pitiless zeal we will scrub Through the whole city for all greasy fellows; burrs too, the parasites, off we will rub. That verminous plague of insensate place-seekers soon between thumb and forefinger we'll crack. All who inside Athens' walls have their dwelling into one great common basket we'll pack. Disenfranchised or citizens, allies or aliens, pell-mell the lot of them in we will squeeze. Till they discover humanity's meaning.... As for disjointed and far colonies, Them you must never from this time imagine as scattered about just like lost hanks of wool. Each portion we'll take and wind in to this centre, inward to Athens each loyalty pull, Till from the vast heap where all's piled together at last can be woven a strong Cloak of State.

MAGISTRATE

How terrible is it to stand here and watch them carding and winding at will with our fate, Witless in war as they are.[21]

Getting pregnant, though, was the absolute priority, despite the young age of most new wives, and the numerous medical risks that brought to mother and baby. The average household had around 4 children, with the average woman enduring six or more pregnancies.

The arrival of a baby was, naturally, cause for great joy and celebration. To announce the birth to the neighbours, a woollen strip was draped over the front door to indicate a girl; an olive branch announced that a boy had been born. The joy was sometimes short lived—even when the baby survived the birth, the fate of the baby was in the hands of the father; if the husband accepted it, it would live, but if he refused it, it would be abandoned, or even killed. Reasons for rejection include illegitimacy, infirmity, deformity, or just gender, as girls were costly, non-productive economically, and needed a dowry down the line. The unlucky babies would be put in a clay pot and abandoned. Legally and religiously, this exonerated the parents because, if the infant was to die, then it died of natural causes.

More happily, when the baby was accepted, there would be celebrations and, for girls, a naming at the *amphidromia*; this was a ceremony held on the fifth or seventh day of the baby's birth, where the girl was named and officially welcomed into the family, and a presentation was made to the gods and goddesses. It was believed that if a baby was going to die, then it was likely that this would happen before the seventh day, so the festival was deferred so that there might be a good chance of the child remaining alive. Much more lavish ceremonies awaited the naming of boys (the *dekate*) on the tenth day after his birth, where all the relatives were fed and entertained.

Seclusion and Exclusion: How much of an Illusion?

Generally speaking, the received wisdom among Greek men was that Greek women should be, and actually were to be, secluded and excluded. As already noted, Thucydides perhaps said it all when he famously asserted that 'a woman's reputation is highest when men say little about her, be it good or evil.' However, we must add the caveat here that he was specifically addressing war widows from the Peloponnesian War, and not women in general; the quotation has been hijacked by those wishing to prove conclusively that women were totally repressed and ignored. Thucydides was not making a generalisation, stereotyping all Athenian women.

Things, however, had been different in the age of the Homeric epics, in Crete, Mycenae and, as we shall see, in Sparta. Penelope, Nausicaa, and Helen all show a degree of social and domestic independence, as well as active involvement in their immediate environments. Penelope gets on with her wool work, but she plays a powerful role in the deflection and deterring of her irritating suitors; Nausicaa too is not confined anywhere—she offers sound advice to the wandering hero Odysseus about how best to manage his homecoming in the face of those annoying suitors; and Helen is pivotal in the circumstances leading up to the Graeco-Trojan war.

The Minoan civilisation on Crete was quite different from the prevailing situation later on the mainland. The Minoans did not conform to the patriarchal society model found elsewhere. Minoan society seems to have been more equal, and archaeological evidence suggests that women played a comparatively important and prominent role in public life. Women were priestesses and public service administrators; women are represented as skilled craftswomen, entrepreneurs, and are found among the highest echelons of political life. The priesthood was dominated by women. Although the palace kings were male, Minoan society was not exclusively patriarchal; unusually, Minoan society may have been matrilineal.

Minoan women took part in sports, usually the preserve of males, particularly boxing and bull-jumping; these were common themes in Minoan wall paintings and vase sculptures. Women in Minoan Crete were allowed the freedom to attend the public games; in the palace at Knossos, a miniature fresco has been discovered, showing a high gallery with roof-top and windows, from which elegant ladies look down over the heads of a crowd of people of both sexes. As noted, Cretan girls and women took a very active part in sport, and in dangerous sport at that. Bull-leapers are always depicted as young, slim, and athletic—boys and girls alike. They wore a loincloth, decorative bracelets, armlets, and ankle-gaiters; they wore their hair long, usually curled. There was nothing combative about the sport; it was not about harming or defeating the bull, it was simply about demonstrating athletic prowess. Perhaps, the finest depictions of the sport are two exquisite ivory miniature works—the Oxford boy and the Toronto girl, representing a boy and a girl 'matador'. Saltman describes exactly what a girl did when bull-leaping:

> Facing the charging bull, a girl athlete seizes a horn, and, as the beast flings up its head, gets enough spring to land on the bull's back, to grip its flanks and turn a back-somersault … the second [movement] being performed by a boy. As the athlete leaves the bull, the second girl catches him to break his fall.

He then goes on to describe the Toronto girl in dramatic detail:

> There is a lovely ivory statuette in Toronto which represents a girl in this exact position. Her face is tense as she waits to catch her comrade; she wears a golden apron protecting groin and belly, over the ribs a corsage held by wide gold shoulder-straps, and a collar. But the breasts, each with a golden stud for a nipple, are bare, following the regular Minoan fashion. Similar is the ivory figure in Oxford of a young boy, clad in a little gold apron, who, with arms raised, awaits the bull's charge.[1]

Back on the mainland, the Bronze Age was marked by the storming and razing of all the major strongholds of Mycenaean power. The site of the Palace of Nestor was never again occupied, after it was sacked in this period. The only consolation to later historians was that a library of clay tablets has surfaced, chronicling the decline and fall of Myceneae. They are made of sun-dried clay and list numerous women with their male and female children, along with occupational names, such as 'bath-pourers', confirming that it was a slave-owning society. These female slaves and their children, it seems, were being transported into what were probably two evacuation centres. Some of the tablet footnotes suggest deployments in what was clearly an emergency, such as, for example, 'sons of the X women, willing to act as rowers'. [2]

Elsewhere, the status and rights of women may have varied from *polis* to *polis*, but, we can draw some general conclusions. For example, we know that women were allowed to own land in Delphi, Gortyn, Thessaly, Megara, and Sparta. On the other hand, because their right to property was limited, Athenian women did not qualify as full citizens, as citizenship and civil and political rights were defined in relation to property. However, women could assert some property rights through gifts, dowry, or inheritance; though her *kyrios* still had the right to dispose of a woman's property as he saw fit.

In the comparatively liberated Gortyn, women were also excused a dowry and were granted a proportion of the father's estate equal to one half of a brother's. An *epikleros*, could sometimes choose her own husband and, on divorce, a woman could keep her own property and half of all the cloth she had woven during the marriage.

When not conceiving or trying to conceive, the wife was, it is commonly believed, confined to a secluded part of the house. On the other hand, slave-girls, *hetairae*, and concubines were at liberty to wander around the house performing their domestic tasks and providing their sexual favours as required, thus relegating the wife and mother of the house to a situation that has been called 'Oriental Seclusion'. This meant that they were confined to specific rooms in their home and denied contact with anyone, especially males, who were not members of the immediate family. The phrase derives from the similarities of this purdah with the situation of women in societies east of Greece.[3]

In reality, there is precious little evidence to support this supposed virtual segregation, relieved only by progenerative copulation and, presumably, sexual gratification sought by the domestic male; this, in fact, appears to be a convenient generalisation.

Homer advocated what he called *homophroneonte* in marriage—thinking along the same lines.[4] Sophocles says likewise, when he asks if there is anyone you argue less with, or turn to, more than your wife to discuss serious issues. Indeed, tombstone inscriptions provide us with unique insight into how women were remembered in death by loving husbands and sons, and occasionally how they themselves wished to be remembered. Loving fathers were able to show paternal and maternal love for deceased sons in this very public, enduring way when they chose the texts for their epitaphs; fourth century BCE Telemachus is typical, 'laid to rest at the right hand side of his mother and not deprived of her love'.

The most famous evidence against the presumption of seclusion, exclusion, and undervalue is in a court case against the *hetaira* Neaera, who masqueraded as an Athenian citizen, in which the jury was asked 'If you acquit this woman what will you say to your wives and daughters?'[5] This suggests that women enjoyed a degree of importance in the Athenian home, where they joined in family discussion on the news of the day, and whose opinions were heard and respected. Our assumption that Athenian houses were physically divided into two demarcated areas, *andron* and *gunaikon* (or *gynaekonitis*) for men's and women's quarters respectively, comes largely from two orators and writers: Xenophon (*c.* 430–354 BCE), and Lysias (*c.* 445–*c.* 380 BCE). Xenophon, in an account of an Athenian showing his new bride around the marital home, demonstrates how the women's apartment is separated from the men's by a bolted door.[6] Many assume the bolt is to keep the wife locked in, but it could just as plausibly be to prevent the servants stealing things from the women's quarters, and from having clandestine sex in there.

The unremarkable truth of the matter may simply be that in some families, the husband and wife slept separately, and in others they slept in the same room. In a case where a client attempts to explain how his wife had been secretly committing adultery in the family home, Lysias describes the woman's apartment upstairs and the man's apartment downstairs. When their baby was born, the accommodation was reversed, so that his wife could breastfeed in the night without the danger of falling down the stairs in the dark.[7] Segregation, however, cannot have been enforced too rigorously if the couple were to fulfil the obligation to have children. Indeed, we hear from Aristophanes of newly-weds sleeping together upstairs with no distinction between men's quarters or women's quarters, and Antiphon tells of a male guest sleeping upstairs.[8]

Aristotle thought that women brought disorder, evil, and were 'utterly useless and caused more confusion than the enemy'; no surprise, then, that he thought keeping women segregated was a good thing. To him, as we have seen, women are failed 'males'; a woman's natural characteristics include envy, shiftiness, a weakness for pity and tears, cunning, despondency, and dishonesty. She eats less because she does much less.[9]

Segregation would be very much in keeping with such extreme views, and cannot be said to reflect the actual layout of houses. Indeed, have no archaeological evidence for the *andron* or the *gunaikon*; so far, no un-covered rooms seem to have belonged exclusively to women, and so, it remains a puzzle how a woman might effectively manage the home if she were excluded from parts of the building. The Socrates household provides further evidence that the ancient Greek home was not segregated; when the philosopher brought an unexpected guest home for supper one evening, his wife lost her temper and tipped over the table at which they were seated. Embarrassing as this no doubt was, Socrates and his male guest went on to have dinner with his wife in attendance, as a matter of routine, and in a part of the house to which his wife had free access.

It seems rather unlikely that women were not only confined within the house, but were also confined to the house. Slaves would run many errands and do the shopping but only, of course, in households that had slaves. Where there were no (or few) slaves, it would sometimes fall to the wife or daughters to fetch the shopping, or get the water. Normally, men would do the shopping, as it was deemed unfitting for women to engage in financial transactions, but how often that happened in actual practice is impossible to say. Non-elite women, of course, in ancient Greece worked for a living to supplement the family income or help with the family business; this, of course, entailed leaving the house. Hippocrates, the father of medicine (*c.* 460–*c.* 370 BCE), describes a case in which a twenty year-old girl (old for an unmarried woman) suffered from fever and headaches, after being accidentally struck on the head while playing with another young woman; the fact that she was playing outside seems to have been quite normal behaviour.[10] Many girls and women must have walked from one place to another, as part of regular social interaction and to partake in education and religious activities. Their work in agriculture, wool-working, midwifery, shop-keeping, business management and wet nursing would have made this a necessity. On the other hand, you could excuse the Athenian girl or woman from venturing out if Theophrastus' Buffoon-flasher was anything like a common sight in the streets—'and the Buffoon is one that will lift his shirt in the presence of free-born women.'

Museums around the world are full of pottery and paintings depicting women outside the home, engaged in various activities. We find them washing themselves, hanging out clothes, swimming, talking with boys, visiting a tomb, or picking apples; there is not much seclusion or confinement here.

In the seventh century, the lyric poet Sappho (*c.* 630–570 BCE) ran an institution known as a *thiasos*—a community in which Greek girls received a basic education and were, at the same time, exposed to homosexual love, sometimes for or from their teachers; Sappho writes of her love for various students, and sometimes their love for each other. As the *polis* evolved, however, marriage as we know it became established as a social norm, marking the end of the *thiasoi*, and with it, some measure of Athenian female independence and homosexual preference, as these had no place within the constraints of this nascent social institution.

The education of girls was rather rudimentary compared with that received by boys – the reason, of course, being that women would never work in local or national government, in the armed forces or in the law. Their education would provide them with enough to be able to manage the household and its budget, and pass on elementary knowledge to their young children. Current affairs may have been picked up piecemeal through eavesdropping on the husband and his friends; better off women would have benefitted intellectually from trips to the theatre. Most girls would have a good working knowledge of local and national religion through their involvement in various festivals; they would learn to sing and dance, as these skills were often needed in a religious context. Spartan girls (and boys) did the *bibasis*, a bizarre dance, typical of the Spartans, which involved striking the posteriors of the other dancers with the flat of the foot as many times as possible. Aristophanes describes the joy and sheer abandon of it at the end of *Lysistrata*:

> Now the dance begin; Dance, making swirl your fringe of woolly skin, While we join voices To hymn dear Sparta that rejoices in a beautiful song, And loves to see Dancers tangled beautifully; For the girls in tumbled ranks Along Eurotas' banks Like wanton fillies throng, Frolicking there And like Bacchantes shaking the wild air To comb a giddy laughter through the hair, Bacchantes that clench thyrsi as they sweep To the ecstatic leap. And Helen, Child of Leda, come Thou holy, nimble, graceful queen, Lead thou the dance, gather thy joyous tresses up in bands And play like a fawn. To madden them, clap thy hands, And sing praise to the warrior goddess templed in our lands, Her of the House of Brass.[11]

Athenians were obsessed with the fear that if a woman committed adultery, this would foster doubt regarding the paternity of her children, and raise questions about inheritance; crucially, if paternity could not be established, then the child could not be a citizen. This often presented a problem, as a husband had to know that he was the father of his child, and a father had to know where his unmarried daughter was, what she was up to, and with whom. The solution, trotted out by centuries of scholars, was seclusion. Furthermore, adultery was thought not just to blemish a woman's chastity, but to corrupt her mind as well.

The court case described by Lysias, *On the Murder of Eratosthenes*, illustrates the ramifications of adultery in the domestic setting. Euphiletos stands trial accused of the murder of Eratosthenes, his wife's lover. According to Athenian law, if a husband caught his wife's lover in the act of adultery, he could either kill him or demand financial compensation. Euphiletos caught his wife with Eratosthenes, and killed him in front of witnesses.

Aristophanes includes a number of references to adulterous relationships; in the *Thesmophoriazusae* we have seen how men typically call women: 'adulterous, lecherous, bibulous, treacherous, and garrulous... Does he not repeat that we are all vice, that we are the curse of our husbands?'[12]

In the *Ecclesiazusa*, 'they receive their lovers in their houses just as they always did,'; then there is 'the woman who spreads open a large cloak before her husband's eyes to make him admire it in full daylight in order to conceal her lover by so doing, and afford him the means of making his escape'.[13]

Citizenship was what Athens was all about. The fuss over Neaera shows us how vital it was that both parents have Athenian citizenship before their offspring can be granted full citizenship. Women were key players in the allocation of citizenship—this was their trump card; to qualify as an Athenian you had to be born of an Athenian father and of an Athenian mother. Without women, citizenship could not exist, so wives had to be denied opportunities for adultery, and girls had to be kept pure until marriage, when they could help produce more legitimate citizens; loose premarital sex and bastard children were anathema to the family- preserving brothers, fathers, and prospective husbands. Therefore, generations of paranoid and insecure husbands and fathers apparently resolved the issue by keeping their wives and daughters secluded and excluded. To some extent, this is true, but not as much as generations of scholars have generalised in the name of academic tidiness, convenience and, at times, their own sexist and prejudicial outlook on life.

If a woman complained about her husband's infidelity, she was unlikely to make much progress, either legally or socially; the perpetrator would be neither prosecuted nor ostracised socially. One woman who tried was Hipparete, the daughter of Hipponicus III, but she may have wished she had not bothered. The story is significant to us because it not only illustrates the elite male's attitude to adultery and how a wife should deal with it (not through the divorce courts), but it also demonstrates that Hipparete was out and about when Alicibiades took the action he did. She was a wealthy Athenian who in about 424 BCE married the Athenian statesman and general Alcibiades. Hipparete loved Alcibiades but she was uncomfortable with his whoring and sued him for divorce. Plutarch tells us how, when the case came to court, 'Alcibiades came up and seized her and carried her off home with him through the market place, no man daring to oppose him or take her from him.' Being hauled off ignominiously over her husband's shoulder through the busy city obviously would have done nothing for her pride and, presumably, the case was dropped; she lived with him until her death and gave birth to a daughter and a son, whom they called Alcibiades.

There are examples of sensible public involvement. Married women were not permitted to participate in, or to watch, the games because athletes competed in the nude. One exception was the priestess of Demeter, goddess of fertility, who was given a privileged seat. Women could, however, participate—but only by proxy; Cyniska, daughter of King Archidamos of Sparta, was the first woman to go down as an Olympic victor. Her chariot won in the four-horse chariot race in the ninety-sixth and ninety-seventh Olympiads (396 BCE and 392 BCE respectively). It was forbidden for women to compete, but in the equestrian events, the victory wreath was awarded to the owner, not the rider, of the horse.

We get an example of overt and obtrusive Olympic cross-dressing with Callipateira, the daughter of Diagoras of Rhodes, the famous Olympic prize-winning boxer. She became the only lay woman to gain access to the Olympic Games. Callipateira's son, Peisírrhodos, her three brothers and her nephew, Euklēs, as well as her father had all won the Olympic Games. Disguised as a man, Callipateira snuck in to watch their next performances, as Pausanias noted:

> There is a mountain with high, precipitous cliffs. It is called Mount Typaeum. It is a law of Elis to throw any women down it if they are caught at the Olympic games, or even on the other side of the Alpheius, on the days prohibited to women. However, they say that no woman has been caught, except Callipateira … She, being a widow, dressed up just like a gymnastic trainer, and brought her son Peisirodus to compete at Olympia. Peisirodus… was victorious, and Callipateira, as she was jumping over the trainers' enclosure, 'bared her person'. So, her sex was discovered.[14]

She was hauled before the *Hellanodíkai* (the judges of the games) on a capital charge of sacrilege. In her defence, Callipateira argued that if there ever was a woman who could be allowed to defy the ban, then it was she—with a father, three brothers, a son, and a nephew who had achieved victory eight times at previous Games. The judges could not help but agree and she was acquitted. They had, nevertheless, learnt their lesson and passed a law stipulating that, in future, trainers should strip before entering the arena. In the event, there was nothing low profile about Callipateira or her aspirations.

If women were excluded from the Olympic Games on pain of death, then there were no such restrictions imposed at the Heraean Games, dedicated to Hera; it was the first sanctioned women's athletic competition to be held in the stadium at Olympia prior to the men's events, as a kind of warm up act. The games date from the sixth century BCE, when Hippodameia gathered the 'Sixteen Women' group of women together and established the Heraea Games, out of Hippodameia's gratitude for her marriage to Pelops. Others maintain that the 'Sixteen Women' were politically astute peace-makers from Pisa and Elis.

The Heraean Games originally consisted of only foot races; champions won olive crowns, beef carved from the beast sacrificed to Hera, and the right to dedicate statues inscribed with their names or place painted portraits of themselves on the columns of Hera's temple – the ancient equivalent of photographs or t-shirts celebrating a victory today. Competitions were in three age groups, probably ranging from six to eighteen, on a track in the Olympic Stadium 158-m long, instead of the 192-m run by the men; the deficit accounted for by women's shorter stride rather than an expression of male chauvinism, as some have suggested. Pausanias describes the women: 'their hair hangs down, a chiton reaches to just above the knee, and the right shoulder is bared as far as the breast.'[15] Men competed nude but women had to be dressed, although by wearing the short chiton they were in effect dressed as men.

The 'politically astute peace-makers from Pisa and Elis' were significant because they provide rare evidence of women participating in political and public affairs. Pausanias, again, tells us what happened:

'They chose a woman from each of the sixteen cities of Elis still inhabited at the time to settle their differences, this woman to be the oldest, the most noble, and the most esteemed of all the women…The women from these cities made peace between Pisa and Elis.'[16]

These early Eleans and Pisans took the highly unusual step of entrusting crucial political decisions and negotiations to their female elders; an indication, surely, that they respected and valued the political *nous*, ability and intelligence of these women. Unfortunately, the political and social status of women there declined markedly after this.

If women were barred from many of the games, they were at least able to enjoy the tragedies of Euripides; Aristophanes alludes to this in the *Frogs*; Aeschylus says, 'Since you persuaded noble ladies, wives of noble men to drink hemlock out of shame because of people like that Bellerophon of yours.'[17]

The comic theatre may have been different. In *Birds*, the wife of the cuckolded top-ranking official is obviously not in the audience; likewise in *Peace* where women are conspicuous by their absence while '*decrepit dotards*' are in the audience when the audience is addressed: 'As for me, I will explain the matter to you all, children, youths, grown-ups and old men, aye, even to the decrepit dotards.'[18]

Solon was no supporter of women's rights. He forbade dowries—the wife was only to possess three sets of clothes, some household effects, and that was all; he would not have marriages contracted for gain or land, but only for pure love, affection, and the birth of children. Draconian as these laws were, they do provide further evidence that love and affection was a factor in Athenian marriages – otherwise why cite it as a legal precondition?

He regulated women's walks, feasts, and displays of mourning, and banned everything that was either unbecoming or immodest; the only other permissible possessions were an obol's worth of meat and drink; and no basket higher than a cubit; and at night women were only to be allowed out in a chariot preceded by a torch. Sacrificing an ox at the graveside was not allowed.

Women, though could excel in the courts of law, as this poor woman shows in Aristophanes' *Thesmophoriazusae*.

> Allow me only to tell you what happened to me. My husband died on Cyprus, leaving me five children, whom I had great trouble to bring up by weaving chaplets on the myrtle market. Anyhow, I lived as well as I could until this wretch [the playwright Euripides] had persuaded the spectators by his tragedies that there were no gods; since then I have not sold as many chaplets by half. I charge you therefore and exhort you all to punish him, for does he not deserve it in a thousand respects, he who loads you with troubles, who is as coarse toward you as the vegetables upon which his mother reared him? But I must now go back to the market to weave my chaplets; I have twenty still to deliver.[19]

Seltman noted in 1955 that earlier and contemporary scholars made much of the fact that, unlike the Romans, Greek women did not join their husbands at dinner parties; he then humorously added that neither did his grandmother in the early twentieth century, by pointing out that women going out to dine was a relatively modern thing. Although Seltman makes no reference to the elite Roman women who attended dinner, he has a point when he asserts that it is of little consequence to women's independence and public activity; moreover, we could ask with some validity why a woman would want to attend a dinner party if it in any way resembled the *symposia* that degenerated into excessive drinking sessions, embroidered with salacious entertainment courtesy of the lady flute players.

Greek girls often received the feminine form of male names, often just adding the letters 'ina' to the end of her husband's name, thus introducing them soon after birth to a life dominated by men. Respectable women were never referred to by their first names, except within the household; women's names were not known or uttered outside of the family. In public, the women were acknowledged as the daughters of their fathers, or if married, as wives of their husbands. Women were thereby robbed of their personal identity and individuality. Socially, women existed in relation to men; women were defined by men. Caution is needed, though, if we try to measure how different and socially restricting that is from our custom of a woman taking her husband's surname when she marries him.

Once the age of sexual activity and attractiveness had passed, it seems that the restrictions on women consorting with men not from their immediate family were relaxed. An elderly woman in Aristophanes' *Plutus* 'enters, dressed as a young girl and trying to walk in a youthful and alluring manner.' She strikes up a lengthy conversation with a stranger, Chremylus, at his house. The story has a surprise, in that the old woman reveals that she enjoys the attentions of a young lover, with whom she conducts a healthy sexual relationship; 'Listen! I loved a young man, who was poor, but so handsome, so well-built, so honest! He readily gave way to all I desired and acquitted himself so well! I, for my part, refused him nothing.'[20]

Ironically, things started to improve for women because of a war, in much the same way as the horrors of the First and Second World Wars tentatively paved the way for increased social and occupational independence for women nearer our own time. The disastrous Peloponnesian War certainly had a social and economic impact, driving women out of the home to work in order to supplement the reduced family income. Demosthenes moaned that women were now finding employment as nurses, wool workers, and fruit pickers.

The chapter on women and work shows how, later, women would excel as surgeons and doctors, midwives, medical writers, and the authors of sex manuals and love poetry. Prostitutes, including urbane *hetairae*, continued to ply their trade, flute girls kept on fluting, and wet nurses went on feeding other women's babies. Tragedians and comic playwrights needed leading roles for women, good and bad, in the drama of the day; Plato included them in his vision of Utopia. All of this was very tentative, but it was progress that gradually displaced the clichéd image of the confined, solitary, and subdued woman of Athens.

One important area in which women could freely assert official importance and status was in the highly visible public pursuit of religious cults (particularly cults of female deities), in which they officiated as priestesses. This is dealt with in the chapter on women in Greek religion and philosophy.

Women and the World of Work

We have seen that the absolute priority for elite women, and probably for women in general, was to marry, get pregnant, take good care of their homes, raise their children, manage the slaves, and balance the housekeeping budget. This respectable behaviour in turn earned them respect. Baking bread and working with wool were important—symbolically and in practice. Working the wool was a badge of the respectable wife; related tasks included wool buying, then cleaning, carding, spinning, weaving, and dyeing—in short, making clothes for the whole household.

There were competitions for various aspects of wool working. A black figure vase from the fifth century BCE bears the inscription, 'I am Melosa's prize'; she was the winner in the girl's carding contest.[1] In fourth-century Athens, Melinna not only raised her children but, 'by her handiwork and skill', raised a memorial to Athena, goddess of handicrafts, and donated a share of 'the possessions she has won'. At around the same time, a relative of Nicarete etched on her tombstone 'I worked with my hands, I was a thrifty woman, I Nicarete lie here.'

We have seen, in the previous chapter, how the chaplet weaver in the myrtle market was ruined by Euripides sacrilegiously telling everyone that there was no god. In other work, a washerwoman called Smikythe offered a tithe in the sixth century, while in the fourth century, a society of clothes washers working on the banks of the river Ilissos set up a tablet to the nymphs and all the gods. The society included Leuce and Myrrhine, as well as eleven men. We hear of three grocers, or wives of grocers: Thraitta, Glycanthis, and Mania. Menander mentions a Woman's Market in his *Synaristosae*.

Less comfortably-off women, to whom slaves were beyond financial reach, would labour alongside men in the fields or on stalls in the *agora* (the market place). They might also offer board and lodge to travellers. Archaeological and literary evidence reveals that poorer women were also involved in ribbon selling and grape picking. We can identify the following occupations taken up by freedwomen in fourth century Athens: sesame seed seller; wet nurse; woolworker; grocer; harpist; horse-tender, pulse vendor; aulos player; perfume seller; honey seller; shoe seller; and frankincense vendor. Children often accompanied the woolworkers to their place of work. Gravestones reveal the following female occupations: wet nurses; cloak seller; unguent boiler; and salt seller.[2]

In his *Helen*, Euripides describes hanging out the washing—'Beside the deep-blue water I chanced to be hanging purple robes along the tendrils green and on the sprouting reeds, to dry them in the sun-god's golden blaze.'[3] In the *Electra*, Electra mentions fetching the water from the well:

> O sable night, nurse of the golden stars! beneath thy golden pall I go to fetch water from the brook with my pitcher poised upon my head, not indeed because I am forced to this necessity, but that to the gods I may display the affronts Aegisthus puts upon me...[4]

Homer tells us about women working in the mills, and the sheer hard work involved:

> And a woman, grinding at the mill, cursed from within the house nearby, where the mills of the shepherd of the people were set. At these mills twelve women in all would ply their tasks, making meal of barley and of wheat, the marrow of men. Now the others were sleeping, for they had ground their wheat, but she alone had not yet finished, for she was the weakest of all.[5]

Aristophanes frequently mentions working women in his plays—all of whom, of course, have to venture out in public.[6]

the *artopolides* – breadwoman.[7]
the *myropolides*—perfume seller.[8]
the *stephanopolides*—wreathmaker.[9]
the *lekithopolides*—pease pudding vendor.[10]
the *lachanopolides*—greengrocer.[11]
the *skorodopolides*—garlic seller.[12]
the *kapilides*—spiv.[13]
the *promnestriae*—a matchmaker.[14]
the *maiai*—midwife.[15]
the *titthai*—nurse.[16]
the *mastropoi*—madam.[17]
the pandokeutriae—hostess.[18]

Aristophanes has a low opinion of them generally. They are abusive, they cheat, and they are degrading.

He elsewhere also refers to women innkeepers, wet-nurses, bakers, myrtle-wreath and vegetable sellers, perfume vendors, unguent boilers, launderers, honey-sellers, wool workers and multi-tasking 'garlic-selling barmaid bakehouse girls'. Some, often foreign immigrants, ran brothels, although many whorehouses were state-owned. As stated, rearing children and running a household earned respect; boiling unguents or selling garlic did not. Water fetching was not always convivial or a wonderful social event:

Or poor Calyce's in flames And Cratylla's stifled in the welter. O these dreadful old men And their dark laws of hate! There, I'm all of a tremble lest I turn out to be too late. I could scarcely get near to the spring though I rose before dawn, What with tattling of tongues and rattling of pitchers in one jostling din With slaves pushing in!.... Still here at last the water's drawn And with it eagerly I run To help those of my friends who stand In danger of being burned alive. (Aristophanes, *Lysistrata* 321f)

Aristophanes describes the scene at the opening of *Lysistrata*, where Lysistrata and Calonice meet to talk, which was surely typical of the daily life for a woman:

If they were meeting up for a Bacchanal, A feast of Pan or Colias or Genetyllis, The tambourines would block the rowdy streets, But now there's not a woman to be seen Except—ah, yes—this neighbour of mine over there.
>Enter CALONICE (Aristophanes, *Lysistrata* 1–3)

In the *The Trojan Women*, Hecabe describes slaves' work as: 'the door, bowing to shut and open … and meal to grind.'[19]
Female slaves would have been kept busy doing the shopping, fetching water, cooking, serving food, cleaning, child-care, and wool-working. Some may have been nurses or wet nurses. Female slaves (and males) would frequently have to endure sexual exploitation and physical abuse. Slaves could not have children; if they did the infants were exposed or abandoned. As Xenophon tells in his *Oceonomicus,* slaves were prohibited from marrying, as marriage was deemed the exclusive privilege of the elite citizens of Athens.

Despite the eternal drudgery experienced by most slaves, some may have been fortunate enough to forge close relationships with their mistresses, as confidantes. Euripides' Medea confided her personal feelings to her nurse, who advised and comforted her at her lowest points; that nurse must have been very busy. In Aristophanes' *Plutus*, the lady listens to the slave Cario.[20] Slaves accompanied their mistresses on trips outside of the home; such relationships are also recorded on tombstones. It is possible that some relationships were forged by a common sense of exclusion and lack of respect from husbands and masters, with these tensions and resentment transcending class boundaries. Such disrespect is typified in Hesiod's *Works and Days*:

First of all, get a house, and a woman and an ox for the plough—a slave woman and not a wife, to follow the oxen as well—and make everything ready at home, so that you may not have to ask of another, and he refuse you.[21]

In the first century BCE, we learn of a female civil engineer; a woman called Phile financed a cistern and water pipes for the city of Priene, in Ionia. She was the first woman *stephanephorus* there, a magistrate with the right to wear a crown (*stephanos*).

Women feature amongst professional sportswomen. Cynisca is covered in the chapter on Sparta, but other female chariot race winners include Zeuxo of Argos, Euryleonis, Bilistiche, Timareta, Theodota, Arstocleia, and Cassia. Spartan Euryleonis was victorious in the two-horse chariot races in the 368 BCE games; she was only the second female stephanite (crown-bearer) in Olympic history. A statue of Euryleonis was erected at Sparta around 368 BCE, and is one of few bronze statues surviving anywhere in the Greek world.[22] Belistiche was a courtesan; she won the four-horse (*tethrippon*) and two-horse (*synoris*) races in the 264 BCE Olympic Games. Ptolemy II Philadelphus was so impressed that he took her as his a mistress, and deified her as Aphrodite Belistiche.[23] According to Clement of Alexandria, she had the further honour to be buried under the shrine of Sarapis, in Alexandria. Aristocleia won a two-horse chariot race in Larisa.[24] The Panathenaic victor lists tell us that Zeuxo was victorious in the four-horse chariot race around 194 BCE.[25]

Spartan women

Sparta was another world; this exceptional *polis* was made up of three groups: citizens—those with the political power; the *perioikoi*—free but with no political rights; and helots—serfs owned by the state to do all of the hard, but necessary, agricultural work, then hand over half of the produce to their citizen masters. The helots outnumbered the citizens by about seven to one; they were a dangerously united community, as they all spoke the same language, shared the same culture, and lived in communities separate from those occupied by the citizens. Rebellion and revolution by the helots was an ever-present threat.

Unlike every other *polis*, women played a vital role in keeping the war machine well-oiled and efficient. Generally, they enjoyed status, power, and respect unheard of in other parts of ancient Greece, or even later in Rome. Since Spartan men were fully occupied with military training, bonding in mess life, and doing battle, it fell to women to run the farms and keep the *polis* going in their absence. This was not without its rewards; it is estimated that, by the fourth century BCE, Spartan women actually owned between 35 and 40 per cent of all Spartan land and property. Indeed, by the Hellenistic Period, some of the wealthiest Spartans were women, controlling their own properties and looking after the properties of male kin who were posted away with the army. Working the wool was never as important a part of the Spartan woman's life as it was in the rest of Greece; she filled her day with many more important things.

Sparta was a military society. In the eighth century BCE, Lycurgus summed it up when he said that Sparta's walls were built of men, not bricks. Women of childbearing age were crucial in keeping the war machine ticking over. The zeal with which they applied themselves to this work for the state may have diminished their natural maternal instinct, if this encounter is anything to go by. When a mother is told of the death of her five sons in battle, she retorts to the messenger, 'don't tell me about that you fool; tell me whether Sparta has won!' Just as sensitive was the wife and mother who, as Plutarch famously recorded, told her son or husband to come home with his shield, or on it.[1] The bereaved mothers of the fallen at the battle of Leuctra in 371 BCE are said to have had smiles on their faces, out of pride.

The production of male children by a woman was on a par with being a male warrior in the Spartan army. Women who died in childbirth and men who died in battle were honoured in the same way, with their names inscribed on their gravestones. By the same token, producing a son who turned out to be a coward was a cause for great shame and sorrow. One traitor, Pausanias, met a terrible end when he took refuge in a sanctuary to Athena. Instead of pleading for his life, his mother, Theano, picked up a brick and placed it in the doorway; very soon others followed her lead and bricked up the temple door, with Pausanias eventually dying inside. Plutarch, in his *Sayings of Spartan Women*, cites three Spartan mothers who killed their cowardly sons with their own hands.

At the siege of Sparta in 272 BCE, King Pyrrhus of Ephesus hesitated with his mercenary troops before attacking the walls of Sparta, because they were defended by women, children and old men.[2] He was less concerned about the real possibility of killing women and children than he was about the fearsome opposition he faced from the belligerent and bellicose women. The Spartan *gerousia* (council of elders) wanted to evacuate their women to Crete for protection; however, this was vetoed by Arachidamia, the former queen and grandmother of the Eurypontid King Eudamidas II, who made it clear that the Spartan women would stay to help protect the city. Arachidamia entered the Gerousia 'with sword in hand', and challenged the proposal, questioning whether the Spartan women were expected to survive the ruin of their own city.

After the arrangements for reinforcing the city's defences were made, the plan was to confound Pyrrhus' terrifying elephants. The older men and the women dug a trench parallel to Pyrrhus' camp, sinking wagons into the ground as obstacles for the elephants—an ancient form of tank trap. They proved a mighty obstacle: 800 feet long, 6 feet deep and 9 feet wide. Arachidamia led the Spartan women and 'completed with their own hands a third of the trench.' The formidable Arachidamia led the Spartan women in the subsequent fighting against Pyrrhus.

On the next day, the Spartans (led by Arcotatus) were encouraged by their women defenders and by the sight of Chilonis, daughter of Leotychidas, who had ostentatiously placed a halter around her neck; she said that she would rather commit suicide than return to her husband, Cleonymus, if Pyrrhus captured the city.[3] Cleonymus, something of a mercenary and a pretender to the Spartan throne, had been refused the throne because of his violent behaviour; to make matters worse, he had been deeply humiliated when Chilonis was seduced by arch-enemy Arcotatus. This drove Cleonymus to leave Sparta and enlist the help of Pyrrhus. Pyrrhus subsequently led the attack on the city, but was repulsed. The Spartans, overjoyed by Arcotatus' superb leadership, jubilantly told him to withdraw from the battle and return to Chilonis, to father more children like himself for Sparta. The next day saw a new Epiriote attack but the Spartans held out; the Spartan women dutifully acted as ammunition loaders, taking away the wounded and providing food and drink for the sick and the fighters. Chilonis and Acrotatus had a child, who later ruled as Areus II, Agiad King of Sparta.

There was another high profile, prominent lady called Chilonis; she was both princess and queen, being daughter, wife, sister, and grandmother to four different Spartan kings (Leonidas II, Cleombrotus II, Cleomenes III, and Agesipolis III respectively). Chilonis became queen of Sparta in 272 BCE, when Leonidas, her father, was deposed from the throne by the ephor Lysander and replaced by her husband Cleombrotus II. Chilonis followed her father into exile, rather than stay in Sparta with her husband, now king.

The next year, when Lysander's year as ephor came to an end, Leonidas returned to Sparta and regained the throne, with a view to sentencing his son-in-law to death. But Chilonis saved him when she successfully persuaded her father to commute the penalty to exile. Chilonis along with their two children followed Cleombrotus out of Sparta.

Arachidamia went on to help her grandson Agis IV, in his attempts to restore old Lycurgan values to a Sparta then riven by wealth and greed. Arachidamia, and her daughter, Agesistrata (both women of some wealth), were among the first to donate their money to a common fund which was to be distributed equally amongst both old and new Spartan citizens. However, their efforts were ruined by the corruption of Agis's uncle and former supporter, Agesilaus, and a rival party, led by the Agiad King, Leonidas II. Leonidas had Agis illegally imprisoned and executed; Arachidamia and Agesistrata were lured into the prison, thinking they were to see Agis, but they too were executed.

We have seen how Spartan men were preoccupied, obsessed even, with their military careers; though usually marrying from their mid-twenties, they did not see very much of domestic or family life before the age of thirty. Their wives therefore played a vital and active economic role in raising their children and managing the household. They were wholly responsible for raising sons until they were aged seven, when they left to join the junior army (*agoge*), the start of their extensive and intensive training. It was, therefore, crucial that women of the citizen class be in the best condition physically and mentally, for conception and motherhood. The wife stayed at home, but was educated in the arts and took training in athletics, dancing, and chariot racing; a strong, fit, and educated mother delivered strong babies for a strong Sparta. It seems that the Spartans went more for quality and caliber, than indiscriminate or indifferent quantity.

Spartan women rarely married before the age of twenty, unlike their precocious Athenian counterparts. Dowries were less important, perhaps to encourage marriages that produced the healthiest babies rather than the best commercial prospects. Divorce was relatively uncomplicated and positively more humane than elsewhere; the woman retained her personal wealth and custody of her children, and she was not coerced into remarriage.

Athenian women wore clothes, veils even, to cover their bodies entirely; the clothes of the socially more liberated Spartan women were, appropriately, much looser and more revealing. However, we do see from various artefacts that Spartan women did, occasionally at least, cover their heads, and sometimes their faces. Furthermore, the nudity amongst Spartans, which the hostile Athenians made so much of, was often reserved for religious ritual; it was never a routine or casual thing.[4] We have noted how Spartan girls, as well as boys, received an education—both physical and intellectual; Plato points out in his *Protagoras* that in Sparta, 'not only men but also women pride themselves on their intellectual culture,' high level education in rhetoric and philosophy.[5]

Girls and women played sport just like the boys, enjoying wrestling, running, discus, and javelin—some of which may have been done in the nude—much to the outrage of the scandalised Athenians. Spartan women competed in the Olympics and other athletic events, where they often featured in wrestling. Religious festivals featured processions, athletic contests, and horse and chariot racing, all for both sexes. A chariot race for women took place at the three-day Hyacinthia. There were also dancing and singing competitions for boys and girls, again, sometimes in the nude.

Controversy continues to rage over whether Spartan society permitted pederasty, as was the norm in other Greek *poleis*. A passage in Xenophon would suggest that pederasty in Sparta was prohibited:

> … [Lycurgus] … ruled that in Sparta lovers should refrain from molesting boys, just as much as parents avoid having intercourse with their children or brothers with their sisters… It does not surprise me, however, that some people do not believe this, since in many other cities the laws do not oppose lusting after boys. (Xenophon, *Constitution of the Spartans* 2)

Aristotle was of the view that everything that was wrong with Sparta could be accounted for by the fact that women were in control, and that this was due to the absence of homosexual practices in Spartan society. Indeed, Aristotle has a lot to say about Spartan women in his *Politics*. Much of it, of course, is propaganda aimed against an enemy *polis*:

> Again, the license of the Lacedaemonian women defeats the intention of the Spartan constitution, and is adverse to the happiness of the state. For, a husband and wife being each a part of every family, the state may be considered as about equally divided into men and women; and, therefore, in those states in which the condition of the women is bad, half the city may be regarded as having no laws … the legislator has neglected the women, who live in every sort of intemperance and luxury. The consequence is that, in such a state, wealth is too highly valued, especially if the citizen fall under the dominion of their wives … many things were managed by their women. But what difference does it make whether women rule, or the rulers are ruled by women? The result is the same. Even in regard to courage, which is of no use in daily life, and is needed only in war, the influence of the Lacedaemonian women has been most mischievous … the disorder of the women, as I have already said, not only gives an air of indecorum to the constitution considered in itself, but tends in a measure to foster avarice … nearly two-fifths of the whole country are held by women; this is owing to the number of heiresses and to the large dowries which are customary. It would surely have been better to have given no dowries at all, or, if any, but small or moderate ones.[6]

We should also point out that Herodotus, ever one for the tabloid and sensational, nowhere describes a pederastic, or even homosexual, relationship in his descriptions of Spartan society. We read about a man lusting a close friend's wife, one who runs off with a rival's bride just before her wedding, or the king who loves his infertile wife so much that he refuses to discard her, even if it means compromising the succession to his throne; all of these feature in the *Histories*, but nothing about a Spartan with a male lover, boy or man.

Although liberal in some ways, in other ways Sparta would appear to have been somewhat more censorious than other city states. This is true with regards to what we would now term pornography. The absence of archaeological evidence from Sparta showing homoerotic pornography is in stark contrast to the wealth of explicitly pornographic art from both Athens and Corinth, for example, where pederasty appears as frequently as heterosexual sex.

What we have found, however, are depictions of romantic scenes in which couples sit next to each other side by side. Elsewhere in Greece, images of couples engaging in sexual intercourse are quite usual, but not in Sparta. Perhaps this was due to Spartan marriage being more of an even-sided partnership, where couples were more equal, both in terms of age and in their role within the family. Xenophon points out that Spartan law permitted men and women to marry in their prime, and not when the girls were so very young. It may also have been the case that these Spartan images imply that women were allowed to enjoy sex as much as men in their relationships, contributing to a balanced and healthy marriage, producing healthy children of positive value to the family and the state.

We saw in the Introduction how the Athenian dramatist Euripides sometimes denigrates women in his plays. The poems of Spartan Alcman (*fl.* seventh century BCE), on the other hand, celebrate and champion women. His sixty or so hymns are actually the lyrics of songs performed at public festivals by choruses of girls—*partheneia* (maiden-songs παρθένος)'. In some of the poems, there is possible evidence of female homoerotic love when the girl choruses exclaim: 'If only Astaphis were mine, if only Philylla were to look my way and Damareta and lovely Ianthemis; no, Hagesichora wears me out with love' and 'I were to see whether she might love me. If only she came nearer and took my soft hand, I would be her suppliant immediately'.[7]

For Alcman, women are part of the beauty that forms the rich tapestry of nature. He describes a woman's hair and the golden chain she wears around her neck in the same breath, as it were, as the purple petals of a Kalchas flower and the purple depths of the sea.

Sparta had no brothels; Spartans were, apparently, without prostitution and adultery, preferring instead to honour the sanctity of marriage and fidelity. Helen of Troy, however, was a Spartan and did her compatriots no favours when it came to sexual *mores*. She was one of the world's greatest adulteresses, and responsible for the outbreak of a major regional conflict.

The relative freedom and respect enjoyed by Spartan women generally, their social obtrusiveness, their education and sexual liberation triggered salvos of misogynistic and abusive slurs aimed at the alleged permissiveness; this is all typified by Euripides in *Andromache*—'Spartan girls could not be chaste even if they wanted to be. They leave home, and with naked thighs and their dresses loose, they share the running tracks and gymnasiums with young men.'

This socially conservative attitude was coloured by the fact that Sparta and Athens were arch-enemies; attacking an enemy's morals through their womenfolk was a popular strategy in the ancient world. As it happened, Sparta was not alone in naked exercising. Athenaeus writes that Ionian Chios shared the custom of exercising in the nude with Sparta.[8]

It comes as no surprise that the conversation in the *Deipnosophistae* by Athenaeus eventually turns to 'love and amatory matters', or, more specifically, to Spartan women and sex:

> At Lacedaemon, all the young women used to be shut up in a dark room, while a number of unmarried young men were shut up with them; and whichever girl each of the young men caught hold of, he led away as his wife, without a dowry. That's why they punished Lysander, because he left his former wife, and wished to marry another who was much more beautiful. But Clearchus of Soli, in his treatise On Proverbs, says,- 'In Lacedaemon the women, on a certain festival, drag the unmarried men to an altar, and then thrash them; in order that ... they may become more affectionate, and in time may start thinking about marriage. (*Deipnosophistae* 13, 2)

By Athenaeus' time, the first anecdote above had become ancient history and only survived as a ritual in Spartan weddings in which the bride's hair would be cut short and, wearing a man's cloak and sandals, would be left alone in a dark room, where she would be 'captured' by her new husband.

> At Athens, Cecrops was the first person to marry a man to just one wife, when before his time relationships were random, and men had wives in common. That's why some people say that Cecrops was called διφυής ['of double nature'], because before his time people did not know who their fathers were because of the numbers of men who might have been so.[9]

However, pre-Cecrops Athenian sexual *mores* were shared by Persians and some Homeric heroes:

> But among the Persians, the queen tolerates the king's having a number of concubines, because there the king rules his wife like her master; and also because the queen, as Dinon states in his history of Persia, receives a great deal of respect from the concubines. At all events they offer her obeisance. And Priam, too, had a great many women, and Hecabe was not indignant. Accordingly, Priam says nineteen of my sons are from one womb; The rest were born to women in my halls.[10]

They were not alone:

But Heracles is the man who appears to have had more wives than any one else, for he was very much addicted to women; and he had them in turn ... And by them he had also a great multitude of children. For, in one week, as Herodotus relates, he relieved the fifty daughters of Thestius of their virginity. Aegeus also was a man of many wives. For, first of all he married the daughter of Hoples, and after her he married one of the daughters of Chalcodon, and giving both of them to his friends, he cohabited with a great many without marriage. Afterwards he took Aethra, the daughter of Pittheus; after her he took Medea. And Theseus, having attempted to ravish Helene, after that carried off Ariadne. (Athenaeus, *Deipnosophistae* 13, 4)

Euripides opens his *Medea* with the nurse telling us that Medea is 'unhinged in her love for Jason'; at this point, she is the perfect Greek wife who did everything her husband asked, making great sacrifices for him. In return, he cruelly betrayed her love, with shocking consequences for their children. For Medea, love was for life; in the *Argonautica* (3, 126-8) she swears, 'in our lawful marriage-chamber, you shall share my bed, and nothing will separate us in our love until the appointed death enshrouds us'.

And so it goes on—an epic catalogue of serial, 'historical' rape and general licentiousness by the heroes of Greece who, before the time Cecrops put their moral house in order enabling them to appropriate the moral high ground, were just as promiscuous as the Spartans ever were.

Plutarch's *Moralia* includes a collection of *Sayings of Spartan Women*, including one attributed to Gorgo, the wife of Leonidas I; when asked by a woman from Attica why Spartan women were the only women in the world who could boss their men, she replied 'Because we are the only women who are mothers of men'. Gorgo is one of the few female historical figures whom Herodotus actually names and was famed for her political judgement and wisdom. She was the daughter of a king of Sparta, the wife of another, and the mother of a third. When she was about eighteen (although Herodotus says eight or nine), Gorgo precociously but astutely told her father, the vacillating King Cleomenes, to dismiss the tyrant Aristagoras of Miletus, who requested military aid from Sparta for his rebellion against Persia:

Aristagoras took the suppliant's branch and went to the house of Cleomenes; and ... asked Cleomenes to dismiss the child and listen to him—the daughter of Cleomenes was standing by him, whose name was Gorgo; as it happened she was his only child, now eight or nine years old. Cleomenes told him to say what he wanted to say, and not to stop because of the child. Then Aristagoras began to promise him money, beginning with ten talents, if he would do for him what he wanted; and when Cleomenes refused, Aristagoras went on increasing the sums of money offered, until at last he had promised fifty talents. At this point the child cried out: 'Father, the strange man will harm you, if you do not leave him and go.' Cleomenes, then, pleased by his child's advice, went out into another room, and Aristagoras left Sparta.[11]

Gorgo also rose to the occasion when a blank wax tablet was sent to Sparta from the exiled king Demaratus, then residing at the Persian court, regarding a Persian attack on Greece:

> He took a folding tablet and scraped off the wax which was on it, and then he wrote the design of the king upon the wood of the tablet, and having done so he melted the wax and poured it over the writing, so that the tablet (ostensibly blank) might not cause any trouble when given to the keepers of the road. Then when it had arrived at Lacedemon, the Lacedemonians were not able to make head or tail of it until at last, as I am informed, Gorgo, the daughter of Cleomenes and wife of Leonidas, suggested a plan of which she had herself thought up, bidding them scrape the wax and they would find writing on the wood; and doing as she said they found the writing and read it, and after that they sent notice to the other Hellenes.[12]

Before the Battle of Thermopylae, knowing that her husband's death was inevitable, Gorgo asked him what she should do in widowhood. Leonidas replied 'marry a good man who will treat you well, bear children for him, and live a good life'—family values prescribed in the most distressing of circumstances.

Polygamy, or wife-sharing was another characteristic of Spartan social life and epitomises the dichotomy within sexual *mores* there. Three or four brothers are known to have shared the same wife, usually to preserve the integrity of their inheritance but also to enhance the quality of the stock; any children belonged equally to all involved. Essentially, if an unmarried man wanted a child but not a wife, he could borrow a wife in order to produce that child.

This became a favourite refrain amongst the Athenians when denigrating the Spartans. However, wife-sharing was by no means exclusive to the Spartans in antiquity; Julius Caesar describes a similar arrangement amongst the ancient Britons in the first century BCE, along with their penchant for long hair, another Spartan trait. We are told by Theopompus how well before that, the allegedly sex-mad Etruscans shared their beautiful, bibulous, and permissive wives too.[13]

But such free love was not universally welcomed. King Agis II (r. 427–401 BCE) was persuaded by the interpretation of an earthquake that he should not sleep with his queen, Timaea. A lusty Alcibiades saw an opportunity there, so persuaded Timaea that he would make a fine father for her offspring in the absence of Agis' attentions. A son, Leotychides, was duly born whom Agis discovered to be illegitimate upon consulting his calendar.[14] The son was disowned and a death warrant sent out for Alcibiades, who managed to avoid execution when warned of the threat by Timaea.[15]

The production of healthy sons in Sparta was amply rewarded. After the birth of the third son, the father was excused military service; after the fourth, he could live free of taxes.

Spartan women were only human though, as the following episode illustrates. Tarentum was one of only two colonies to be established by the Spartans; the other was Cyrene. Its founders were the Partheniae, traditionally believed to be the sons of virgins; they were the sons of Spartan women and Perioikoi, free men who were not officially citizens of Sparta, whom the women of Sparta turned to when their husbands were in the Messenian Wars in eighth century. Womanly needs apart, the Spartan women had a duty to increase the Spartan birthrate, and thereby the number of recruits to the Spartan military, during these Messenian Wars; therefore, they slept with the Perioikoi. However, the marriages were later annulled, and the sons were forced to leave Greece. Phalanthus, the Parthenian leader, consulted the oracle at Delphi about how to handle this unfortunate situation; he was told that Tarentum was to be the new home of the exiles.[16] Things evidently went well there; Tarentum grew in stature and, by the time Roman power was spreading south, had become a major commercial and military force among the cities of Magna Graecia in southern Italy.

Financially, Spartan daughters were better off than their Athenian sisters. The Spartan daughter inherited half of what a son would inherit; although part (if not all) was in the form of a dowry delivered to them at the time of their marriage, this beneficence gave Spartan women a lot more wealth than their Athenian counterparts. Unlike in Athens, a Spartan dowry often included land. Land could be given away or bequeathed, but it could not be sold; despite this, some women became major landowners and enjoyed considerable wealth as a result. There were restrictions though; slaves were state-owned so could not be freed or sold. Laws limited spending on weddings and funerals, and restricted the amount of jewellery that could be worn.

As liberated as women were in Spartan society, some took it one stage further and carved out a life of exceptional achievement and determination. We have touched on how Cynisca excelled at the Olympic Games. Cynisca (born *c.* 440 BCE) was the wealthy daughter of the king of Sparta, Archidamus II; her name means 'female puppy'.[17] Xenophon tells us that she was urged by her brother, Agesilaus II, to compete in the Olympic Games, participating in the prestigious four-horse chariot race as an owner and trainer of horses. Agesilaus was ever keen to instill bravery and belligerence in the Spartans, and to raise the profile of women at the same time. An alternative explanation is that he wanted to discredit the sport by having a woman win it.[18] Cynisca duly won the four-horse race (*tethrippon*, τέθριππον) in both 396 BCE and 392 BCE. She was honoured with a bronze statue of a chariot and horses, a charioteer, and a statue in the Temple of Zeus in Olympia. The inscription read that she was the only woman to win in the chariot events at the Olympic Games. Pausanias reminds us that usually, only Spartan kings were honoured in this way. This is what the statue tells us:

> My fathers and brothers were Spartan kings. I won with a team of fleet footed horses and put up this monument. I am Cynisca: I declare that I am the only woman in Greece to have won such a wreath.[19]

Given what we know about Spartan women, it comes as no surprise that Spartan women were slurred and vilified by the men of other *poleis*, not least by their arch-enemy, the Athenians. Wife sharing, bigamy, financial independence and wealth, intellectual development and education, even the Doric *peplos*, all served to attract sexual spitefulness and enmity. The *peplos* had a long slit up one side, to enhance mobility, and was termed φαινομηρίδες 'thigh-showing'. Alongside the bronze figurines showing Spartan female athletes competing in a tunic that exposed one breast, and Plutarch's report that Spartan girls performed ritual dances nude in public with nude boys, then the more socially conservative and dominating Athenian male, whose women were altogether less revealing, was always going to be outraged by (and no doubt sexually fascinated by) a Spartan woman.[20] Known best for his pederastic poems, we have the lyric poet Ibycus (*fl.* second half of sixth century BCE), to thank for the thigh-showing epithet, quoted by Plutarch as evidence of permissive morals among Spartan women. Sophocles, with just a hint of prurient indignation, joins in the outrage when he describes Hermione, daughter of Helen, as a 'young girl, whose tunic, still unsewn, lays bare her gleaming thigh Between its folds'.

No history written by a Spartan survives; therefore, we have to rely on the undoubtedly biased, xenophobic, and hostile writings of other Greeks for our picture of Sparta and Spartan society. Polemic and propaganda taint what has come down to us. Anton Powell puts it best: 'to say that the written sources are 'not without problems'... as an understatement would be hard to beat'.[21]

Dressing down and making up

Dress was very important to the ancient Greek. The typical 'wardrobe' comprised the *chiton*, *peplos*, *himation*, and *chlamys*, with men and women alike wearing two pieces of clothing: an undergarment (*chiton* or *peplos*) and a kind of cloak (*himation* or *chlamys*). Clothes were usually homespun out of linen or wool, with little cutting or sewing involved; they were both held on and kept together with ornamental clasps or pins, and a belt or girdle (*zone*).

The *peplos* was a large rectangle of wool fabric fastened at the shoulder with a pin or brooch and with armholes on each side. The *chiton* was made of linen, long and wide and girded around the waist. The chiton came in two types: the Doric chiton and the later Ionic chiton. The Doric was simple and had no sleeves. It was a single rectangle of woollen or linen fabric; it was pinned with περόνη (*perone*), sewn, or buttoned at the shoulder. It could be worn on its own, or with an overfold (an *apotygma*), which was more common with women. The Ionic version was more elaborate, made from a wider piece of fabric, and pinned, sewn, or buttoned all the way from the neck to the wrists; a large belt (*zoster*) could be worn over the chiton, under the breast. The blousing or excess material was known as *kolpos*, κόλποις. There was also a double-girdled style. The chiton was often worn with the heavier *himation* on top as a cloak. When the *himation* was worn without a chiton, it was called an *achiton*. On its own, the chiton was known as a *monochiton*. A long chiton that extended to the heels was called a *chiton poderes*, while a longer one that dragged on the ground was a *chiton syrtos* or an ἑλκεχιτώνες. A woman would always wear her *chiton* ankle length. Initially, men wore the long *chiton*, but later wore it at knee length, except for priests and charioteers, and the elderly.

The *peplos* (πέπλος) was a body-length tubular cloth, with the top edge folded down about halfway, so that the top of the tube was below the waist, and the bottom reached to the ankle. It was gathered at the waist and the folded top edge pinned over the shoulders. The most famous and familiar examples of the *peplos* in statuary are those worn by the caryatids, in the porch of the Athens Erechtheum.

The *peplos* had deep religious significance; on the final day of the Pyanepsion, the priestess of Athena Polias and the Arrephoroi set up the loom, on which the enormous *peplos* was to be woven by the Ergastinai, a group of girls selected to pass nine months making the sacred *peplos*. Their task was to weave a theme around Athena's defeat of Enkelados, and the Olympians' vanquishing of the Giants. The *peplos* was changed annually during the Plynteria; it also had a role in the Great Panathenaea. A special *peplos* would be woven by young women nine months before the festival, at the arts and crafts festival called Chalkeia. This *peplos* had myths woven into it and was placed on the statue of Athena during the festival procession. The *peplos* usually consisted of purple and saffron yellow cloth. Women sometimes wore an *epiblema*, a shawl, over the *peplos* or *chiton*. A *tainia* (ταινία) was a head band or ribbon worn at Greek festivals.

There was little or no difference between men and women' clothing; clothes might double up as bedding. Most clothing was un-dyed white, although we have evidence of decorated borders (usually purple) and vividly coloured patterns, especially for women.

Women would also wear a *strophion*, breast band or bra, which was a wide band of wool or linen wrapped across the breasts and tied between the shoulder blades. It differs from modern attire in that it was worn on the outside rather than as underwear. There were hairnets (*sakkos*) and stretchy socks (*sokkoi*). Men and women might also wear triangular loincloths (*perizoma*); women did so when menstruating. The *perizoma* originated from Minoan culture and can be seen on participants in the Bull Leaping fresco.

Both sexes wore leather sandals, slippers, soft shoes, or boots for outside; at home, they usually went barefoot. The *carbatine* was a sandal that featured a single piece of leather secured to the sole of the foot with laces, which pulled the tops of the shoes together when tied, leaving the toes exposed.

In Crete, a tightly hemmed waist was the fashion for women and girls. Skirts were full and long, being heavily flounced in the Late Minoan period; sometimes, an embroidered double-apron was worn over the skirt. A short-sleeved jacket, open in front and leaving the breasts bare might be worn. We have seen how Spartan women incurred the disgust of other Greeks with their thigh revealing split *chitons* and breast exposing *chitoniskos*.

We know from statuary that Greek women, particularly the elite, sometimes covered both their head and face with a veil when out in public.[1] This included Spartan women, despite their reputation for attire that was more liberal and revealing.

For women, the apparent blandness of most clothes was offset by flashy jewellery, fetching hair styles and make-up. The cult of Helen of Troy was of special significance in Sparta. Excavations at sites where her cult was practiced have revealed mirrors, eye-liners, combs, and perfume bottles, indicating the importance of cosmetics to the ancient Greek woman. The word 'cosmetic' comes from the Greek *kosmetikos,* which means a sense of harmony, order, and tranquillity. Mirrors reflect a concern about personal appearance; ancient burials have revealed a large number, particularly in the graves of women. Many have been made with great attention to detail and decoration; excavations show that the Greeks developed one of the first compacts, a box mirror made from two hinged metal discs.

Cosmetics in ancient Greece can only be described as bordering on the industrial. Light skin was craved, so women painted their faces with (toxic) white lead (lead carbonate) called *fucus* (φῦκος, a life-shortening habit), or ψιμύθιον, cerussa; where there was no lead, chalk was used but that was nowhere near as effective or enduring. Lead-based facial masks were applied to remove blemishes and impurities from the skin. Many Greek women died, unknowingly from lead poisoning, after applying this noxious substance. Pliny did not mince his words, pointing out 'it is useful for giving women a fair complexion; but like scum of silver, it is deadly poison.' Even when the health risks were known in Roman times, women continued to apply it; such are the lengths to which women would go for the sake of beauty.

For a smooth foundation and moisturizer, women used creams made from honey mixed with olive oil, added to make it shine. Minoan women are said to have bathed in honey and milk. Cheeks were rouged with red-coloured pastes—ἄγχουσα (*anchousa*)—obtained from the root of a plant.[2] Lipsticks were made with a dangerous combination of red iron oxide and ochre clays, or olive oil with beeswax. *Paideros* (παιδέρως, a vegetable dye), *sukaminon* (συκάμινον, mulberry), and focus (φῦκος, a seaweed) produced rouge.[3]

We met Ischomachus earlier, looking for a light-headed woman whom he could mould and train the Ischomachus way. Here he is again describing to Socrates how his wife is what today we might call 'tarted up':

> Ischomachus then said, 'One time, Socrates, I saw that my wife had clarted her face with white lead, so that she would seem to have a paler complexion than she really had, and put on thick rouge, so that her cheeks would seem redder than they really were, and high boots, so that she would seem taller than she actually was'. (Xenophon, *Oeconomicus* 10, 2)

Ischomachus is not too concerned about the unfortunate impression his wife may be giving, made up in such a way. On the contrary, he sees this as an opportunity to explain to his wife the difference between true beauty and the appearance of beauty. Her appearance was presumably quite usual and normal, telling us how young Greek women made up and dressed to enhance their attractiveness.

From Lysias' speech on the murder of Eratosthenes, we learn that the wife made herself up before visiting her lover, a fact which did not go unnoticed by her husband. Apparently, red wine, beetroot, and mastic (an aromatic resin) were used. Olive oil mixed with ground charcoal produced eye shadow. The eyebrows and eyelids were stained black with asbolos (ἄσβολος), made from soot, or kohl (στίμμι) eye shadow—toxic antimony trisulphide has since been used in safety matches, ammunition, explosives and fireworks. Such dark powders were used to make the fashionable unibrow, where the eyebrows are joined up. The versatile and ubiquitous olive oil was also used as a moisturiser and a skin cleanser.

Female slaves wore their hair short; free women had long hair, worn loose while they were single, and tied up, usually in a chignon or bun, upon marriage. When in mourning, they cut their hair short. Straight hair was often curled. Diadems, jewelled combs, hair pins, scarfs, and other hair accessories were popular. Dark hair was lightened to achieve the much sought after blonde look, by applying vinegar and sitting in the sun. Urine may have been used to rinse hair because of the bleaching power of the ammonia. Tans were avoided by wearing broad-brimmed hats; these also helped in lightening a woman's hair when she pulled her hair through the top of the hat, leaving the rest to the sun. Olive oil was used as a conditioner, to keep hair soft. Sappho celebrated Kleis' hair:

My mother used to say, when I was just your age, that a girl who bound her hair with a purple band wore the most becoming thing that any girl could wear. But for the girl whose hair is more yellow than torches wreathes of flowering buds are more becoming by far. Not long ago I had a broad embroidered band from Sardis. But for you Kleis, I have no coloured band, nor do I know where I shall get one.[4]

Indeed, the literature is replete with references to cosmetics and hairstyles. Here are just a few which will give an idea of how important they were at various stages of ancient Greek history.[5]

These crocus-gowns, this outlay of the best myrrh, slippers, cosmetics dusting beauty, and robes with rippling creases of light.[6]

Dear Spartan girl with a delightful face, washed with the rosy spring.[7]

With smooth roses powdered on our cheeks, our bodies burning naked through the folds of shining Amorgos' silk, and meet the men with our dear Venus-plaits plucked trim and neat.[8]

I am but a servant, and yet I have poured on my hair the most exquisite essences.[9]

For unmarried girls before their marriage will cut their hair for you.[10]

You who, before your daughter's death was decided, as soon as your husband had started from home, were adorning the golden locks of your hair at the mirror. A wife who decks herself out for beauty, when her husband is gone from home–strike her off the list as worthless. There is no need for her to show her pretty face out of doors, unless she is seeking some mischief.[11]

Therewith she anointed her lovely body, and she combed her hair, and with her hands plaited the bright tresses, fair and ambrosial, that streamed from her immortal head.[12]

Perfumes were big business in antiquity, as now. Although four hundred years apart, both Theophrastus (in his *De Odoribus*) and Pliny (in his *Natural History*) catalogued the various origins of different perfumes and scents, as well as recipes for specific fragrances and ointments. Specific fragrances were produced for application on different parts of the body, both to conceal unpleasant odours as well as to provide pleasant ones. Fragrances were also added to wines. This is an example of how certain perfumes are made:

> For making each perfume, they put in the suitable spices. Thus to make kypros, they put in cardamom and aspalathos, having first steeped them in sweet wine. To make rose-perfume, they put in ginger-grass aspalathos and sweet-flag: and these are steeped as in the case of kypros. So too into each of the others are put the spices which suit them. Into rose-perfume moreover is put a quantity of salt: this treatment is peculiar to that perfume, and involves a great deal of waste, twenty-three gallons of salt being put to eight gallons and a half of the perfume.[13]

The stock characters in New Comedy were made more recognisable by the fashions typically projected through their masks, hair styles, and costumes. Certain kinds of complexion, styles of hair, and eyebrows were the preserve of particular classes. White or grey hair was the sign of old age. Red hair indicated a rascally slave. Thick, curly hair denoted strength in a man. Misers wore their hair close-cropped, while soldiers were distinguished by long manes. Courtesans usually bound up their hair with blingy ornaments or brightly colored bands. Beards were worn by middle-aged men to denote their manhood or middle age. A white complexion denoted effeminacy; pale complexions indicated love or ill-health. Colours were special too and so were appropriated by specific characters: white was for old men and slaves, purple for young men, black or grey taken up by parasites. Pimps wore a bright, multi-colored tunic and cloak. Old women were typically dressed in green or light blue, young women and priestesses in white. Procuresses sported a purple head band. Pimps carried a straight staff, an oil flask, and a flesh-scraper. Heiresses were recognisable by fringes on the hems of their dresses.

The pursuit of beauty among women was relentless, perhaps even obsessive. Thargelia, the Milesian, was so beautiful and accomplished that she had fourteen different husbands.[14] Anutis, the wife of Bagazus and sister of Xerxes, was reputedly the most beautiful and the most permissive of all the women in Asia. Timosa, the concubine of Oxyartes, surpassed all women in beauty. Xenopitheia, the mother of Lysandrides, was said to be the most beautiful of all the women in Peloponnese; the Spartans killed her and her sister Chryse. Pantica of Cyprus was also a very fine looking woman—she was with Olympias, the mother of Alexander the Great, when Monimus asked for her hand in marriage; as she was reputedly a very licentious woman, Olympias said to him: 'O you wretch, you are marrying with your eyes, and not with your brain'[15].

Some places boasted a surfeit of beautiful women. Hesiod, in the third book of his *Melampodia*, and Theophrastus, call Chalcis in Euboea 'Land of fair women'. Nymphodorus, in his *Voyage Around Asia*, says that the women in Tenedos, an island near Troy are the most beautiful of all.[16] There was also Helen of Troy, famous for having a face that launched a thousand ships.

The first beauty contests took place in Greece. One winner was Herodice; the women who contested were called 'gold-bearers' (χρυσοφόροι). In some places, Theophrastus tells us, perhaps with a twist of irony, 'there are contests between the women for modesty and good management, as there are among the barbarians ... the honour paid to modesty ought to be higher'.[17]

Beauty, of course, elides into sexuality; at what point this actually happens is probably very much, as beauty, in the proverbial eye of the beholder. One of the more erogenous of zones in a woman is the buttocks—both sexual, and a symbol of fertility and beauty. Statues created as early as 24,000 BCE, such as the *Venus of Willendorf* found in Austria, have exhibited exaggerated buttocks, hips, and thighs. Pygophilia is sexual arousal caused by the buttocks.

Athenaeus tells of the well-read *hetaira* Mania, mistress of Philip II, quoting Sophocles:

Mania once was asked, by King Demetrius, for a perfect sight of her fair buttocks;
and she, in return, demanded that he should grant her a favour. When he agreed, she
turned her back, and said—'O son of Agamemnon, now the Gods grant you to see
what you so long have wished for.'[18]

Gnathaena gives us more buttock exposure, or at least a request for it, and an exquisite put-down:

They say that one fine day a youth from Pontus was sleeping with Gnathaena, and in
the morning he asked her to show her buttocks to him. But she replied, 'You have no
time for that now, it's time for you to feed the pigs.' (Athenaeus, *Deipnosophistae* 13,
580f, 581a)

Demophoon, a friend of Sophocles', was also partial to his *hetaira's* buttocks: 'And it is said this woman had fair buttocks, And when Demophoon tried to hold them, 'A pretty thing,' said she, 'that what you get From me, you may present to Sophocles.'' (Athenaeus, *Deipnosophistae* 13, 582 [after Machon]).

In the boundless pursuit of physical beauty, the buttocks were crucial. The ideal was portrayed on a Greek bronze, but this is now lost; a fine first-century BCE Roman copy in marble called the 'Kallipygean Venus' can be seen in the Naples Archaeological Museum. Athenaeus tells the story of a Syracusan farmer with had two daughters who could not agree on which had the best buttocks, so they enlisted the opinion of a young boy passer-by. He preferred the buttocks of the older sister and fell in love with her. His inquisitive younger brother fell likewise for the younger sister; the two married their callipygian girls, commissioned a temple to the Kallipygean Aphrodite, and erected a cult statue. The Christian Clement of Alexandria was later to describe the masterpiece as 'shamefully erotic examples of pagan religious art.'

Educated Women:
Poets, Philosophers, Painters,
Physicists, and Prostitutes

This chapter looks at women's education and the surprising number of ancient Greek women who were highly educated and excelled in the arts (poetry, philosophy, painting and sculpture) and in the sciences. It also covers that educated breed of socialite, the sophisticated and urbane prostitute, the *hetaira*. Given that most Greek women were largely uneducated—except in household matters—there is a remarkable number of educated women proficient in, and excelling in, the arts and sciences; although admittedly small numbers in terms of the general population, they were still significant, and act as more evidence that ancient Greek women were not as socially or intellectually suppressed, as is often argued. Precious little has survived, but we do have fragments and citings from later writers.

Generally speaking, Greek women were home educated by a mother, another close relative, or perhaps by an educated slave. The days of the *thiasoi* were short lived and long-gone by the classical age. Girls received tuition in reading, writing, arithmetic, spinning, weaving, embroidery, singing, dancing, and playing a musical instrument. Spartan girls, as we have seen, were much luckier; they received a formal education more akin to that which a boy received in other parts of Greece, to equip them to raise Spartan boys for the army, and girls to raise successive generations of boys for those armies. When Macedonia emerged as a powerful political and military force, Macedonian girls too seem to have received a broader and more extensive education, enabling the top echelons of women to operate at the highest levels of government, even in the military, and to participate in their culture generally.

In the rest of Greece, resulting low levels of literacy (especially in the lower classes) would have had a harmful effect on female employment prospects outside the home; however, despite this and the male contention that women belonged in the home, we do know that women did go out to work, as we have shown.

The most famous of the educated women we know of is Sappho. Sappho was a Greek lyric poet (*c.* 620–570 BCE), born on Lesbos. She was the daughter of aristocratic parents Skamandronymos and Cleis. Her poetry was well-known in classical times and admired, but most of it has since been lost; nevertheless, her reputation endures through surviving fragments. Sappho was commonly regarded in antiquity as one of the greatest lyric poets and was called 'the tenth muse' by Plato. Details of her life are unclear; she was probably married and had a daughter, Cleis. One story from

Menander says that Sappho committed suicide by jumping off the Leucadian cliffs for love of Phaon, a ferryman, though perhaps this was an attempt to heterosexualise her.[1]

In her poetry, Sappho focuses on love for both men and women. Of the 12,000 lines of poetry she is thought to have composed, many of which described her love for other women, about 600 lines have survived. As a result of her fame in antiquity, she and her island have become emblematic of love between women. Our word lesbian derives from Lesbos, while her name is also the origin of the word Sapphic, though neither word was applied to female homosexuality until about 1890. The Christians visited a kind of *damnatio memoriae* on her, attempting to extinguish all record of her poetic output.

What the surviving fragments do show is a unique intimacy inspired by a world from which men were excluded; *Parting* is significant as it is written by a woman for a woman:

'The truth is, I wish I were dead.' She left me, weeping all the time, and she said, 'Oh what a cruel fate is ours, Sappho, yes, I leave you against unwillingly.' And I answered her: 'Good-bye, go and remember me, for you know how we cared for you. 'If you do remember, I want to remind you ... and were happy ... of violets ... you set beside me and with woven garlands made of flowers around your soft neck and with perfume, royal, rich ... you anointed yourself and on soft beds you would drive out your passion 'and then ... sanctuary ... was ... from which we were away ...'[2]

As we have seen, Sappho is believed to have run a *thiasos*—a community in which Greek girls could receive a basic education. There, they could also be exposed to homosexual love; sometimes that love was aimed at their teachers, and sometimes at each other. Sappho's contemporary, Alcaeus, described her as 'Violet-haired, pure, honey-smiling Sappho.'[3]

Of the 200 or so fragments of Sappho's poetry, *Fragment 16* and *Fragment 44* are lyric retellings of Homer—both allude to scenes originating in the *Iliad* that Sappho expands on; *Fragment 16* characterises Helen, while *Fragment 44* describes the domestic joy leading up to the wedding of Hector and Andromache.

Sappho's reception down the ages has sadly been hijacked by moralists, most of whom have missed the finer points of her verse. The Poetry Foundation puts it well:

Much of the history of Sappho's reputation, though, is the story of her appropriation by moralists. Those New Comedians who picked up the strain of abuse initiated by the Anacreontic fragment mentioned earlier rendered the poet a popular burlesque comic figure on the stage. A good many plays centered around Sappho, though most were wholly unrelated to her life or her poetry. Later Christian censors in various ages in Alexandria, Rome, and Constantinople condemned her in words such as those of Tatian, who called her 'a whore who sang about her own licentiousness.' Saint Gregory of Nazianzus and Pope Gregory VII ordered her works to be burned.[4]

Parts of two previously unknown poems by Sappho were published in February 2014 in the *Times Literary Supplement*.

Anactoria is mentioned by Sappho as one of her a lovers in *Fragment 16*, otherwise known as *To an Army Wife, in Sardis*. *Sappho 31* is usually called the *Ode to Anactoria*, although her name appears nowhere in it. Algernon Charles Swinburne wrote a long poem called *Anactoria*, in which Sappho addresses Anactoria with imagery that includes sadomasochism, cannibalism, and dystheism—the belief that a god, goddess, or just God is not completely good and may even be evil.

Erinna was a contemporary and friend to Sappho; she was from Rhodes and was active about 600 BCE. She is famous for the *Distaff* (Ἠλἄκάτη)—300 dactylic hexameter lines written in Aeolic and Doric Greek. In the poem, the traditional female activity of weaving is a metaphor for writing poetry and alludes to the thread of life spun by the Fates. Importantly, it gives us a girl's view of her relationship with her mother. In 1928, a papyrus (*PSI* 1090) was found, comprising fifty-four fragmentary lines, now in the Biblioteca Medicea Laurenziana. The poem is a lament (θρῆνος) on the death of her friend Baucis, a disciple of Sappho, just before her wedding. Apparently, she died a virgin at the age of nineteen.

Cleitagora or Clitagora was a Spartan lyric poet referred to by Aristophanes in his *Wasps* and his lost play *Danaids*. She is also variously represented as a Thessalian, and a Lesbian; she was even called a 'female Homer.' Megalostrata was another Spartan poet, much admired by Alcman, who describes her as a golden-haired maiden enjoying the gift of the Muses. Athenaeus tells us that Megalostrata could talk a man into bed; she attracted lovers with her urbane conversation.

Cleobulina of Rhodes (*fl. c.* 550 BCE)—whose father was Cleobulus, one of the Seven Sages of Greece—specialised in riddles or enigmas written in hexameters. Aristotle quotes her in both his *Poetics* and the *Rhetoric*; she was satirized in a play by the comic playwright Cratinus. Plutarch tells us that Thales praised her as being a woman with 'a statesman's mind'; some say she was Thales' mother.

Corinna is traditionally placed in the sixth century BCE, but some scholars now put her much later. According to Plutarch and Pausanias, she came from Tanagra in Boeotia, where she was a teacher and rival to Pindar. Pausanias says she beat Pindar in a poetry competition; she had a monument erected to celebrate this. Pindar jealously put her success down to her beauty and her use of the local Boeotian dialect, as opposed to Pindar's Doric Aelian. She defeated Pindar five times; Pindar uncharitably called her a sow. Antipater of Thessaloniki counted her in his catalogue of nine mortal muses.

Her *Minouaie* (*The Daughters of Minyas*) is about the three adult daughters of King Minyas of Orchomenus: Leukippe, Arsippe, and Alkathoe. *Koronaie* (*The Shuttle Maidens*) tells of Orion's two daughters Menippe and Metioche, who cut their throats with their shuttle, 'accepting death for their neighbours' sake'.

Praxilla of Sicyon (fifth century BCE) was a contemporary of Telesilla; Antipater of Thessalonika lists her first among his canon of nine 'immortal-tongued' women poets. She was celebrated by her contempories—Lysippus made a bronze statue of her; a vase has been found with the first four words from one of her poems; Aristophanes parodied lines from her poetry in the *Wasps* (l. 1238) and the *Thesmophoriazusae* (l. 528), indicating clearly that his Athenian audience would recognise the allusions. She wrote drinking songs (*scolia*), hymns, and dithyrambs—choral odes performed at festivals of Dionysus. She composed a hymn to Adonis in which he replied to a question from the ghosts in the underworld—'What was the most beautiful thing you left behind [on earth]?' He answers 'finest of all the things I have left is the light of the sun, Next to that the brilliant stars and the face of the moon, Cucumbers in their season, too, and apples and pears'.

The fact that Praxilla composed drinking songs that would have been sung at *symposia*, from which respectable women were excluded, has led some to conclude that she may have been one of the many *hetairae*, urbane courtesans who attended such parties.

Telesilla (*fl.* 510 BCE) was from Argos; she is just as famous for her military prowess and soldierly activities as she is for her poetry. Apparently, as a young woman, Telesilla was so sickly that she went to the Pythia for some medical advice; Pythia told her to 'serve the Muses' ('τὰς Μούσας θεραπεύειν'), and so began Telesilla's career in poetry.

Moero was a poet of the third century BCE from Byzantium. She was the wife of Andromachus Philologus, and the mother of the tragedian Homerus of Byzantium. Antipater of Thessaloniki lists Moero in his list of famous female poets; she wrote epic, elegiac, and lyric poetry. Athenaeus quotes from her epic poem, *Mnemosyne* (*Μνημοσύνη*); two of her dedicatory epigrams are included in the *Greek Anthology*. She also wrote a hymn to Poseidon, and an anthology of poems called *Arai*.

Hedyle (*fl.* third century BCE) was an Athenian iambic poet, daughter of Moschine and mother of Hedylus, also poets. We know her from a poem called *Scylla*, from which a passage is cited by Athenaeus in a characteristically detailed discussion on the different types of fish available. Interestingly, Hedyle's Scylla is not the monster we know and fear from Greek epic, but an object of love to the merman Glaucus:

But Hedylus of Samos (or Athens) declares that Glaucus cast himself into the sea through love of Melicertes; and Hedylê, this poet's mother, who was the daughter of Moschinê, the Attic poetess of iambic verse, records in the poem entitled Scylla that Glaucus, in love with Scylla, entered her cave carrying 'gifts, either cockleshells from the Erythraean crag, or the still wingless young of halcyons—toys for the nymph before whom he was diffident. But even the Siren, virgin neighbour, pitied his tears; for she was swimming back to those shores and the borders of Aetna'.[5]

Nossis (*c.* 300 BCE) was an epigrammist who lived in Locri, southern Italy. Her work was inspired by Sappho, whom she claims to rival. Twelve epigrams of hers are in the *Greek Anthology*. Meleager includes her among the most distinguished Greek singers, and Antipater ranks her among the nine poets who compete with the Muses.

We have more complete poems by Anyte of Tegea than by any other Greek poet, since the nine books of Sappho survive only in fragments. Anyte (*fl.* early third century BCE) was an Arcadian poet, admired by her contemporaries and later generations for her delightful epigrams and epitaphs; Antipater counted her as one of the nine earthly muses. She may well have been the leader of a school of poetry and literature on Peloponnesus, which also included the poet Leonidas of Tarentum. Eighteen of her Doric dialect epigrams survive in the *Greek Anthology*, with an additional six tentatively attributed to her. Her verses focus on pity for the deaths of young women and animals, and take delight in children; Marilyn Skinner described her as 'the acknowledged inventor of the pastoral epigram, introducing evocations of peaceful idyllic landscapes into the repertoire of themes'. Boeo was a Delphic priestess, known to us only through four lines quoted from a hymn she composed to Apollo, in Pausanias's description of the Delphic oracle.

Melinno probably lived in the second century BCE, and came from Epizephyrian Locris, in Magna Graecia. She is known for five Sapphic stanzas, an *Ode to Rome* addressing the deity Roma. This is a Hellenistic attempt to revive the moribund Sapphic stanza in Greek, keeping alive a tradition that was later translated in to Latin by Catullus and Horace.

Female philosophers were no less numerous. Themistoclea (*fl.* sixth century BCE) was a priestess at Delphi and Pythagoras' teacher. Diogenes Laërtius (third century CE) quotes Aristoxenus (fourth century BCE) when he asserts that Themistoclea taught Pythagoras most of what he knew; Porphyry (233—305 CE) says the same.[6]

Timycha of Sparta (early fourth century BCE) was part of a band of Pythagorean pilgrims with her husband Myllias of Croton; it was attacked by Syracusian soldiers on their way to Metapontum as they had snubbed the tyrant Dionysius the Elder. One avenue of escape for them was through a field of beans, but they had to reject this since beans were taboo and off limits to them. Instead they fought and died; the only survivor was the pregnant Timycha and her husband, who were taken prisoner. Dionysius interrogated her about the bean taboo, but she refused to answer, in keeping with the well-attested Pythagorean inclination to be secretive and mysterious. Instead, she bit off her own tongue and spat it at his feet in a magnificent gesture of defiance.

These were not the only Pythagoreans who died from a fear of a field of beans, as beans were the death of Pythagoras. Enemies of the Pythagoreans set fire to Pythagoras' house, sending him running out towards a bean field; when he realised where he was, he stopped, declaring that he would rather die than go through the field—the mob promptly slit his throat. The beans taboo was to avoid favism, in which susceptible people may develop hemolytic anemia as a result of eating beans, or even of walking through a field where bean plants are in flower. Alternative explanations for the Pythagorean phobia are rather more magico-religious, including the idea that beans represent the potential for life and resemble the kidneys and genitalia, as well as a belief that beans and human beings were created from the same material. According to Diogenes Laërtius, the fava bean was sacred to the Pythagoreans because they have hollow stems; it was believed that souls of the dead would travel through the ground, up the hollow stems, and lodge in the beans.[7]

Pythagoreanism welcomed women philosophers; some of the first female philosophers that we have extant texts from followed Pythagoras. Some of these thinking women were major contributors to the works of the Pythagorean school, and entered the Pythagorean society on an equal basis with men. Pythagoras has been called the 'feminist philosopher' because much of his *oeuvre* was influenced by various women; Pythagoras was respected enough for men to give over their wives to the school to learn his doctrines. After his death, his wife Theano took charge of the school and their three daughters (Arignote, Myia, and Damo) were educated there and continued its teaching.

However, they did not espouse equality as we understand it; they taught that women were responsible for creating harmony and justice in the home, in much the same way as men did in the public arena and in the state.

Apart from the contribution made by involvement, participation, and teaching, gender had a central role in Pythagorean doctrine. Numbers were at the root of all things in the universe, and since numbers include both odd and even, all things must have a contradiction. Male and female were two of those contradictions that were implicit in all things, like light and dark, good and evil; these created harmony. In relation to human behaviour, harmony came from acting temperately or by exhibiting moderation. Much of the work of Pythagorean women demonstrated that life was harmonious; there was a direct relationship forged between a woman's soul, fidelity, bringing up children, respect to parents, religiousness, and public behaviour. When things went wrong, there was discussion and correspondence about women's chastity, women's responsibilities, and how a woman should react in the face of a husband's infidelity.

What we know about the female philosophers in Pythagoras' immediate family bears this out. Theano expatiated on number theory, explaining it as a principle to create order that helped to differentiate one thing from another. A maxim attributed to Theano concerns the immortality and transmigration of souls. She confirms for us that the Pythagoreans believed in divine justice, the afterlife, and metempsychosis— the transmigration of souls after death into a new body, not necessarily human. She also described the *mores* a woman should adopt in her day to day life. In *On Piety*, she explains how men and women have very different natures; the special virtue of women is temperance, whereby a wife's sexual activity must be restricted to pleasing her husband, for example. By having sex with her husband, a woman remains pure, whereas a woman can never be pure if she has sex with someone other than her husband. It fell to a woman to uphold law, justice, and domestic harmony; failure to do so led to chaos and disorder of society—a woman must be aware of her actions and the consequences of those actions in society.

Damo inherited her father's body of work, which she refused to sell, living a life of poverty as a consequence. The third daughter was Myia (*fl. c.* 500 BCE); she married Milo of Croton, the famous athlete, worked as a choir leader, and was noted for her exemplary religious behaviour. In his *In Praise of a Fly*, Lucian (*c.* 125 CE) states that he would be happy to say many things about Myia the Pythagorean, if her life story was not so well known already.[8]

Myia focussed on female temperance. She applied the principle of harmony to a woman's daily life through the care and upbringing of a newborn in the *Letter to Phyllis* attributed to her; she recommends that the woman who raises a child must be modest, well-disposed, and temperate, applying moderation in feeding, clothing, and bathing the child. If a nurse is employed, then it is critical that the nurse must not be permitted too much sleep or drink, and must keep her husband's sexual appetite in check. The child's wellbeing must remain the first priority, to promote harmony and help bring up a well-raised child.

Abrotelia (*fl.* fifth century BCE) was one of fifteen women included in the *Life of Pythagoras*, written by Iamblichus (*c.* 245–*c.* 325 CE).[9] Aesara of Lucania (fourth or third century BCE) was also a Pythagorean philosopher, and author of *On Human Nature*, from which a fragment is preserved for us by Stobaeus.[10] Aesara may be the same woman as Aresa, another daughter of Pythagoras and Theano. Aesara taught that, by the study of human nature and the human soul, we can understand the philosophical basis for natural law and morality—'Human nature seems to me to provide a standard of law and justice both for the home and for the city'. She divides the soul into three parts: the mind that delivers judgement and thought, the spirit that contains courage and strength, and desire which provides love and amity.

Phintys (fourth or third century BCE) was also a Pythagorean philosopher. Two fragments survive, which argue that it is necessary for a woman to be chaste, otherwise she wrongs the gods and natural law. A woman's greatest honour is to bear children that resemble their father, and that she must dress in moderation and not be flamboyant. Many Greek men would have applauded such sentiments, but Phyntis also argues that it is vital for a woman to practise philosophy because courage, justice, and intelligence are common in both men and women:

> Now some people think that it is not appropriate for a woman to be a philosopher, just as a woman should not be a cavalryman or a politician...I agree that men should be generals and city officials and politicians, and women should keep house and stay inside and receive and take care of their husbands. But I believe that courage, justice, and intelligence are qualities that men and women have in common... Courage and intelligence are more appropriately male qualities because of the strength of men's bodies and the power of their minds. Chastity is more appropriately female.

Ptolemais of Cyrene (*fl.* third century BCE) was a harmonic theorist, and author of *Pythagorean Principles of Music* (Πυθαγορικὴ τῆς μουσικῆς στοιχείωσις); we know her from references in Porphyry's commentary on Ptolemy's *Harmonics*.

Melissa (*fl.* third century BCE) is familiar to us only from a letter written to a Clareta, in which she asserts, somewhat like Phintys, that a wife must be modest and virtuous, and that she should obey her husband. Melissa believed that when it came to clothing, the only red that should be worn should be modest as in blushing, since that is the colour of virtue. Some scholars have argued that all this must have been written pseudonymously by a man.

Nicarete (*fl.* 300 BCE) was a philosopher of the Megarian school, said by Athenaeus to have been a *hetaira* of good family and education; 'she was very well calculated to excite affection by reason of her accomplishments, and she was a pupil of Stilpon the philosopher.'[11]

Diogenes Laërtius states she was Stilpon's mistress, even though he was married.[12] The Epicureans also welcomed women, and slaves. Leontion (*fl.* 300 BCE), an adherent of Metrodorus of Lampsacus, was one such philosopher and said by some to have been a *hetaira*—although this might just be the usual male denigration of clever women, or an expression of hostility toward Epicureans.[13]

Leontion was obviously talented. Diogenes Laërtius has a line from a letter that Epicurus wrote to Leontion, in which Epicurus praises her well-reasoned arguments.[14] Pliny says that she was painted by Aristides of Thebes in a work entitled *'Leontion thinking of Epicurus'*.[15] Cicero records that Leontion published arguments criticizing Theophrastus:

> Leontion, a mere courtesan, who had the temerity to write a riposte to Theophrastus—mind you, she wrote elegantly in good Attic, but still, this was the sort of licence which went on in the Garden of Epicurus.[16]

Pliny was likewise surprised that a woman could critique Theophrastus.[17]

Themista of Lampsacus, the wife of Leonteus, was another student of Epicurus, from the early third century BCE. Cicero scorns Epicurus for writing 'countless volumes in praise of Themista,' when he could have been writing about worthy men such as Miltiades, Themistocles or Epaminondas.[18] Themista and Leonteus named their son Epicurus.[19]

Arete of Cyrene (*fl.* fifth–fourth century BCE) was a Cyrenaic philosopher, and the daughter of Aristippus of Cyrene from whom she learned her philosophy and who in turn was taught by Socrates. Arete taught her son—Aristippus the Younger—philosophy, winning for him the nickname 'Mother-taught' (μητροδίδακτος). Arete may have succeeded her father as head of the Cyrenaic school. The Cyrenaics were a sensual hedonist school of philosophy which taught that the only intrinsic good is pleasure. The school died out within a century and was superseded by Epicureanism.

Among the spurious 'Socratic epistles' there is a fictitious letter from Aristippus addressed to Arete in which Arete is described as living a comfortable life in Cyrene. Aristippus makes the suggestion that, after his death, she should 'go to Athens, after you have given Aristippus [the Younger] the best possible education … and live with Xanthippe and Myrto [Socrates' two wives], and that she should regard Lamprocles [their son] as if he were her own child'.

She taught natural and moral philosophy in the schools and academies of Attica for thirty-five years, was the author of forty books, and had 110 philosophers as pupils. Her tomb bore an epitaph that described her as the splendour of Greece, with the beauty of Helen, the virtue of Thirma, the pen of Aristippus, the soul of Socrates, and the tongue of Homer; high praise indeed.

Arignote or Arignota (*fl. c.* 500 BCE) was a student and daughter of Pythagoras and Theano, and perhaps of their daughter Aesara too. According to the *Suda*, she was the author of a *Bacchica* describing the mysteries of Demeter, also called *The Sacred Narrative*; other possible works by her include *The Rites of Dionysus*; while Clement of Alexandria mentions a Τελεταί & Διονυσίου, *Dionysus and his Initiations*. Porphyry knew her work. Arignote reinforced and reiterated the importance of the number theory and its contribution to harmony:

The eternal essence of number is the most providential cause of the whole heaven, earth, and the region in between. Likewise, it is the root of the continued existence of the gods and daimones, as well as that of divine man.[20]

It was not always so easy, though, for aspiring female philosophers. Lastheneia was one of Plato's women students. She was born in Mantinea in Arcadia and was forced to study at Plato's Academy dressed as a man, such was the antipathy towards women students.[21] When Plato died, she continued her studies with Plato's nephew Speusippus, with whom she had an affair.[22] A papyrus fragment from Oxyrhynchus says that 'in her teens, she was lovely and full of unstudied grace.'[23]

Hipparchia of Maroneia (*fl. c.* 325 BCE) was a Cynic philosopher born in Maroneia; when her family moved to Athens, she met Crates, the famous Cynic, fell in love with him and his ways, and married him, despite her parents' opposition. She left her parents little choice in the end, threatening to kill herself if they stopped her. Crates did not help; he stood in front of Hipparchia, took off his clothes, and announced, 'Here is the bridegroom, and these are his goods.' Hipparchia obviously liked what she saw and embraced the Cynic *modus vivendi*; she took to wearing the same clothes as Crates (men's clothes) and appeared everywhere with him in public, even having the temerity to go out to dinner with him.[24] Crates unflatteringly called their marriage 'dog-coupling' (cynogamy), which may say something about the passion with which they conducted their sex life together.[25]

Hipparchia spurned all other suitors, eschewing their wealth, family connections, and good looks—all consistent with the Cynic doctrine of despising wealth and high birth. Moreover, Crates himself was no Adonis, as people mocked him when they saw him exercising.

Enforced destitution was the name of the Cynics' game. In his *Lives and Opinions of Eminent Philosophers* (in which Hipparchia is the only woman with an entry, out of eighty-two entries), Diogenes Laërtius (*fl. c.* third century CE) told that they scratched a living in the mean streets, stoas and porticoes of Athens.[26] The Roman prose writer Apuleius (*c.* 124–*c.* 170 CE) described how they routinely had sex in public, in the broad daylight.[27] Public fornication chimed well with Cynic shamelessness (*anaideia*), but, when added to Hipparchia's cross-dressing, and the fact that she lived on equal terms with her husband, the couple's blatant rejection of conventional values would have outraged most of Athenian society. The role model was Diogenes the Cynic, who is reputed to have practised 'everything in public, both the works of Demeter and those of Aphrodite', and attracted censure not only for masturbating in public, but also for eating in the agora.[28]

Hipparchia could clearly hold her own, even in a male dominated environment. Once she went to Lysimachus' house for a symposium, where she floored Theodorus, nicknamed the Atheist, with the following argument:

If it is not wrong for Theodorus to do a particular act, then it is not wrong for Hipparchia to do it. So, if Theodorus gives himself a slap he does nothing wrong: ergo, if Hipparchia slaps Theodorus she does nothing wrong either.

Theodorus was dumbstruck and reacted by trying to lift up her cloak; Hipparchia refused to be intimidated 'as most women would have been'. Theodorus persisted with his attempt at humiliation by sneering:

> 'Is this the woman 'who left her carding combs next to her loom'?' 'Yes, Theodorus,' she retorted, 'it is I. But do you think I have made a bad decision if instead of wasting my time at the loom I have used it for philosophy?'[29]

Exposing other people's genitals seems to have been a habit of the Cynics; Theodorus recalls Diogenes, who refused to answer a question put to him by a smartly dressed student unless he lifted his cloak to discern whether he was male or female.[30]

Hipparchia had at least two children, a daughter and a son named Pasicles. When Pasicles came of age, his father took him to the house of a prostitute and told him, 'this is what your father's wedding was like.'[31] In the first century BCE, Antipater of Thessaloniki describes Hipparchia's philosophy on life:

> I, Hipparchia, have no use for the works of deep-robed women; I have chosen the Cynics' virile life. I don't need capes with brooches or deep-soled slippers; I don't like glossy nets for my hair. My wallet is my staff's travelling companion, and the double cloak that goes with them, the cover for my bed on the ground. I'm much stronger than Atalanta from Maenalus, because my wisdom is better than racing over the mountain.[32]

Diogenes of Sinope (412 or 404 BCE–323 BCE), a founding Cynic, leaves us with this anecdote addressed to the people of Maroneia from the *Cynic Epistles* that, even if apocryphal, tells us something about the influence Hipparchia had:

> You did well when you changed the name of the city and, instead of Maroneia, called it Hipparchia, its present name, since it is better for you to be named after Hipparchia, a woman, it's true, but a philosopher, than after Maron, a man who sells wine. (Pseudo-Diogenes, *Epistle* 43, from Abraham J. Malherbe, (1977), *The Cynic Epistles: A Study Edition.*)

Perictione (*fl.* fifth century BCE) has the distinction of being the mother of Plato. She was a descendant of Solon, and was married to Ariston, by whom she had three sons— Glaucon, Adeimantus, and Plato—and a daughter, Potone. After Ariston's death, she remarried to Pyrilampes, an Athenian statesman who was also her uncle; she had her fifth child, Antiphon, with him. Antiphon appears in Plato's *Parmenides*.

Perictione has been associated with two spurious works which have survived in fragments—*On the Harmony of Women* and *On Wisdom*. The former describes the duties of a woman to her husband, her marriage, and to her parents; the latter gives a philosophical definition of wisdom.

Aspasia merits inclusion here as she appears to have flirted with philosophy, or just with philosophers, to some degree or other, either as a subject of study or as a philosopher of sorts herself. Aspasia is mentioned in the philosophical works of Plato, Xenophon, Aeschines Socraticus and Antisthenes. Plato apparently admired her intelligence and wit, and modelled Diotima in the *Symposium* on her. According to Plutarch:

> Now, since it is thought that he proceeded thus against the Samians to gratify Aspasia, this may be a fitting place to raise the query what great art or power this woman had, that she managed as she pleased the foremost men of the state, and afforded the philosophers occasion to discuss her in exalted terms and at great length.[33]

In his *Menexenus*, Plato lampoons Aspasia's relationship with Pericles, and quotes Socrates when he claims ironically that she was a prolific trainer of orators.[34] Martha Rose reminds us that 'only in comedy do dogs litigate, birds govern, or women declaim'.[35] Xenophon refers to Aspasia in his Socratic works, in *Memorabilia* and *Oeconomicus*, where her advice is recommended to Critobulus by Socrates.[36] Aeschines Socraticus and Antisthenes both named a Socratic dialogue after Aspasia; they survive only in fragmentary form. In the former, Socrates recommends Callias send his son Hipponicus to Aspasia for tuition. When the boy recoils at the prospect of a female teacher, Socrates reminds him that Aspasia had influenced Pericles and Lysicles. He himself visited her with his acolytes and their wives, even though she ran 'a disreputable business'. Lysicles was a former sheep-seller, and became a celebrity on account of his liaison with Aspasia. Cicero features Aspasia as a 'female Socrates', advising first Xenophon's wife and then Xenophon himself (not the famous historian) about acquiring virtue through self-knowledge.[37] Aeschines describes Aspasia as a teacher and inspirer of excellence, despite her sideline as a *hetaira*. To Antisthenes, Aspasia embodies a life of sexual abandon.

Writing in the second century CE, Aspasia is the apogee of wisdom to Lucian:

> We could choose no better model of wisdom than Milesian Aspasia, the admired of the admirable 'Olympian'; her political knowledge and insight, her shrewdness and penetration, shall all be transferred to our canvas in their perfect measure. Aspasia, however, is only preserved to us in miniature: our proportions must be those of a colossus.[38]

In more recent times, Aspasia has won much admiration from modern scholars. Although it is probably going too far to agree with the belief that Aspasia opened an academy for elite young women or even invented the Socratic method, others such as Cheryl Glenn are more sober; she believes that Aspasia 'seems to have been the only woman in classical Greece to have distinguished herself in the public sphere and must have influenced Pericles in the composition of his speeches'.[39]

Kagan sees Aspasia as 'a beautiful, independent, brilliantly witty young woman capable of holding her own in conversation with the best minds in Greece and of discussing and illuminating any kind of question with her husband'.[40] Roger Just believes that Aspasia was 'an exceptional figure, but her example alone is enough to underline the fact that any woman who was to become the intellectual and social equal of a man would have to be a hetaira'.[41] Sister Mary Prudence Allen, a philosopher and seminary professor, believes that 'Aspasia moved the potential of women to become philosophers one step forward from the poetic inspirations of Sappho'.[42] All things considered, Aspasia failed miserably with Thucydides' dictum that women should not encourage men to talk about them.

Diotima was a female philosopher and priestess prominent in Plato's *Symposium*, especially influential in the definition of the concept of Platonic love, 'a teacher in the art of love'.[43] In addition, by having the Athenians offer sacrifices ten years before the plague engulfed the city, she apparently managed to delay its onset. In the *Menexenus*, Plato had Socrates declare that he learnt rhetoric from Aspasia. He also concedes that Aspasia was an authority on household management, agreeing that the key to a successful *oikos* was the result of a joint effort between the breadwinning husband and the household-managing wife.

Although women philosophers were a minority both among women and philosophers, their contribution to the life of women in general was considerable. Their tenets, particularly those of the Pythagoreans, obviously reflected the contemporary social status of women all around them; this explains the preponderance of philosophy relating to a harmonious management of the household, and a child-raising regime conspicuous for its emphasis on moderation, all the while staying faithful to the husband and keeping him happy, in and out of bed.

But, just as importantly, the philosophy delivered by the women adherents to the various schools would have offered invaluable advice to other literate women on how to survive on a day to day basis, how to practice moderation and achieve at least a modicum of harmony while running the household and raising the children, often while pregnant with the next one. Perhaps a fitting conclusion is *The Grecian Girl's Dream of the Blessed Islands* by Thomas Moore:

> *Oh! There I met those few congenial maids*
> *Whom love hath warm'd, in philosophic shades;*
> *There still Leontium, on her sage's breast,*
> *Found lore and love, was tutor'd and caress'd;*
> *And there the clasp of Pythia's gentle arms*
> *Repaid the zeal which deified her charms.*
> *The Attic Master, in Aspasia's eyes,*
> *Forgot the yoke of less endearing ties,*
> *While fair Theano, innocently fair,*
> *Wreath'd playfully her Samian's flowing hair,*
> *Whose soul now fix'd, its transmigrations past,*
> *Found in those arms a resting-place at last;*
> *And smiling own'd, whate'er his dreamy thought*

In mystic numbers long had vainly sought,
The One that's form'd of Two whom love hath bound,
Is the best number gods or men e'er found.

Women too were represented as eminent and gifted practitioners of the visual arts. Alcisthene was a painter mentioned by the Roman Pliny the Elder (*c.* 23–79 CE) who includes her in his list of notable female painters, and mentions in particular one of her pictures portraying a dancer. Pliny also mentions Eirene, the daughter of a painter, and famous for painting an image of a girl from Eleusis.[44] Boccaccio included Eirene in *De mulieribus claris* (*On Famous Women*); some paintings he credits to Eirene are of an older Calypso, the gladiator Theodorus, and a famous dancer called Alcisthenes.[45] Anaxandra (*fl. c.* 220 BCE) was the artist daughter and student of Nealkes, a painter of mythological scenes. She is mentioned by Clement of Alexandria, the second century CE Christian theologian, in a chapter in his *Stromateis* (*Miscellanies*) entitled *Women as Well as Men Capable of Perfection*. Clement cites a lost work by the Hellenistic scholar Didymus Chalcenterus (first century BCE) as his source.

Kora or Callirhoe (*c.* 650 BCE) was the daughter of Butades. Butades and Kora can be credited with the invention of modeling in relief. Pliny the Elder and others tell us that Kora drew the profile of a man she loved on a wall with charcoal; her father then modeled the face of the man in clay based on this outline, thus creating the first relief.[46] The relief was preserved at the Nymphaeum in Corinth for almost 200 years, before it was unfortunately destroyed by fire.

Timarete, or Thamyris, or Tamaris (fifth century BCE), was an ancient Greek painter, the daughter of the painter Micon the Younger of Athens. According to Pliny, she 'scorned the duties of women and practised her father's art.' She was best known for a panel painting of the goddess of Diana which was displayed at Ephesus for many years.[47]

Agamede (*fl. c.* twelfth century BCE) is one of our first woman scientists; according to Homer, she was a physician with encyclopedic knowledge, specialising in the healing powers of plants—'golden-haired Agamede, who knew the virtues of every herb which grows upon the face of the earth.'[48] She hailed from Elis, the eldest daughter of Augeas, King of the Epeans, and was married to Mulius, the first ever man to die in battle, killed by Nestor during a war between Elis and Pylos. Propertius and Theocritus both call her Perimede.[49] By the Hellenistic period, Agamede was seen as a sorceress, much like Circe or Medea.

The remarkable story of Agnodice, the first professional gynaecologist and midwife of ancient Greece, is also told in my *In Bed with the Ancient Greeks*. Here is a summary of her professional achievements.

Agnodice was the first professional gynaecologist and midwife of ancient Greece, practising around 500 BCE. Her desire to study medicine was ignited when she saw more and more women around her dying in childbirth or undergoing unnecessarily painful deliveries. One of the problems was that women, not unnaturally, disliked being treated by male doctors. In Hippocrates' day, women were allowed to learn and practice obstetrics, gynaecology, and midwifery but, when it was later discovered that some women were performing illegal abortions, it was made a capital crime for women to practice medicine. Agnodice, however, was determined to help her fellow women, so she cut her hair and masqueraded as a man to pursue her medical training. She then left Athens to study medicine in Egypt, where it was quite legal for women to study and practice medicine, training at Alexandria, under Herophilos, a leading anatomist of her day. Once qualified, she continued to masquerade as a man in order to treat the women back in Athens.

However, Agnodice became the victim of her own success when she was rejected by women patients because they thought she was a man. Hyginus tells us how:

> she heard a woman crying out in the throes of labour so she went to her assistance. The woman, thinking she was a man, refused her help; but Agnodice lifted up her clothes and revealed herself to be a woman and was thus able to treat her patient.

Agnodice, as a man, was then tried by the Areopagus, on behalf of jealous husbands and rival doctors, for seducing the women of Athens. To prove her true identity, she again lifted up her tunic, only to be condemned on pain of death for deceit and false pretenses, allegations which she was, fortunately, able to disprove. Her opponents then condemned her for violating the law against women practicing medicine, but she was saved by a group of influential Athenian women who protested and had the law repealed. Hyginus again: 'you men are not spouses but enemies since you are condemning the woman who discovered health for us.'

Salpe was a first century BCE midwife from Lemnos whose work was a major source for Pliny the Elder. Athenaeus records that Salpe wrote *paignia*—trifles. From Pliny, we learn about Salpe's remedies for sunburn, stiffness, dog bites, and sore eyes. There is also information on an aphrodisiac, a topical depilatory cream, and a procedure for stopping a dog from barking. Her pharmacopeia included saliva and urine, which were believed to have both natural and supernatural powers. Salpe is often associated with Laïs, as both agreed on the magical powers of menstrual fluid against rabies and fever.

Aglaonice was a Thessalian astronomer of the second or first century BCE, mentioned by Plutarch and in the scholia to Apollonius of Rhodes.[50] Inevitably, her association with lunar matters attracted accusations of witchery and a reputation for being a sorceress. She could make the moon disappear from the sky, and predict when and where a lunar eclipse would take place—standard skills for the witch in antiquity. Plutarch wrote that Aglaonice was:

> Thoroughly acquainted with the periods of the full moon when it is subject to eclipse, and, knowing beforehand the time when the moon was due to be overtaken by the earth's shadow, imposed upon the women, and made them all believe that she was drawing down the moon.[51]

A number of other female astrologers from the third to first centuries BCE were associated with Aglaonice and were known as the 'witches of Thessaly'. In Plato's *Gorgias*, Socrates refers to 'the Thessalian enchantresses, who, as they say, bring down the moon from heaven at the risk of their own destruction.' Algaonice lives on in the name of a crater on Venus, and is a character in the Jean Cocteau film *Orpheus*.

Pythias (*fl. c.* 330 BCE) was a biologist and embryologist. She was Aristotle's first wife. Aristotle and Pythias had a daughter whose third husband was Metrodorus, the physician. Apparently, Pythias and Aristotle worked together on an encyclopedia from the live specimens they gathered on their honeymoon on Mytilene.

Pamphile of Kos was the first person to spin silk in the Greek world; she also invented the technique of preparing a thread from cotton wool for spinning on a distaff, and weaving from cotton thread. Pliny the Elder remarks that Pamphile discovered the technique of weaving like a spider's web, and that she should not be cheated of the glory of making a silk dress that covers a woman but reveals her charms. Aristotle also links Pamphile with inventing the concept of weaving silk. To be a pioneer of anything relating to spinning, weaving, or wool-working in the ancient world would be of inestimable importance and prestige, given just how central these skills were to women's work in the eyes of both women and men.

In Aegea in Macedonia, Eurydice, mother of Philip II, was a superb role model, and her influence obviously rubbed off on her son and on her grandson, Alexander the Great. According to Plutarch, despite being 'an Illyrian and a complete barbarian', she believed her children's education was important; she dedicated an epigram to the Muses of Hierapolis—'when she had satisfied her desire to become learned, for she worked hard to learn letters, the repository of speech, because she was the mother of growing sons.'[52]

Some women, of course, were experts in the performing arts. Xenophon saw this exceptional hoop-spinning dancer that led Socrates to believe that a girl can be taught anything, just as a man can:

> At that, the other girl began to accompany the dancer on the flute, and a boy at her elbow handed her up twelve hoops. She took these and as she danced kept throwing them whirling into the air, observing the proper height to throw them so as to catch them in a regular rhythm. As Socrates looked on he remarked: 'This girl's feat, gentlemen, is only one of many proofs that woman's nature is really no inferior to man's, except in its lack of judgment and physical strength. So if any one of you has a wife, let him confidently set about teaching her whatever he would like to have her know.[53]

Then, there is the award-winning Theban harpist from 86 BCE:

> The city of Delphi has decreed: whereas Polygnota, daughter of Socrates, a Theban harpist having come to Delphi, at the appointed time of the Pythian games, which could not be held on account of the present war, began on that very day and gave

a day's time and performed at the request of the archons and the citizens for three days, and won the highest degree of respect, deserving the praise of Apollo and of the Theban people and of our city-she is awarded a crown and 500 drachmas. With good fortune. Voted: to commend Polygnota, daughter of Socrates, the Theban, for her piety and reverence towards the god and for her dedication to her profession; to bestow on her and on her descendants the guest-friendship of the city, the right to consult the oracle, the privileges of being heard first, of safety, of exemption from taxes, and of front seating at the games held by the city, the right of owning land and a house and all the other honours ordinarily awarded to other benefactors of the city; to invite her to the town hall to the public hearth, and provide her with a victim to sacrifice to Apollo. To the god. With good fortune. (Pleket 6. G)

The rewards for her skill and professionalism, as we can see, were considerable, raising her well above the norm for privileges usually accorded to women.

High class prostitutes, *hetairae*, were usually educated and witty, as clever conversation went with the job. The best known description is by Athenaeus:

And there were other courtesans who had a great opinion of themselves, paying attention to education, and spending a part of their time on literature; so that they were very ready with their rejoinders and replies.[54]

He tells of one courtesan from the late fourth century BCE, Gnathaenion; one night at a symposium she observed another courtesan picking up leftover food to take home to her mother and said 'If I had known you were going to do this I would have had dinner with your mother instead of coming here.' Another courtesan, Glycera, when accused by a teacher of corrupting the students, replied tartly, 'It makes no difference whether a student is corrupted by a philosopher or a courtesan.' Complimented on the coolness of the wine she was serving up to a playwright, another replied, 'I just put in one of your prologues.' The cheek and wit of these ladies tells us just how self-confident and socially prominent they often were.

Lamia of Athens (*fl.* 300 BCE) was another celebrated, influential courtesan, and mistress of five-times married Demetrius Poliorcetes, also known as Demetrius the Besieger. Lamia was previously a flute-player on the stage, having some success. She then graduated to a career as a *hetaira*, and ended up on board a ship in the fleet of her lover, Ptolemy I, at the battle of Salamis in 306 BCE. Here, she met the dashing young Demetrius Poliorcetes who was smitten with her, even though she was past her best. She apparently owed her appeal to wit and talent, qualities celebrated by contemporary comedy playwrights and historians. Demetrius obviously wasted no time taking Lamia.

The opulence and magnificence of the banquets that Lamia threw in honour of Demetrius are legendary. She reputedly used the treasures lavished upon her by building a splendid painted portico for the citizens of Sicyon; Sicyon was a base in Ptolemy I's campaign of 309.[55] The Athenians and the Thebans, pandering to

The snake goddess from Knossos, in around 1600 BC, or maybe a court lady on coloured faience. The skirt is full length, and has seven flounces. She wears a polonaise (double apron) over the skirt. The bodice has elbow-length sleeves, leaving the breasts and neck exposed. From Heraklion Archaeological Museum.

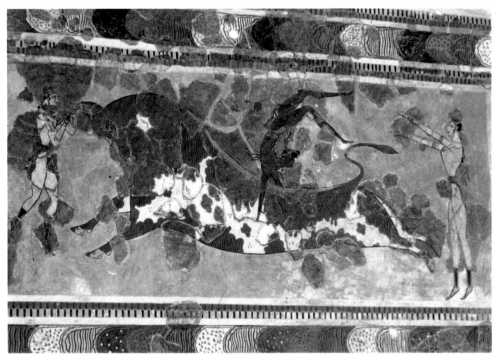

Ταυροκαθάψια (bull-leaping), originally from the upper-story portion of the east wall of the palace at Knossos in Crete, 1700–1400 BC. The Cretan girl is doing the dangerous and difficult bit in the bull-leaping, as depicted here; modern attempts to recreate the leaping on today's cattle have resulted in a number of deaths. From Heraklion Archaeological Museum.

Left: A bust from Mycenae, seventh century. Originally from a Doric temple, the top of the pediment is above the head. The hair resembles an Egyptian wig—two rows of curls over the forehead, falling onto the shoulders.

Below left: Electra at the Tomb of Agamemnon by Frederic Leighton, *c.* 1868.

Below right: Nausicaa by Frederic Leighton, *c.* 1879.

Above left: Pandora—the woman who started it all—with her box of baneful tricks. Dante Gabriel Rossetti, 1870. The model was Jane Morris, the wife of William Morris.

Above right: A copy of a 475 BC Attic *oinichoe* (wine pitcher), painted by P. Vaglis. The original is now in the Athens National Museum. It depicts a woman about to start working the wool, with her *kalathos* (basket) on the right. Wool-working was a powerful symbol, indicating respectability in a woman, and the proper observance of wifely duties. It all started with Penelope, in Homer's *Odyssey*. The peacock in close attendance was sacred to Hera, goddess of all things womanly.

Iphigénie by Louis Billotey, 1935. It depicts Iphigenia (centre) in an embrace with Clytemnestra, with Artemis gazing at the girl. In Euripides' *Iphigeneia in Aulis*, Iphigenia was turned into a deer, to save her from being sacrificed, so that the Achaean fleet could sail for Troy.

A first century AD depiction of the sacrifice of Iphigenia, from the Casa Vetti in Pompeii.

Captive Andromache by Frederic Leighton *c.* 1886. From City of Manchester Art Galleries, Manchester.

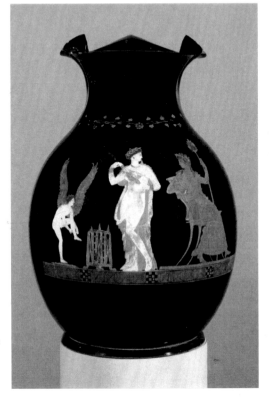

Above: Scene from Menander's *Synaristosai* (*Women Who Do Lunch*), by Dioskourides of Samos, 2nd century BC; it is one of the famous Menander mosaics from the Villa of Cicero in Pompeii.

Right: Terracotta Attic red figure *oenochoe*, from the mid-fourth century BC. Women played a leading role in many religious festivals. Pompe, the female personification of a procession holds a wreath and looks toward Dionysus, seated and wearing a diadem. The winged Eros adjusts his sandals, as though preparing to depart. The gilt openwork basket on the ground is the type used in religious processions to carry sacrificial implements to the place of sacrifice, and is part of an Athenian festival in honour of Dionysos, probably the Anthesteria, which culminated in the sacred marriage of the god to the wife of the archon basileus. © The Metropolitan Museum of Art, Accession Number: 25.190.

Left: Ivory decorative plaque from the second half of the seventh century BC. This plaque illustrates the arrival of Dionysos in Greece. The two daughters of King Proitos of Argos refused to recognize his divinity, were driven insane, and committed violent and unseemly acts until they were healed by the seer Melampos. Here, in their madness, they have unpinned their clothes and stand half naked. © The Metropolitan Museum of Art Accession Number: 17.190.73

Below A Spartan Woman Giving a Shield to Her Son by Jean Jacques François Lebarbier, 1805. The subject of this painting is a Spartan woman bidding her son, or husband, farewell in the traditional manner, 'Return carrying your shield or on it'; all elements of the painting reinforce its message of civil duty. The children playing with the warrior's lance allude to Spartan military training, which began in infancy. The simplicity of the stone-walled interior underscores the austerity of Spartan existence, while the dog is both a symbol of fidelity and a reference to the famed dogs of Sparta. © The Portland Art Museum, Ohio.

Above: Terracotta red figure Attic *kalpis* (water jar) from the fifth century. One woman holds a casket, the other a *lekythos* (oil flask). Such a scene is probably a wedding scenario, although the same figures appear during the late fifth and fourth centuries BC on marble grave reliefs. © The Metropolitan Museum of Art Accession Number: 41.162.87

Right: Female Figurine from a Vessel. This figure is from a type of vase that occasionally took the form of a female head. 3rd century BC. © Walters Art Museum, Baltimore.

Woman decorating a gravestone with garlands, on an Attic white-ground *lekythos*, *c.* 420–410 BC.

Greek Girls Playing at Ball by Frederic Leighton 1889; inspired, no doubt by Homer's description of Nausicaa in the *Odyssey*.

Above: Fourth century tombstone
inscription: a bereaved husband
acknowledges Melite, his wife, as good
and loving, a love that was reciprocated:
'You were the best, and so he [Onesimus]
laments your death, for you were a good
woman.' The picture shows her holding out
her hand to him as she says 'and to you
farewell, dearest of men; love my children.'
[CEG 530]

Right: Perseus and Andromeda by Frederic
Leighton. Andromeda is chained to the
rock, while Perseus on his winged horse
flies above. Perseus approached Cetus while
invisible and slew the monster. From the
Walker Art Gallery, Liverpool.

Left: Antigone Strewing Dust on the Body of Polyneices in a bid to effect proper burial rites, a painting by the late nineteenth century artist Victor J. Robertson.

Below: Perseus and the Graiae by Edward Burne-Jones (1833–1898). Perseus sought out the Graeae, sisters of the Gorgons, to demand the location of the Hesperides, the nymphs tending Hera's orchard. The Graeae were three perpetually old women, who shared one tooth and a single eye. As the women were passing the eye from one to another, Perseus snatched it and held it for ransom until they revealed the location of the nymphs. From the Tate Britain.

Above: The Three Fates: *from A Golden Thread* by J. M. Strudwick, in the Tate Gallery, London. First exhibited in 1885. The three Fates are spinning the thread of life. Their spindles show part gold and part grey threads. The gold part will measure out the allotted span of a person's life.

Right: Greek terracotta dolls with movable arms and legs, with holes for strings to operate the limbs. Dolls like these would be donated by brides to Athena on marriage.

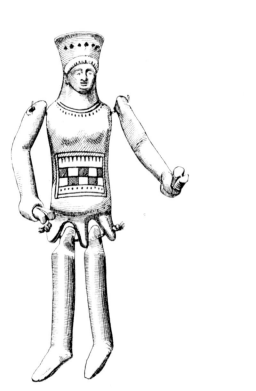

Left: A Spartan girl training for athletics, running with her right breast uncovered, much to the outrage of some Athenians.

Below: Reliefs from the Ludovisi Throne (470–460 BC). The relief on the left side depicts a woman playing a double flute; the one on the right side shows a woman burning incense. Lower relief: the birth of Aphrodite; Aphrodite is clothed by the Horai (Seasons) as she is born from the sea. From the Museo Nazionale Romano.

Illustration from a vase depicting a scene from a mock-tragedy, with a fight between Ares and Hephaestus, watched by a masked Hera.

An *epinetron* or *onos*, used to separate fibres in the wool before it was placed on the distaff; it was semi-cylindrical and placed on the knee. There is a woman's head at the end, with illustrations that helpfully show the *epinetron* in use. In the British Museum.

Sappho and Alcaeus by L. Alma Tadema, 1881. It illustrates a passage by Hermesianax of Colophon (*fl. c.* 340 BCE), a Hellenistic elegiac poet and a pupil of Philitas of Cos, that was preserved in Atheneaus, *Deipnosophistae*, book 2, line 598. On the island of Lesbos in the late seventh century BC, 'Sappho and her companions listen rapturously as the poet Alcaeus plays a *kithara*. Striving for verisimilitude, Alma-Tadema copied the marble seating of the Theatre of Dionysos in Athens, although he substituted the names of members of Sappho's sorority for those of the officials incised on the Athenian prototype.'

A *stela* from Chrysapha, 550–540 BC, Sparta. The relief shows a seated couple and two worshippers. The two figures are shown in profile; they are seated on a throne with a 'palmette' finial, and lions' paws for legs. The man turns his head towards the observer, holding a *kantharos* in his right hand; the other is extended in prayer. His upper lip is shaven, according to Spartan custom. The man's short beard is sharply outlined, and was painted. The woman, presumably his wife, is represented in complete profile, with a pomegranate in her right hand; her left hand lifts her veil-cloak from her face. A big bearded snake, indicative of heroes, stands on its curled tail behind the throne. Two small worshippers are approaching the deified pair, and carry offerings of a cock, an egg, a blossom, and a pomegranate. Berlin, Antikensammlung.

Right: A *stela* depicting the nymph Leucothea dandling baby Dionysus, but intentionally reminiscent of a scene in everyday Greek life. The lady, for whom the monument was erected, is the deceased.

Below: The *Sarcophagus of the Mourning Women* or *Les Pleureuses*. Mid fourth century BC, found in the royal cemetery of Sidon. Eighteen mourning women are depicted with hunting scenes and a funeral procession, indicative of the important role women played in funerals.

Above: Attic Red Figure *kylix c.* 480–470 BC by the Painter of Philadelphia 2449 and the potter Hieron Chiusi, Italy; MS 2449. A scene from the *gynaikonitis*: an elegant woman, holding a box, lifts the lid of an inlaid chest. Courtesy of Penn Museum, Philadelphia; image #163983

Right: The Grave Stele of Hegeso, probably sculpted by Callimachus, is by common consent one of the finest Attic grave *stelae* surviving today (*ca.* 410–*ca.* 400 BC) and is at the National Archaeological Museum in Athens (NAMA 3624); it was found in 1870 in the Kerameikos in Athens, where a replica can be seen. It shows an Athenian woman (Hegeso) wearing a *chiton* and *himation*, seated on a chair, with her feet resting on an elaborate footstool. In her left hand, she holds an open *pyxis*, and in her right, a piece of (missing) jewellery. On the left, stands a maidservant wearing a tunic and a headdress (*sakkos*). On the epistyle, there is the epitaph, ΗΓΗΣΩ ΠΡΟΞΕΝΟ, announcing that the deceased is Hegeso, daughter of Proxenios.

Demetrius, consecrated a temple in honour of Lamia, under the title of Aphrodite. According to Athenaeus, she had a daughter by Demetrius, who was named Phila.[56]

Apart from being a woman's name, a lamia was a bloodsucking man-eater, so a hetaira might adopt a professional name to attract patrons looking for a fetishistic element of excitement and danger from their whores. Lamia was also the name of a celebrated Roman bogeywoman, the equivalent of the Greek Mormio, a sexy Libyan woman whose children by Zeus were murdered by Hera; like Mormio, she too was a cannibal and exacted revenge by murdering other women's babies, eating them alive. Lamia was sometimes described as a *phasma*—a ghost, or nightmare.

Thais was an Athenian *hetaira* and companion to Alexander the Great on his campaigns in Asia Minor. She is remembered for her presence at a *symposium,* urging the burning down of the palace of Persepolis in 330 BCE; the palace was the main residence of the defeated Achaemenid dynasty. Thais made a speech that persuaded Alexander to raze the palace; while Cleitarchus says that it was done on a whim, Plutarch and Diodorus believe that it was retribution for when Xerxes burnt down the old Temple of Athena on the Acropolis in 480 BCE during the Persian Wars. This is how Diodorus describes the incident, and Thais' role in it:

> When the king [Alexander] was inflamed by their words, they all leaped up from their couches and passed the word along to form a victory procession in honour of Dionysus. Promptly many torches were gathered. Female musicians were present at the banquet, so the king led them all out for the comus to the sound of voices and flutes and pipes, Thaïs the courtesan leading the whole performance. She was the first, after the king, to hurl her blazing torch into the palace. As the others all did the same, immediately the entire palace area was consumed, so great was the conflagration. It was remarkable that the impious act of Xerxes, king of the Persians, against the acropolis at Athens should have been repaid in kind after many years by one woman, a citizen of the land which had suffered it, and in sport.[57]

Thais was also the lover of Ptolemy I Soter, one of Alexander's generals and may also have been Alexander's lover, if Athenaeus's statement that Alexander liked to 'keep Thais with him' means any more than he simply enjoyed her company. On Alexander's death, Thais married Ptomely and bore him three children, two boys and a girl: Lagus, Leontiscus, and Eirene. Thaïs was never Ptolemy's queen, nor were their children heirs to his throne. Ptolemy, of course, had other wives: Eurydice of Egypt, and Berenice I of Egypt.

The memory of Thais endured into the Roman republic and early empire, and beyond into the Middle Ages. Terence has a female protagonist who is a courtesan named Thais in his *Eunuchus,* and Cicero quotes Thais' words in *De Amicitia.* In Ovid's *Remedia Amoris*, Thais' behaviour and *mores* are contrasted with Andromache's; Andromache is the epitome of the loyal and chaste wife, while Thais is the embodiment of sex and is what his art is all about, says Ovid.[58] In Dante's *Divine Comedy*, Thais is down in Hell, in the circle of the flatterers, immersed in an excrement-filled trench for having told her lover that she was 'marvelously' fond of him; Thaïs' words here derive from Cicero's quotations from Terence.[59] She emerges with Alexander, conjured up by Faustus in Marlowe's *Doctor Faustus*, and appears as Alexander's mistress in Dryden's *Alexander's Feast*, or The *Power of Music* (1697), in which Alexander is enthroned with 'the lovely Thaïs by his side' who sat 'like a blooming eastern bride'. The poem later became an oratorio, *Alexander's Feast*, by Handel. Robert Herrick (1591–1674) comes to the happy conclusion in his *What Kind of Mistress He Would Have* that 'Let her Lucrece all day be, Thaïs in the night to me, Be she such as neither will, Famish me, nor overfill.'

Rhodopis was a famous sixth century BCE *hetaira* from Thrace, and shares the distinction of being one of only two *hetairae* mentioned by name by Herodotus as being with Archidike. Rhodopis means 'rosy cheeks'—a professional pseudonym. Herodotus says she was a fellow-slave of Aesop, with whom she had a clandestine love affair; Rhodopis ended up in Naucratis in Egypt, during the reign of Amasis II, where she continued to work as a *hetaira* for the benefit of her master and met Charaxus, Sappho's brother. Charaxus fell in love with her, and paid a handsome price when he ransomed her from slavery; Sappho later wrote a poem accusing Rhodopis of stealing Charaxus' property. In any event, she tithed part of her income to the temple at Delphi; Herodotus actually saw the ten iron spits dedicated in her name.

Somewhat less credible is the legend that Rhodopis built the third pyramid at Giza. Herodotus rubbishes the story, but to Pliny the Elder, it was established fact.[60] Another fantasy related by Strabo and Aelian makes her queen of Egypt. One day, Rhodopis was bathing when an eagle picked up one of her sandals, flew away with it, and dropped it into the lap of the Egyptian king at Memphis. He was fascinated and set about finding the owner; when he discovered her, he made her his queen. The story of Rhodopis is, then, the earliest version of the Cinderella story.

Hetairae still had their critics and detractors; this is how Anaxilas vents his spleen around 525 BCE:

> *The man whoe'er has loved a hetaira,*
> *Will say that no more lawless, worthless race*
> *Can anywhere be found: for what ferocious*
> *Unsociable she-dragon, what Chimaira*
> *Though it breathe fire from its mouth, what Charybdis,*
> *What three-headed Skylla, dog o' the sea,*
> *Or hydra, sphynx, or raging lioness,*
> *Or viper, or winged harpy (greedy race),*
> *Could go beyond those most accursed harlots?*
> *There is no monster greater. They alone*
> *Surpass all other evils put together.*

Anaxilas, Hetairai 1-11

In 350 BCE, Eubulus is more restrained, but still talks of the make-up running down the *hetaira*'s face:

> *By Zeus, we are not painted with vermilion,*
> *Nor with dark mulberry juice, as you are often:*
> *And then, if in the summer you go out,*
> *Two rivulets of dark, discolored hue*
> *Flow from your eyes, and sweat drops from your jaws*
> *And makes a scarlet furrow down your neck,*
> *And the light hair which wantons o'er your face*
> *Seems gray, so thickly is it plastered o'er.*
>
> Eubulus, *The Reproach of the Hetairai* 1-8

But, of course, it was by no means all sophistication and smart dinner parties. The best *hetairae* could set their prices according to the sexual positions they were good at. One who excelled in twelve positions charged the most for a position called *keles*— 'racehorse'—in which the woman was on top.

For the low rent *khamaitypés* (χαμαιτυπής), the options were much less comfortable and considerably less dignified; they had to perform 'in the dirt' as they had no beds or rooms. We know of one vase that shows a prostitute standing in dog-style, holding on to a tree for support. Her legs are spread, the man enters her from behind, his hands on the sides of her buttocks; she responds to the thrusting. The artist has painted a smile on the prostitute's face, suggesting that she was enjoying it, or just as likely, pretending to. Another vase demonstrates the *cyon*, or the 'dog', which shows the woman on all fours and the man entering from behind; this is what the Roman Lucretius (in the first century BCE) was to describe uncharitably as *more ferarum*—'the way that animals do it'. On a vase in the British Museum, we can see a *hetaira* sitting on her client's lap facing him; she is assisted by two girls, to rise and fall on her client's penis. The 'leapfrog'—an act of sodomy where the woman is 'folded in two' with her hands flat on the ground—appears on yet another vase. The depiction of women in the visual arts is examined in the next chapter.[61]

Women in the visual arts

We have seen how some women were serious practitioners of the visual arts. Women, or the bodies of women, were often the subject of the visual arts—particularly statuary. A female deity forms one of the truly iconic representations of ancient Greece. When Phidias, sculptor extraordinaire, became superintendent of public works in Athens, he also created the symbol of Athens, the colossal statue of Athena Parthenos; it was completed and dedicated in 438 BCE, made of gold and ivory, standing thirty-eight feet high. The magnificent goddess stands tall, wearing a tunic, aegis, and helmet and holding Nike in her outstretched right hand and a spear in her left; a decorated shield and snake were by her side. Phidias was also responsible for the Athena Promachos, a colossal bronze statue of Athena that stood between the Parthenon and the Propylaea.

In 1958, archaeologists discovered the workshop at Olympia where Phidias made the gold and ivory Zeus. Shards of ivory, as well as terracotta moulds and other equipment for a large female statue, were excavated along with a black glaze drinking cup with the inscription 'I belong to Phidias'.

The statue of Athena stood in the Parthenon until the fifth century CE, when it was removed by the Romans to Constantinople. In 1197, Constantinople was devastated by fire, but the destruction wrought by the fire was nothing compared to that visited on the city by the Crusaders. In January 1204, the protovestiarios Alexius Murzuphlus provoked a riot, it is presumed, to intimidate Alexius IV, but only succeeded in destroying Phidias' Athena that stood in the forum.

But the best, most vivid, and enlightening picture of everyday life involving the ancient Greek woman comes courtesy of two hundred years of Greek vase painting from 600 BCE to 400 BCE. The vases provide an ongoing commentary of what the Greek woman did with her life; this extensive ancient panoramic film strip suggests a lot more than solitary seclusion and confinement. We find the ancient Greek woman both happy and sad: grieving at tombs; waving their husbands goodbye as they go off to war; playing with her children; waited on with clothes and jewellery by slaves; girlish brides gazing into mirrors; excited bridesmaids; applying make-up; washing hair; and bathing naked. They go out to the well to fetch water; they visit the shoemaker, they rejoice at weddings and gloom at funerals; they are tidying their rooms; and they hand baby over to the nurse. These myriad images are surely reflective not just of an active and very public female social life, but also of the joy and respect of the vase painters themselves for their womenfolk.

If you look at the Parthenon, you can see what Seltman calls the 'strong streak of feminism in Greek religion' reflected in its sculpture, reminding us that the Panathenaic procession pouring from the western city gate was headed by a crowd of girls.[1]

The house of Macedon is well represented in statuary; Eurydice I's statue, together with those of her most famous son Philip II, Philip II's wife, Olympias, her grandson (Alexander the Great), and her husband (Amyntas III), were all created by the Athenian sculptor Leochares in ivory and gold. They were placed in the Philippeion, a rotunda in the Altis at Olympia, erected by Philip II in celebration of his victory at the Battle of Chaeronea in 338 BCE.

Eurydice's tomb has been found and confirmed by the Greek archaeologist Manolis Andronikos in 1987 in Vergina (ancient Aigai), a UNESCO World Heritage Site, along with other royal Macedonian tombs. In the summer of 2001, the tomb of Eurydice was unfortunately robbed and seven marble figurines were stolen. Fortunately, two skeletons and an inscribed pot fragment, dating from 344/3 BCE were left inside the tomb.

Women and women's sexuality feature on countless vases. Every conceivable position of copulation and other sexual activity is depicted: vaginal, anal, contact on the thighs, male on female fellatio, cunnilingus, masturbation, use of dildos, troilism, *soixante-neuf*, sado-masochism, orgies, and bestiality.[2]

It is interesting to note that erotic images of the sixth century differ from those of the fifth and fourth centuries BCE, reflecting shifts in social acceptability. In the sixth century, the scenes depicted, initially on black-figure and later on red-figure vases, include only vaginal and anal intercourse with no scenes of oral sex or orgies; they were obviously not considered appropriate for public consumption through vase and other ceramic painting.

By the end of the sixth century, scenes of fellatio, cunnilingus, and group sex start appearing, mainly on cups, *kylikes,* probably in use in *symposia*, which were more private, tolerant and discreet environments. One of the most famous erotic vases by Pedeius Painter shows a *hetaira* tilted on a stool, taking a man's penis in her mouth while another man enters her from behind. Cunnilingus was generally frowned upon, as was fellatio, since it was considered to compromise male supremacy. To compensate, the artists often depicted women kneeling in submission. The missionary position of coitus is absent: women are usually shown having sex on their knees, bent forward, or on their backs, with their legs resting on the man's shoulders. Anal intercourse is depicted; at the very least, it offered an effective means of contraception.

It was not unheard of for statues of women to attract some unhealthy, unrequited attention. Agalmatophilia—from the Greek agalma 'statue', and -philia (φιλία, love)—is a paraphilia involving the sexual attraction to a statue, doll, or mannequin that usually involves a desire for sexual contact with the object.[3] Athenaeus, quoting Philemon, describes such an instance in his *Deipnosophistae*, unfulfilling as it was:

> Cleisophus of Selymbria ... fell in love with a statue of Parian marble that then was at Samos, and shut himself up in the temple to gratify his affection; but when he found that he could make no impression on the coldness and unimpressibility of the stone, then he discarded his passion.

Athenaeus corroborates the story with 'Alexis the poet mentions this circumstance in his drama entitled *The Picture.*' Just to prove that female statues did not have all the fun, one man got away lightly, perhaps, for his 'transgression'; Athenaeus again, quoted Philemon:

> At Delphi, in the museum of the pictures, there are two boys wrought in marble; with one of which, the Delphians say, a visitor fell in love so strongly, that he made love to it, and shut himself up with it, and presented it with a crown; but when he was discovered, the god ordered the Delphians, who consulted his oracle about it, to let him off.[4]

If nothing else, it shows just what clever people find to talk about at dinner parties.

The Greek connection lives on to this day: the article cited in footnote 3 points out, 'the agalmatophiles' descendents are those today whose desires are reserved for artificial females (or males) in the form of realistic life-size dolls (pediophilia, from the Greek *pedio*, doll; not to be confused with pedophilia)'.

Female Greek statuary was also responsible when agalmatophilia first became a subject of clinical study with the publication of Richard von Krafft-Ebing's *Psychopathia Sexualis*. In 1877, he recorded the case of a gardener falling in love with a statue of the Venus de Milo, who was found doing his best to have sex with it.

Women in religion and
in philosophy

It has already been noted how religion liberated women to some extent; it got them out of the house, and gave them a relatively rare role outside in the societies of ancient Greece. For most Greeks, the anthropomorphic, incestuous, and often rapacious gods in the extensive pantheon were all-powerful, all-seeing and all over their lives. Adulation and respect to these gods and goddesses was paramount, despite the rampant incest, bestiality, duplicity and adultery; whatever the Greeks may have thought about the gods as role models, mortal *hubris* was to be avoided at all costs, as it invited the worst possible divine retribution.

The Greeks knew that the gods were rarely over-worked with the actions of men and women, but they honoured the gods all the same in hope of currying favour, and deflecting divine anger. As there was no dogma or creed in Greek religion, it was left to individuals or *poleis* to work out and pursue what they believed to be the right thing to do. Citizens paid homage and tribute to their patron gods by cult worship and regular ritualistic activities, and organised festivals funded by public contributions. In Sparta, for example, even with the emphasis on military, defence and male camaraderie, it is interesting to note that such a patriarchal society might appoint female deities as high-ranking patrons. But Athena and Artemis got significant attention from Sparta in the form of temple dedications, festivals, and ritualistic sacrifice.

Religious festivals are estimated to have taken up around half the days in the year, with some of them lasting two or three days, with multitudes of celebrants. Worship was community business and not a personal thing; it is probably not surprising then that women, who of course made up half of the population, were heavily involved. Herodotus describes how various women established new religious rites, founding oracles in Libya and Dodona, and introducing the festival of Demeter, the Thesmophoria, from Egypt to Greece. One form of participation was as a chorus where women of all ages assembled and recited stories from the lives of the gods and goddesses through song and dance. In many ceremonies, girls or women were the highly visible stars of the show; for any public sacrifice, the *Kanephoros* was the maiden chosen to lead the procession. For major festivals, she would hail from the wealthiest class, but on family occasions (like weddings), the *Kanephoros* would be an unmarried daughter and friend of the bride and groom; she carried a basket on her head to the altar. Euripides sums up the likely situation— 'We women play the most important part [in religion] ... women have a rightful share in the service of the gods. Why is it then that women must have a bad reputation?'[1]

For the *Arrephoria*, two girls aged between seven and ten were selected from among the richest families; they too carried a basket on their heads during a night-time fertility rite, processing into a sanctuary beneath the Acropolis. They spent a year here, until it was their turn to carry the baskets back to the surface; if any of the girls had the temerity to look in the baskets, the gods killed them.[2] According to the lexicon of Harpocration (s.v. Arrêphorein), there were four *Arrephoroi*, two of whom supervised the weaving of the Panathenaic *peplos*.

The *Arkteia* involved even more girls. Dedicated to Artemis at the sanctuaries of Brauron and Mounychion in Attica, it was a mandatory pre-nuptial festival which originated in the Archaic age and continued into classical times; it illustrates well the involvement of girls and women in Greek mythology and the religion which required them to disport themselves in public, for all to see and fraternise with each other. Artemis kept a pet bear in her sanctuary at Brauron. This bear once mauled a young maiden to death after she started to tease it; her brother took his revenge by killing the beast. Artemis was not pleased and sent a plague, only agreeing to lift it in return for the sacrifice of a virgin. One man offered up his daughter, but craftily sent instead a goat wrapped in a blanket. He got away with his deception, and the 'sacrifice' was celebrated for centuries all over Greece. The festival featured girls between the ages of seven and ten racing, dancing, and mimicking the actions of a bear. A set of ceramics called *krateriskoi* depict the girls wearing short tunics, the *chiton*, or performing in the nude. Aristophanes describes the process in *Lysistrata*:

> At seven I carried the holy vessels; then I pounded barley. At the age of ten, and clad in yellow robes. Soon after this, I was Little Bear to Brauronian Artemis; Then garlanded with figs, grown tall and pretty, I was a Basket-bearer.[3]

Greeks apparently saw similarities between girls and wild animals. *Parthenoi* were women who were sexually mature but unmarried, and were thought to be full of lust and a danger to themselves and to society; as such, they were in need of taming. The saffron-coloured robed girls in the *Arkteia* acted as wild animals (*arktoi*); this festival could have been an opportunity for single men, acting like beasts themselves, to inspect the next crop of potential brides.

Women were associated with dogs. Ancient literature emphasises two things about dogs; their voracious sexual appetites, and the ease with which they give birth. Both are reflected in language; the Greek word for 'dog' or 'bitch', *kuos*, is also slang for the genitalia of either sex, while *kuein* means 'to be pregnant'. Hesiod remarks that the world's first woman, Pandora, has the mind of a bitch, with its overtones of sexual permissiveness, and the fecundity required to keep civilisation alive. Women are likewise associated with sexual licence and fertility, and share with dogs their liminal position in society, only half tamed. Agamemnon says in the *Iliad* that there is nothing more like a bitch than a woman.[4]

The *Thesmophoria* was a three day fertility festival in honour of Demeter, open only to married women but paid for by men, thus underlining the importance that fertility held. Slaves and unmarried women were also banned, on pain of severe punishment. On the first day, the women of Athens left their homes and congregated on a hill west of the Acropolis. The second day saw them fasting, while on the third day, they feasted and celebrated. The event was shrouded in mystery and details were (unsuccessfully) kept secret; men were banned.

The *Adonia* was a two day festival honouring the death and rebirth of the vegetation god, Adonis. Aphrodite, the goddess of sex, took Adonis at his birth and, although smitten by his beauty, entrusted him to Persephone in the Underworld for safe-keeping; she too was enthralled by Adonis and refused to return him. After Zeus intervened, Adonis was allowed to spend four months of the year with Aphrodite, four months with Persephone, and four months wherever he wished; Aphrodite and Adonis had an affair. A week or so before the *Adonia*, Athenian women sowed seeds in baskets that they then carried to the roofs of their houses, leaving them there without water. The seeds germinated in the normal manner, but the resulting plants withered and died for lack of water. On the first day of the *Adonia*, these women wailed and flailed themselves, while statues of Adonis, along with the baskets of Adonis, were laid out in the streets like corpses at a funeral. The second day was somewhat lighter, and more permissive, with much merry-making as the women celebrated the resurrection of Adonis, and the renewed growth of vegetation.

Drums were banged by women in the worship of Bacchus and Cybele; women visited the shrine of Aesculapius in thanks, no doubt, for safe deliveries and recovery from illnesses. Aristophanes tells of clandestine worship of Hecate in *Lysistrata*.[5] In *Plutus*, (768ff) we find a woman bringing the nuts and figs (*katachusmata*) to shower over Plutus, to celebrate the restoration of his eyesight, and an old woman processes with the pots to be used in the consecration of the statue of Plutus (1197–1207).[6]

Demeter and Persephone were also involved in the Eleusinian Mysteries, in which girls and women played a part as *mystae* as described here in Aristophanes' *Frogs*:

> In the sacred round dance of the goddess, in the flower-bearing grove sporting with all who partake in the festival dear to the goddess I will go with the women and girls where they dance all night for the goddess, to bring the sacred torch.[7]

Women were also prominent at the *Scira*, a festival held in Pyanepsion in honour of Athena Sciras, where the wives of the state's prominent men had the privilege of sitting in the front row seats at the *Stenia*. Married women were spectators at the Rural Dionysia and participated in the Panathenaic Festival while metic wives acted as *hydroapheroi* (water carriers) and *diphropheroi* (seat carriers) for the *kanephoroi*. Metics were foreigners resident in Greece who enjoyed some of the privileges of citizenship. Women celebrated Pan in fittingly boisterous style, and celebrated *Genetyllis*, goddess of birth and fertility—a less salacious version of the cult of Aphrodite, celebrated by prostitutes on the Colias promontory.

The *Thargelia* was an important Athenian festival held in honour of the Delian Apollo and Artemis on their birthdays, the sixth and seventh of the month of Thargelion (24 and 25 May). All the people offered the first fruits of the year to the gods, to avert them from spoiling the harvest. The most important, and bizarre, ritual involved the two ugliest men, or the ugliest man and the ugliest woman, that could be found (the *Pharmakoi*); they were chosen to die, one for the men, the other for the women. They were led round with strings of figs round their necks, and whipped on the genitals with rods of figwood and squills. On reaching the place of sacrifice on the shore, they were stoned to death, their bodies set on fire, and the ashes thrown into the sea, or over the land as a fertilizer.

The *Gerarai* were priestesses of Dionysus who presided over sacrifices, and participated in the festivals of Theoinia and Iobaccheia, taking place over three days during the month of Anthesteria (around the time of the January or February full moon). The three days of the feast were called Pithoigia, Choës, and Chytroi, and celebrated the start of spring, particularly the maturing of wine stored at the previous vintage and whose *pithoi* (wine jars) were now opened with due ceremony. During the feast, social order was turned on its head, not just because of the fallout from the drinking contests it inspired, but also because slaves were allowed to join in, uniting the household. There were fourteen *Gerarai* selected and sworn to secrecy by the Athenian *basilinna*, the ritual queen, or her husband, the *archon basileus*. The queen married Dionysus in a ceremony that may have involved them having sex with each other. The word *Gerarai* derives from γηράσκω, gerasko ('I grow old'), because more mature women were preferred for the role.

The temples and sanctuaries of a goddess were usually presided over by a priestess, and those of a god by a priest. Chief priestesses were important officials in the community, and were exempt from the rule that no woman's name should be spoken in public. A chief priestess could sign contracts and conduct business appropriate to her office, unlike all other women. She was responsible for animal sacrifices, libations, running cults, and managing temples. Young women about to be married regularly gave their toys and other childhood property to the local temple, and several wealthy women are known to have donated considerable sums in their own names to a god or goddess.

Nothing exemplifies the awe and respect in which women priestesses and seers were held better than the office of priestess of Delphi (also known as the Delphic oracle or the Pythia). The revered Temple of Apollo at Delphi was situated on the slopes of Mount Parnassus, beneath the Castalian Spring; the job was for life, and it was exclusively held by a woman.

Matters of state with the direst of consequences were referred to the Delphic priestess by Greeks and Romans alike for centuries. It is thought to have started in the eighth century BCE; the earliest account of the origin of the Delphic oracle is in the *Homeric Hymn to Delphic Apollo* (c. 580–570 BCE), and the last utterance was in about 395 CE to Emperor Theodosius I, after which he closed down the pagan temples. Pythia comes from pythein (πύθειν, 'to rot'), an allusion to the decomposing carcass of the monstrous Python after he was slain by Apollo. Pythia was the House of Snakes. The possession and frenzy displayed by the priestess is described best by Lewis Farnell in 1907:

> The great moment when the Pythoness ascended into the tripod, and, filled with the divine afflatus which at least the latter ages believed to ascend in vapour from a fissure in the ground, burst forth into wild utterance, which was probably some kind of articulate speech, and which the Ὅσιοι [Osioi], 'the holy ones', who, with the prophet, sat around the tripod, knew well how to interpret.... What was essential to Delphic divination, then, was the frenzy of the Pythoness and the sounds which she uttered in this state which were interpreted by the Ὅσιοι and the 'prophet' according to some conventional code of their own.[8]

Between 535 and 615 of the oracles of Delphi are known to have survived, of which over half have been shown to be historically accurate.

Diodorus tells how, originally, the Pythia was a modestly dressed young virgin, a reflection of the Oracle's chastity and the purity required for communion with Apollo. However, Echecrates the Thessalian spoiled all that when he came to consult and was so entranced by the virgin's beauty that he carried her off and raped her. The Delphians were horrified and, in order to avoid a repeat, enacted a law stipulating that henceforth the prophesying virgin would be replaced by an elderly woman of fifty who would simply declare the Oracles; she would be dressed in the costume of a virgin, as a nostalgic memory of the prophetess of old. Phemonoe was the first Pythia, a post-Homeric poet who invented hexameter; as well as being the source of the phrase 'know thyself' (γνῶθι σεαυτόν), which is inscribed at the entrance to the Temple of Apollo at Delphi, she was also the daughter of Apollo.[9]

On the death of her predecessor, the new priestess would be selected from a guild of priestesses of the temple, all natives of Delphi who could point to having lived a sober and respectable life. Some were married but, on taking on the role of Pythia, they renounced all family, marital obligations, and individual personal identity; it was most definitely a full time job. In the early days, the Pythia was probably always chosen from an elite family, educated in geography, politics, history, philosophy, and the arts. Later though, uneducated peasant women got the job when the priestess's responses would be rendered into hexameters by a priest.

Up to three women might serve as Pythia at any one time, with two taking turns in prophesying, and the third kept in reserve.[10] There was a very small window for consultations, with only one day per month on which the priestess might be consulted. Other sources add that prophecies were only available during the nine warmest days of each year. During the winter, Apollo decamped and was replaced by his half-brother Dionysus. Apollo came back at the beginning of spring on his birthday, the seventh day of the month of Bysios. Once a month, the oracle would be ritually purified, to ready Pythia for communication with the divine. On the seventh day of the month, she would bathe in the Castalian Spring, then would drink the sacred waters of the river Kassotis, where a naiad possessing magical powers lived.

A priestess could attend public events; she was paid a salary with housing provided by the state, and gold crowns. However Plutarch, who served as a priest during the late first and early second century CE, records that the physical demands of the job, and the exhaustion that comes with all the possession and frenzy involved, shortened the Pythia's life, with some dying prematurely through exhaustion; Plutarch's *Why the Pythia Does Not Now Give Oracles in Verse* expatiates on his life as a priest. Moreover, Pythia was routinely drugged with toxic laurel leaves laced with henbane to induce her mind-expanding, hypnotic trance.

The rape referred to above was not the only disaster at Delphi. Plutarch tells us how, on one consultation, the omens were bad, but the oracle was consulted regardless. The priests received the prophecy, but this led to an uncontrollable reaction in the priestess, who died soon after. Pausanias describes how the petulant Hercules caused mayhem with the Pythia, Xenoclea.[11] Hercules went to Delphi to consult the oracle shortly after murdering Iphitus; he had thrown him off a wall in Tiryns, while Iphitus was staying with him as an honoured guest. Hercules was having nightmares as a result, and sought advice on a cure at Delphi. However, a shocked Xenoclea was reluctant to help, because Hercules remained unpurified from the blood and death of Iphitus. She bluntly told him 'you murdered your guest, I have no oracle for the likes of you'. Hercules was so angered by this that he sacrilegiously grabbed the priestess's tripod, took it away with him, and refused to return it until Xenoclea had agreed to a consultation. The tripod was duly returned and, after bathing in the Castalian Spring, Xenoclea pronounced that Hercules would be purified of the death of Iphitus (thus curing his nightmares), but only if he spent a year as a slave; his value when sold was donated to the children of Iphitus as compensation for the loss of their father. Hercules accepted this oracle and served Omphale, queen of Lydia, for one year.[12] The incident can still be seen; an ancient vase shows Hercules carrying off the sacred tripod, while Apollo, holding a branch of laurel, struggles to recover it, and Xenoclea looks on, terrified by the commotion.[13]

In the Mycenaean state of Pylos, Eritha was a high profile priestess from the thirteenth or twelfth century BCE, and was in charge of a sanctuary dedicated to the goddess Potnia. She was also involved in a dispute with the local authorities over the taxable assets of the sanctuary. Potnia was goddess of nature, birth, and death, thus a mother goddess. The priestesses of Pylos were invested with considerable power, and exerted significant influence over the local economy; they controlled land, textile production, and all workers. They enjoyed high status in Mycenaean society along with another local priestess, Karpathia. Eritha would have been assisted in her land management and running the economic resources of the sanctuary by a number of sacred servants. Eritha's dispute with the local authorities (the *damos*) revolved around her claim that the land of the sanctuary should be exempt from taxation as a privileged site, and not as a regular leasehold subject to taxes. We do not know how the matter was resolved, as Pylos and its palace were razed to the ground by invaders in the early twelfth century BCE.

The priestesses of Hera at Argos and their work were so important that they gave their names to significant events in ancient Greek history. Thucydides in Book II dates the start of the Peloponnesian War when Chrysis was priestess at Argos; at the outbreak of the war in 431 BCE, Chrysis was in the forty-eighth year of her tenure as head priestess of Argos.[14] Lysimache (meaning 'she who dissolves the battle') was priestess of Apollo for sixty-four years, and is the model for Lysistrata in Aristophanes' play of the same name.

The Hellespontine Sibyl, born during the lifetimes of Solon and Cyrus the Great, was the priestess who presided over the Apollonian oracle of Apollo at Dardania; she is sometimes known as the Trojan Sibyl. She is particularly famous for her prediction of Christ's crucifixion, and is usually depicted standing next to a cross.

Greek mythology has a good number of priestesses, including Admete; Callithyia; Hero; Io; Iodame; Iphigenia; Nicippe; Phemonoe; Pygmalion; and Xenoclea. Women priestesses were a common feature of everyday Greek life; they had a role to play in politics and dynastic machinations. In real life, in the second half of the third century and first half of the second century BCE, Berenice was a Greek princess from Asia Minor, daughter of Ptolemy II of Telmessos. Ptolemy II was able to cement his friendly relations with Antiochus III, when Berenice was appointed by Antiochus III as chief-priestess of the Carian Satrapy, of the Seleucid Royal Cult of Laodice in 193 BCE. Laodice was a Seleucid queen and the cousin-wife of Antiochus III.

Chrysis is best known as an accidental arsonist when she accidentally started a fire that led to the destruction of the temple at Argos. According to Thucydides in Book IV, Chrysis carelessly placed a candle near a curtain and then, even more carelessly, fell asleep. She did, however, escape the fire, and fled from Argos to nearby Phlius.[15] According to Pausanias, Chrysis then reached Tegea, where she found asylum at the sanctuary of Athena Alea.[16] The fire at Argos was later deliberately misconstrued by the Christian theologians Clement of Alexandria and Arnobius, who contended that Chrysis had died in the fire and her death was an example of the impotence of heathen gods.

Women get a mixed reception from Greek philosophers. Plato nails a problem, in some ways our problem too, when he describes how women in different places can act, and are treated, very differently:

Shall it be that of the Thracians, and many other tribes, who employ their women in tilling the ground and minding oxen and sheep and toiling just like slaves? Or that which obtains with us and all the people of our district? The way women are treated with us[Athenians] at present is this—we huddle all our goods together, as the saying goes, within four walls, and then hand over the dispensing of them to the women, together with the control of the shuttles and all kinds of wool-work. Or again, shall we prescribe for them, Megillus, that midway system, the Laconian [Spartan]? Must the girls share in gymnastics and music, and the women abstain from wool-work, but weave themselves instead a life that is not trivial at all nor useless, but arduous, advancing as it were halfway in the path of domestic tendance and management and child-nurture, but taking no share in military service; so that, even if it should chance to be necessary for them to fight in defence of their city and their children, they will be unable to handle with skill either a bow (like the Amazons) or any other missile, nor could they take spear and shield, after the fashion of the Goddess (Athena), so as to be able nobly to resist the wasting of their native land, and to strike terror— if nothing more—into the enemy at the sight of them marshalled in battle-array? If they lived in this manner, they certainly would not dare to adopt the fashion of the Sauromatides, whose women would seem like men beside them.[17]

Plato projects an ambivalent attitude to women, to say the least. He advocates a more equable role for women in some of his works and in the *Republic* crucially foresees an upper tier of 'guardians' in which the chattel status of women is abolished so that the wife is no longer just the property of her husband.[18] As guardians do not own property, and child-care is a communal responsibility, the *oikos* (and by extension, marriage) were to be abolished under this regime, freeing women up to play a civic, and actively political, role in society. Standing shoulder to shoulder with men, female guardians could safeguard the city and ensure the existence of a just society.

Moreover, and just as importantly, Plato recommends that women receive exactly the same education and training as men: 'It won't be two different kinds of education that will produce our men and our women for us, especially since it will be entrusted with people of the same nature? It must be the same education.'[19] CCW Taylor summarises it:

Since the function of a wife in Athenian society was confined to the private sphere, female guardians are not in the conventional sense wives of their male counterparts. Rather they are comrades whose shared social role includes temporary sexual liaisons, the function of which is the perpetuation of the guardian class, itself required for the continued existence of the ideal state. Plato's attitude to the emancipation of women has to be understood in the context of the complex moral and political theory in which it is embedded.[20]

For Plato here, physical strength is the only differentiating factor between men and women. In all other matters they are equal, because intellectually they are on a par with men and must be treated with equal respect. Plato asks:

So shall we assign everything to men, and nothing to a woman? How could we? No, because, as we'll agree, one woman has a natural ability for medicine, and another not, and one for music, another not. So there is also a woman equipped to be a Guardian, and another who isn't. Isn't that sort of natural potential that we selected in our male guardians too? (Plato *Republic* 5, 456a)

Significantly, Guardian status was a paramilitary position that was at the pinnacle of citizenship. Plato not only refuses to consign women to a life of housework and baby production, but also argues that women are just as capable of filling the role of highest of citizens. A long way from the voteless, powerless, non-citizen and unobtrusive little woman cultivated by many of his contempories.

Progressive and liberal as all this may sound, it is important to remember that Plato's concern in the *Republic* was the establishment and preservation of an ideal state, not the status of women; get the role of women right, among any other things, and you are a step nearer getting the state right. Nevertheless, an ambivalence lurks within Plato's argument relating to relative physical strength; women can, and should, be Guardians, but only as a lesser form, a Guardian-lite:

[The Guardians] should share all activities—except that we employ the females as weaker animals, the males as stronger ... are you aware of any practice cultivated by humans in which the male sex is not superior to the female in all ... ways ... ? Or do we have to spend time discussing weaving and the preparation of cakes and vegetables ... It's true that the one sex is greatly surpassed by the other in virtually everything. (Plato, *Republic* 5, 454d)

His conflicting ideology is encapsulated in the statement: women must be allotted lighter tasks than the men, because of the weakness of their sex. This, if anything, torpedoes the argument held by some that Plato was a feminist.

Moreover, there is no escaping the biological fact that only women can give birth and nourish babies; therefore, to produce the best, Plato has a eugenicist solution in which women are seen as the means of reproduction and not as objects of sexual desire, or indeed as recipients of sexual pleasure:

It follows from our previous agreements, first, that the best men must have sex with the best women as frequently as possible, while the opposite is true of the most inferior men and women, and, second, that if our herd is to be of the highest possible quality, the former's offspring must be reared (as guardians) but not the latter's. And this must all be brought about without being noticed by anyone except the rulers, so that our herd of guardians remains as free from dissension as possible.[21]

Marriage or a similar relationship, then, was to be founded on the likely quality of offspring, with those unfortunate children who did not make the grade being exterminated at worst or, at best, exposed—a practice (*ékthesis*) that prevailed in the real world in Greek, and Roman and so-called barbarian societies.

Women were eligible not just for the position of guardian but, by definition, as philosopher- leaders too—the heads of state. Because women had access to the studies described in book 6 of the *Republic*, by acquiring a knowledge of mathematics and dialectic, they presumably qualified as philosopher-leaders. Diogenes Laërtius gives us the names of two women who attended Plato's Academy:

> His disciples were Speusippus of Athens, Xenocrates of Chalcedon, Aristotle of Stagira…and many others, among them two women, Lastheneia of Mantinea and Axiothea of Phlius who is reported by Dicaearchus to have worn men's clothes.[22]

The policy on education and women also appears in the *Laws*—nothing will 'withdraw our recommendation that so far as possible, in education and everything else the female sex should be on the same footing as the male'.[23] In the *Timaeus*, Plato concedes that women are inferior to men due to a degeneration from or corruption of the pinnacle of perfect human nature:

> 'It is only males who are created directly by the gods and are given souls. Those who live rightly return to the stars, but those who are 'cowards or [lead unrighteous lives] may with reason be supposed to have changed into the nature of women in the second generation'. This degeneration may continue through successive reincarnations unless reversed. In this situation, obviously it is only men who are complete human beings and can hope for ultimate fulfilment; the best a woman can hope for is to become a man'.[24]

The views on women of Plato's student, Aristotle, can be found, among other places, in his Politics; 'the male, unless constituted in some respect contrary to nature, is by nature more expert at leading than the female, and the elder and complete than the younger and incomplete'. (Aristotle, *Politics,* 6, 1259a41)

To Aristotle, it is natural for the male to rule and for a female to be ruled:

> 'The relation of male to female is by nature a relation of superior to inferior and ruler to ruled' The slave is wholly lacking the deliberative element; the female has it but it lacks authority; the child has it but it is incomplete'.
> Woman may be said to be an inferior man.[25]

The female is, as it were, a deformed male.[26]

Females are weaker and colder in nature, and we must look upon the female character as being a sort of natural deficiency.[27]

What difference does it make whether women rule, or the rulers are ruled by women? The result is the same.[28]

The courage of man is shown in commanding, of a woman in obeying.[29]

The female is softer in disposition than the male, is more mischievous, less simple, more impulsive, and more attentive to the nurture of the young; the male, on the other hand, is more spirited than the female, more savage, more simple and less cunning. The traces of these differentiated characteristics are more or less visible everywhere, but they are especially visible where character is the more developed, and most of all in man...Woman requires a smaller quantity of nutriment.[30]

In other words, women are defective, second rate and should not concern themselves with public affairs.[31]

[Women are] more mischievous, more complicated, more impulsive ... more compassionate ... more easily moved to tears ... more jealous, more argumentative, more likely to scold and to hit out... more prone to depression and less hopeful ... more shameless, lacking in self-respect, bigger liars, more deceptive, of more retentive memory ... also more wakeful; more shrinking, more difficult to rouse to action.[32]

Women were on a par with slaves and children.

Aristotle believed in what Robert Garland neatly called 'a hierarchy of physical perfection, with male human beings at the summit'.[33] To him, being a woman was the first step on the road to deformity, although he did concede that women were a necessary evil; they are 'required by nature', because 'the race of beings which is separated into female and male has to be preserved'. This leaves us with the feeling that Aristotle would have preferred a world made up entirely of men were it biologically viable. Aristotle trots out the old cliché that women are born from the left testicle and grow on the left side of the womb, with all the sinister connotations of left-sided badness and evil.

Only fair-skinned women, not darker-skinned women, produced a sexual discharge and had orgasms. Aristotle was not impressed by a woman's sexual discharge, likening its relative impotency to that of an infertile male. Both sexes contributed to reproduction, but the female's contribution was in her defective semen rather than anything to do with the ovaries.[34]

Aristotle, in his *Politics*, claimed that 'A man would seem a coward if he had only the courage of a woman: a woman a chatterer if she were no more reticent than a good man.'[35] Here, women are stereotyped as cowardly and garrulous; Aristotle is obviously of the opinion that compared to men, women cannot possibly exhibit positive traits, such as bravery or discretion.

There is nevertheless some better news for women in Aristotle's *Economics* (Οἰκονομικά; *Oeconomica*). He discourages male promiscuity ('random intercourse'), not least because any bastard children will have a right to the legacies of his lawful children, and his wife and sons will be dishonoured by his behaviour. The husband should honour his wife and talk civilly to her with reason. He believed that a woman responded best when shown respect, and when she saw that her husband was faithful to her. Aristotle wrote that a husband should endeavour to cultivate harmony, loyalty, and devotion in his wife; he should also show her that they had interests in common, and instil in her the notion that, when he is away from her, absence really does make the heart grow fonder. In the *Rhetoric*, he asserts that a society cannot be happy unless its women are happy too.

The Stoic philosophers were nothing if not socially unconventional. They argued for equality of the sexes; sexual inequality to them was contrary to the laws of nature. In teaching this, they followed the Cynics, who believed that men and women should dress identically, and be educated in the same way. Stoics saw marriage as companionship between equals, rather than a biological or social necessity, and practiced this as well as preaching it.

As we have seen, women successfully took up philosophy; the Pythagorean school was particularly welcoming to women philosophers. Pythagoras' wife and daughters may have authored one of the sacred discourses attributed to Pythagoras. Themistoklea is said to have influenced Pythagoras, not the other way around, while Plato's Diotima of Mantinea was the teacher of Socrates, not Plato himself.

Death and the woman

If women enjoyed an uncharacteristically high profile part in aspects of ancient Greek religion, the same can be said of them in their role in death, especially death in the family. What some Greeks believed happened after death is first described by Homer in the *Odyssey*. As he says, and as we might suspect, hell (Hades) was not a happy place:

> His wife, Persephone, reigned over countless drifting crowds of shadowy figures—the 'shades' of all those who had died. It was not a happy place. Indeed, the ghost of the great hero Achilles told Odysseus that he would rather be a poor serf on earth than lord of all the dead in the Underworld.[1]

The underworld and chthonic *topoi* enjoy an established place in Greek poetry, so any literate Greek, anyone who had the time to listen to poetry recitations, or anyone who attended religious rites and ceremonies, would be well aware of what was in store.

We can only speculate on which of the Cyclic Epics featured *katabaseis* or *nekyiae*, descents to the underworld or audiences with the raised dead, but we know that the one surviving fragment of the *Minyad* describes Charon, and that Virgil was familiar with descents to the underworld by Orpheus, Dionysus, and Hercules, possibly through epic poems.[2, 3] Indeed, Greek and Roman literature up to Virgil and beyond is replete with stories of and references to underworld journeys, chthonic topology, eschatology, and the like.

Homer has a number of infernal references apart from Odysseus' *katabasis* in Book 11: Proteus predicts Menelaus' destiny in Elysium; Circe instructs Odysseus to visit the Underworld; the twin gates of dreams are described; Odysseus buries his comrades at sea; and in the last book, Homer depicts the souls of Penelope's suitors, Achilles and Agamemnon, in Hades.[4] In the *Iliad*, he describes the ghost of Patroclus.[5]

In *Works & Days*, Hesiod outlines the afterlife of the different ages of man; in the *Theogony*, he describes Tartarus and its inhabitants in some detail.[6] Pindar deals with judgement of the dead and metempsychosis in his second *Olympian Ode*, and two fragments reveal coverage of Elysium as well as more on the transmigration of souls.[7]

Aristophanes has his celebrated *katabasis* of Dionysus in the *Frogs*, which features grumpy old Charon; in Sophocles' *Oedipus*, Creon elaborately describes the setting for a necromancy, in which a multitude of ghosts are summoned, including Laius. Aeschylus raises the ghost of Darius, after Atossa's libations to the gods of the underworld in the *Persae*.[8]

Herodotus describes Melissa's *nekuomanteion* and Periander's necrophilia in his *Histories*.[9] Diogenes Laërtius leaves a fragment of Empedocles' that refers to a necromancy.[10] Plato expatiates on the immortality of the soul (*Phaedo*)—the nature of death, judgement of the dead (*Gorgias*), Orphism (*Cratylus*), and metempsychosis (*Phaedrus*).[11] His *Myth of Er* describes Er's experience in the underworld.[12] Ovid describes Pythagorean and Orphic beliefs on the afterlife that prevailed in ancient Greek days.[13]

To the Greeks, life on earth came to an end when the *psyche*, or spirit of the dead, left the body as a short exhalation of breath. The destination thereafter was not gender specific; men and women all ended up at the same place, before segregation according to the life lived. Back on Earth, after 1100 BCE, Greeks began to bury their dead in individual graves rather than group tombs. The Athenians, however, normally cremated their dead, and placed their ashes in an urn.

The role and function of women in the ceremony of the dead was crucial. The deceased was readied for burial according to ancient ritual. A proper burial and its attendant rites was absolutely paramount; its neglect or absence was an affront to human dignity.[14] Women had a particular responsibility to attend to these rites: the *prothesis* involved the laying out the body by women in the family and placing it on a bed within the house. The body was cleaned, anointed, adorned with a wreath, dressed in new or clean clothes, and placed on a clean funeral cloth. Aristophanes describes the process in the *Ecclesiazusae*: 'first spread out a layer of oregano on four pieces of wood; tie fillets round your head, bring phials of scent and place a bowl filled with lustral water before your door.'[15]

Women made the honey cake that was offered to the deceased. A coin might be placed on the deceased's tongue, as payment for Charon, the ferryman, for passage over the Styx, transfering from the world of the living to the world of the dead. Similarly, those initiated into the mystery religions might be decorated with a gold tablet, placed on the lips or positioned on the body; this provided a route map for navigating the afterlife, and for appropriately addressing the rulers of the underworld, Hades and Persephone. The Germans call this *totenpass*. The ferryman, Charon, was notoriously saturnine, unbending, and officious. During the *prothesis*, relatives and friends came to mourn and pay their respects, somewhat like a wake; lamentation of the dead and mourning can seen on early Greek geometric vases. The fact that the Greeks believed that a person was polluted after touching the body may have something to do with the fact that these tasks were delegated (and relegated) to women.

After the body was made ready and laid out for viewing on the second day by kinswomen, wrapped in dark robes who stood round the bier; the chief mourner, often a mother or wife, was at the head, and others behind. Women led the mourning by chanting dirges, tearing at their hair and clothing, and beating their breasts. The *prothesis* was originally an outdoor ceremony, but Solon decreed that the ceremony take place indoors.

After the *prothesis*, the body was taken to the cemetery in a procession (the *ekphora*) usually just before dawn. The women headed the group, while the male relatives followed behind; this was another of the rare occasions when the women were allowed to lead the way in a public event. Women brought the *choai*—libations of honey, milk, water, wine, perfumes, and oils all mixed up—and the *haimacouria*, blood propitiation. One of the women dedicated a lock of hair, along with the *choai*, followed by a prayer and the *enagismata*; these were offerings to the dead that included milk, honey, water, wine, celery, *pelanon* (a concoction of meal, honey, and oil), and *kollyba* (small round cakes), the first fruits of the season and dried and fresh fruit.

If it was an interment, a few favourite objects were placed in the grave to make the afterlife more accommodating. Monumental earth mounds, rectangular tombs, and marble *stelai* and statues were sometimes erected for the elite dead; this was to mark the grave and enshrine the memory of the deceased relative, the observance of which helped to ensure immortality. At cremations, the body was placed on a pyre of flammable reeds or wood, set alight, and doused with wine after the body had been burned.

With burial or cremation over, the house and household objects were thoroughly cleansed with seawater and hyssop (named from azob, a holy herb used for cleaning sacred places); the women most closely related to the deceased took part in the ritual washing in clean water. A funeral feast followed (the *perideipnom*), at which the deceased was the (absent) host.

A woman's subordinate status lived on with her in death. The etching on her tombstone was the first publication of her name; she was identified by her given name and patronymic, and sometimes her demotic, or 'deme' name, all illustrating the superiority of the men in her life. She was never described as a mother here, as this would imply that she had authority over any sons in the family.

Images on white-ground *lekythoi* show us that it was the women who regularly visited graves with offerings, including small cakes and libations. Neglect of the dead by the living might excite ghosts, so ongoing maintenance and visiting through graveside offerings, including hair clippings from the closest survivors, was very important. The dead were commemorated at certain times of the year, such as Genesia, but the memories of most faded after a couple of generations into the collective dead, 'thrice-ancestors' (*tritopatores*), who also had annual festivals devoted to them. The object of Genesia was to avert the nemesis of the dead who punished the living if their cult had been neglected.[16]

Conduct at funerals, and women's conduct in particular was of sufficient concern in Solon's time to attract the attention of the authorities. In his *Life of Solon*, Plutarch records laws enacted around 590 BCE, restricting funeral expenses and clamping down on ostentatious behaviour at Athenian funerals. Wailing and lacerating the flesh by Athenian women was prohibited, and the graveside sacrifice of oxen was criminalized; no more than three garments could henceforth be buried with the body, and the number of female relatives allowed to attend was limited. Transgressors were punished for womanly and weak behaviour, and for carrying their mourning to extravagant lengths. The consequences of this desperate legislation were profound; in reality, Solon was denying women one of the few ways in which they were able to express themselves, to take control and assume responsibility in a good and honorable ritual. Lamentation and the like were seen by the state as subversive, seditious, and Siren-like; it had to stop:

> These are the laws concerning the dead: bury the dead person as follows: in three white cloths-a spread, a shroud, and a coverlet-or in fewer, not worth more than 300 drachmas. Carry out [the body] on a wedge-footed bed and do not cover the bier with cloths. Bring not more than three chous of wine to the tomb and not more than one chous of olive oil, and bring back the empty jars. Carry the shrouded corpse in silence all the way to the tomb. Perform the preliminary sacrifice according to ancestral customs. Bring the bed and the covers back from the tomb inside the house.[17]

The officious minutiae associated with this severe, draconian legislation would have been sharpened by the fact that women's conduct at funerals had precedent in the revered verses of Homer's *Iliad*, in Andromache's and Hecabe's reaction to the death of their beloved Hector. In accordance with traditional funerary custom, Andromache reacts with a spontaneous and impulsive outburst of grief; the final stage of this was the communal grieving (*thrēnos*), when Hector's body was returned to her.

> Now, among the women, Hecabe raised loud lament: 'My child, how wretched I am! Why should I live on in suffering now you are dead? You were my pride of Troy, night and day, a saviour, greeted as a god, by every man and women in this city, surely their great glory while you lived. But now death and fate overtake you. Hecabe wept, but Andromache, Hector's wife, as yet knew nothing, no one had even told her that her husband had stayed outside the walls. She was at work in an inner room of the lofty palace, weaving a double-width purple tapestry, with a multicoloured pattern of flowers. In all ignorance she had asked her ladies-in-waiting to set a great cauldron on the fire so that Hector would have hot water for a bath, when he returned… she ran through the halls, her heart pounding, beside herself, and her ladies followed. When they came to the wall…Darkness shrouded her eyes, enfolding her, and she fell backward, senseless. From her head fell the bright headdress, the frontlet and netted cap, the plaited strands, and the veil that golden Aphrodite had given her.[18]

There are similar pathetic scenes at the end of the *Iliad*, before Hector's body is cremated and Andromache, Hecabe, and Helen all lament:

Soon the city emptied. Plunged in unbearable grief, all ran to the gate, and close beyond them met Priam, bringing home his dead. Hector's beloved wife and royal mother flung themselves at the cart. Clasping Hector's head, they wailed and tore their hair, while the great host of people wept. And they'd have been there, outside the gate, lamenting him the livelong day till the setting of the sun, if old Priam had not called out to them from the chariot: 'Let the mules pass, and when I have brought him to the palace then you can take your fill of lament.'

Solon was rewriting women's history, and erasing revered aspects of the Greek past in legislation that had a profound impact on the freedom of women and their expression.

Woman as witch

Generally, the ancient Greeks (like the Egyptians before, and the Romans after them) were, by nature, very superstitious. Societies have dabbled in the dark arts for as long as religions have been practised; ancient Greece is no exception. The Greeks had to keep the Olympians on side, but at the same time watch out for malevolent curses, voodoo dolls, and witches lurking in the background. Magic was in the air.

The first witch we have the misfortune to meet in ancient Greece is in the *Odyssey*, when the hero meets Circe, a witch. Her name is derived from *kirkoô* (meaning 'to secure with rings' or 'encircle'), and that is exactly what she did in a magical way; she ran rings around everyone. Homer lists her divine credentials:

A goddess with braided hair, with human speech and with strange powers; gloomy Aeetes was her brother, and both were radiant Helios' the sun-god's children; their mother was Perse, Okeanos' daughter. (Homer, *Odyssey* 10. 135f)

Home for Circe was the island of Aeaea.[1] This is the first sight and sound Odysseus and his men, having disembarked, get of the beautiful witch-goddess:

And now they could hear Circe within, singing with her beautiful voice as she moved to and fro at the wide web that was more than earthly—delicate, gleaming, delectable, as a goddess' handiwork needs must be—a goddess or a woman, moving to and fro at her wide web and singing a lovely song that the whole floor re-echoes with. (Homer, *Odyssey* 10, 225f)

Circe provided a meal, but the food was drugged. She changed his crew into swine (and later back again), with the practiced wave of a staff, a single spell, and a simple potion. She confined them in a pig sty, obviously wanting to keep a ready supply of men to satisfy her voracious sexual appetite. Odysseus himself escapes the form-changing experience because 'golden wanded' Mercury, in his counter role as a male sorcerer, had prescribed him *molu*, a kind of snowdrop that acted as an antidote with mystical properties, with the following advice:

I will tell you of all her witch's arts. She will brew a potion for you, but with the good things she will mingle drugs as well. Yet even so, she will not be able to enchant you; my gift of the magic herb will thwart her. I will tell you the rest, point by point. When Circe strikes you with the long wand she carries, draw the keen sword from your side, rush upon her and make as if to kill her. She will shrink back, and then ask you to sleep with her. At this you must let her have her way; she is a goddess; accept her bed, so that she may release your comrades and make you her cherished guest. (Homer, *Odyssey* 10. 277 ff)

Odysseus complies. After a refreshing bath, he convinces Circe that his men need to be restored to their previous form; she does this, with the added bonus that they each re-emerge rejuvenated, 'younger than they were before, and much taller, and better looking'. Immune from the porcine magic himself thanks to Mercury, Odysseus succumbs to Circe's obvious physical charms, and the two begin a divinely approved, yearlong torrid affair in Circe's 'sumptuous bed.' Part of the package is Circe's revelation of what the future holds for the hero, including his pending appointment with dead people in his necromancy.[2]

Circe is a *pharkamkis* (witch) or *pharmakeutria* (poisoner); she is *polu pharmakos* (expert in the arts of the sorceress) and she uses *pharmaka* (drugs)—a veritable expert in spells, potions, and mind altering drugs. Her skills are a perfect exposition of the three-way association between drugs, spells, and medicine prevalent in antiquity. She has other witchy attributes: she can render herself invisible and she can fly through the air; she has the power to emasculate her lovers; she can literally run rings round her victims. She is also versed in the art of chthonic communication with the souls of the dead; she demonstrates this when she sends Odysseus to his *nekuia*, or necromancy, with impressively precise instructions.

Go forward, and dig a trench a cubit long and a cubit broad; go round this trench, pouring libations for all the dead, first with milk and honey, then with sweet wine, then with water; and sprinkle white barley-meal on top. Then with earnest prayers to the insubstantial dead you must promise that when you have come to Ithaca you will sacrifice in your palace a calfless heifer, the best you have, and will load a pyre with precious things; and that for Teiresias and no other you will slay a ram that is black all over, the pick of the flocks of Ithaca. When with these prayers you have made appeal to the noble nations of the dead, then you must sacrifice a ram and a black ewe; bend the victim's heads down towards Erebos, but turn your own head away and look towards the waters of the river. At this, the souls of the dead and gone will come flocking up to you. With commanding voice you must call your comrades to flay and burn the two sheep that now lie before them, killed by your own ruthless blade, and over them to pray to the gods, to resistless Hades and dreaded Persephone. As for yourself, draw the sharp sword from beside your side; then, sitting down, restrain the insubstantial dead from drawing nearer to the blood until you have questioned

> Teiresias. Then, King Odysseus, the seer will come to you very quickly, to prophesy the path before you, the long stages of your travel, and how you will eventually reach home over the teeming sea. (Homer, *Odyssey* 10. 520ff)

Later in the poem, Odysseus tries to justify his year-long delay, blaming it all on 'the cunning knot which Circe had brought to his knowledge in other days', and 'subtle Aiaian Circe [who] confined me in her palace and would have had me for husband'.[3] Aeschylus' lost satyr play *Circe* also told the story of Odysseus' encounter with Circe; contemporary vase paintings suggest that Odysseus' pig-men formed the chorus in place of the usual Satyrs.

Circe's reach was long, and her influence over Odysseus and his family did not end when he sailed for Ithaca. First, one of her acolytes turns Odysseus in to a horse in his dotage:

> There is … a Tyrrhenian poisoner; she worked for Circe and fled from her mistress. It was to her, says the author, that Odysseus came [at the end of his life]; with the aid of her drugs, she changed him into a horse and kept him with her until he died of old age. (Ptolemy Hephaestion, *New History* Book 4 (summary from Photius, *Myriobiblon* 190))

Then, Circe married Telemachus, Odysseus' son by Penelope, and they in turn have a son called Latinus who gave his name to the Latin language; Telegonus, Circe's son by Odysseus, married Penelope.[4]

It is, however, the lost epic *Telegony* to which we turn to learn the unspeakably tragic disaster that befell the house of Odysseus; Circe finally told Telegonus who his absent father was, prompting him to find Odysseus, taking a poisoned spear provided by Circe. It is with this that he unwittingly killed his father. Telegonus returned to Aeaea with the corpse, accompanied by his stepmother and stepbrother, Penelope and Telemachus; Circe buried Odysseus and made the other three immortal. However, that was by no means the end for Odysseus. Circe used her magical herbs to reanimate Odysseus, who, fully restored to life, gave Telemachus to Circe's daughter, Cassiphone, in marriage.[5] Later, according to this source, Telemachus quarrelled with mother-in-law Circe and slew her; Cassiphone then killed Telemachus to avenge her mother's death. Odysseus died of grief.

Of course, Odysseus was not the only lover to be ensnared by Circe in one form or another. Parthenius, a Greek mythographer from the first century BCE, tells us how hapless Calchos fell under her uncompromising spell, literally and metaphorically, in his *Love Romances*:

> Calchos the Daunian [in southern Italy] was greatly in love with Circe…He handed over to her his kingship over the Daunians, and employed all possible blandishments to gain her love; but she felt a passion for Odysseus, who was then with her, and

loathed Calchos and forbade him to land on her island. However, he persisted and could talk of nothing else but Circe, and she, being very angry with him, laid a trap and had no sooner invited him into her palace but she set before him a table covered with all manner of food. But the meats were full of magical drugs, and as soon as Calchos had eaten them, he went mad, and she drove him into the pig-sties. After some time, however, the Daunian army landed on the island looking for Calchos; she then released him from the spell but not before binding him by oath that he would never set foot on the island again, either to woo her or for any other reason.[6]

Ovid gives us the tragic story of Circe's passion for Picus, and the magical lengths to which she goes to get him.[7] One day, Picus went out boar hunting; Circe was in the same area collecting strange herbs when she saw Picus and was entranced. She dropped the herbs and 'like blazing fire a thrill of ecstasy raced through her veins'. Circe could not get to him because he rode so fast, and cried out 'you won't get away', calling on the powers vested in her herbs and spells. She conjured up an image of a boar, which Picus pursued on foot into a dense part of the wood, believing it to be a real boar. Then, Circe resorted to prayers, incantations, and chants to unknown gods, eclipsing the moon and blotting out the sun. The heavens went dark; the earth breathed vapours as she finds him groping in the darkness and cries 'oh, by your eyes, those eyes of yours,' she said, 'that captured mine, and by your beauty, loveliest of kings, that makes me here, a goddess, kneel to you, favour my passion... and harden not your heart to Circe Titanis' love.' Picus, however, was singularly unimpressed, and declared his love for Canens Janigena; in response, Circe repeatedly pleaded, screaming 'You'll pay for this, never again will Canens have you; now you will find out just what a wronged woman is capable of'. Picus fled but Circe turned him into a woodpecker as he ran, leaving him nothing but his name, which is Latin for woodpecker. His men frantically searched for him, but could only find Circe, whom they implicated in Picus' disappearance. This undiplomatic move brought out the worst in Circe, who responded with a show of her most horrific witch-like skills:

> She sprinkled round about her evil drugs and poisonous essences, and out of Erebos and Chaos called Nox and the Di Noties [Gods of Night] and poured a prayer with long-drawn wailing cries to Hecate [her mother]. The woods (wonder of wonders!) leapt away, a groan came from the ground, the bushes blanched, the spattered sward was soaked with gouts of blood, stones brayed and bellowed, dogs began to bark, black snakes swarmed on the soil and ghostly shapes of silent spirits floated through the air.

Picus' retinue was aghast, stunned by such hellish sorcery, but Circe was far from finished; she touched their faces with her poisoned wand, turning each of them into a wild beast. Back home, Canens waited in vain. Elsewhere, Circe purifies Jason and Medea after their murder of Apsyrtus, and helps them to lay his ghost; when the Argonauts met Circe, she was washing her hair, surrounded by congenitally malformed monsters:

Here they found Circe bathing her head in the salt water. She had been terrified by a nightmare in which she saw all the rooms and walls of her house streaming with blood, and fire devouring all the magic drugs which she used to bewitch her visitors. But she managed to put out the red flames with the blood of a murdered man, gathering it up in her hands; and so the horror passed. When morning came she rose from bed, and now she was washing her hair and clothes in the sea. A number of creatures whose ill-assorted limbs declared them to be neither man nor beast had gathered round her like a great flock of sheep following their shepherd from the fold... The Argonauts were dumbfounded by the scene.

The purification rites are duly performed:

She set about the rites by which a ruthless slayer is absolved when he seeks asylum at the hearth. First, to atone for the unexpiated murder, she took a suckling pig from a sow with dugs still swollen after littering. Holding it over them she cut its throat and let the blood fall on their hands. Next she propitiated Zeus with other libations … she herself stayed by the hearth, burning cakes and other wineless offerings with prayers to Zeus, in the hope that she might cause the loathsome Erinyes to relent, and that he himself might once more smile upon this pair, whether the hands they lifted up to him were stained with a kinsman's or a stranger's blood.[8]

Another story concerning Circe is that, in jealousy against a rival, she poured the juice of poisonous herbs into the sea where Scylla used to bathe, changing her into the repellent monster we know.

Circe embodies everything a witch needs to practise effectively: magical skill and accoutrements, mystical plants, erotic magic, rejuvenation skills, and a working knowledge of eschatology. She was, of course, a member of that satanic family, the unholy trinity, which boasted Hecate as Circe's mother, and Medea as her sister:

[Medea] said [to the Argonauts] that she had brought with her many drugs of marvellous potency which had been discovered by her mother Hecate and by her sister Circe; and though before this time she had never used them to destroy human beings, on this occasion she would, and by means of them easily wreak vengeance upon men who were deserving of punishment.[9]

A lost play about Circe by Anaxilas describes the transformation of one the characters who subsequently complains that he is unable to scratch his face now that he is a pig, thanks to Circe; Ephippus of Athens also wrote a *Circe*.

Homer's Circe was later interpreted as a moralising cautionary tale on the perils of inebriation, as Odysseus' crew drank Pramnian wine provided by Circe; Ovid's Picus added uncontrollable jealousy to the witch's list of character defects, which already included sexual attraction and deception. The metamorphoses she inflicted on men were interpreted as male emasculation by a vengeful woman.

Circe has been well remembered. Boccaccio collected the known facts about Circe in his *De Mulieribus Claris* (1361–1362), admitting with a sense of resignation that there now exist many more temptresses like her, all intent on leading men astray. In botany, the Circaea are plants belonging to the Enchanter's Nightshade genus; the name was given by botanists in the late sixteenth century who believed that this was the herb used by Circe to charm Odysseus' companions; however, it is no relative to the nightshade family, which includes the deadly nightshade. Medical historians believe that the transformation to pigs is an instance of anticholinergic intoxication, the symptoms of which include amnesia, hallucinations, and delusions. Moly, as given to Odysseus by Mercury, is a snowdrop that contains galantamine, an anticholinesterase inhibitor, and is effective as an antidote for anticholinergics.

Medea came with the finest pedigree a witch could ask for. Medea is seen by many as the archetypal witch, and frequently appears in any ancient literature that describes the supernatural. As early as the fifth century BCE, an obscure writer called Pherecydes of Athens tells how Medea murdered her brother, Apsyrtus, to help the Argonauts against the Colchians; this version is supported by Sophocles and Apollonius of Rhodes, although here it is Jason who deals the fatal blow. Pindar cannot resist including Medea in a scene in which Aphrodite, paradoxically, uses magic to help Jason win Medea's heart. Sophocles describes Medea in the *Rhizotomoi* as she harvests her roots naked, her hair in disarray; the other 'root-cutters' of the play's title are a chorus of witches. Euripides, of course, has his *Medea*. Menander's lost plays *Deisidaemon* and *Theophoroumenos* both included magic; Pliny the Elder reports that Menander's *Thessala* featured Thessaly, infamous for its many witches.

Apollonius of Rhodes depicts Medea and her *pharmaka* in detail in his epic poem, the *Argonautica*. He ascribes to her the traditional nefarious abilities of being able to pervert the course of nature, interfere with the moon and stars, and tame snakes with a hypnotic melange of herbal drugs and spells. Medea's bewitching and wrecking of the bronze Talos is achieved through trance-like possession, incantations, invoking ghosts, and an evil glare (an early glimpse, or glance, of the evil eye); her instructions to Jason, for the invocation of Hecate from Hades, recall the underworld myth of Orpheus and Eurydice—don't look back.

It is the Apollonius version that best illustrates Medea's superlative skills as a sorceress. Medea first got involved with Jason when he arrived at Colchis, to claim his inheritance and throne by retrieving the golden fleece. Medea fell hopelessly in love with him and promised to help him achieve his objective, on the condition that if he was successful, he would take her away with him and marry her; Jason agreed. Medea's father, Aeëtes had his conditions too, and promised to give Jason the fleece, on completion of some very challenging tasks. Firstly, Jason had to plough a field with fire-breathing oxen; Medea provided a magic lotion as antidote against the bulls' fiery exhalations. Secondly, Jason was required to sow the teeth of a dragon in the ploughed field, teeth which inconveniently changed into an army of warriors; Medea advised Jason to hurl a rock into their midst, which sent them into confusion so that they attacked and killed each other. Finally, Aeëtes demanded Jason fight and slay the sleepless dragon that guarded the fleece; Medea put the beast to sleep with her narcotic herbs.

Having completed the tasks, Jason took the fleece and sailed off with Medea, as promised. Medea had distracted the pursuing Aeëtes by killing her brother Absyrtus; she dismembered his body and scattered the body parts, knowing that her father would delay to retrieve them for proper burial; in some versions, Medea and Jason visit Circe, so that Medea could be ritually cleansed after the murder, thus absolving her of blame for the deed. *En route* back to Thessaly, Medea prophesied that Euphemus, the helmsman on the Argo, would one day rule over all Libya. This transpired through Battus, a descendant of Euphemus.

The Argo then reached Crete, famously guarded by the bronze man, Talos, an oddity who had one vein extending from his neck to his ankle, plugged by a single bronze nail. Medea hypnotized him from on board the Argo, driving him so mad that he pulled out the nail, causing ichor to gush from the wound; he bled to death, clearing the way for the Argo to land.

Jason celebrated in Crete with the Golden Fleece, but could not help noticing that his father, Aeson, was too old and ill to join in. Medea had a witchy solution; she drew out the blood from Aeson's body, infused it with magical herbs and transfused it back in to his veins—this is known in the witch trade as jugulating. Aeson was a new man; when the daughters of king Pelias saw this, they demanded the same revivifying procedure for their aging father, the very man who had despatched Jason to get the fleece in the first place (in the hope that he would thereby not depose him). As it happened, Hera wanted Pelias dead because he refused to give up his throne, so Medea conspired to have Pelias' own daughters kill him. This would be gorily achieved by changing an old ram into a young ram, by chopping up an old ram and boiling it in a cauldron of magic herbs. The old ram was boiled up, and a live, young ram leapt from the pot; the gullible girls then hacked their father into pieces and threw him into a pot in the hope of achieving the same result.

Jason and Medea fled to Corinth, where he soon abandoned Medea for the king's daughter, Glauce. Horrified and distraught at this betrayal, Medea exacted her revenge when she sent Glauce a dress and golden coronet smeared with poison, killing both the princess and the king, Creon. According to Euripides, Medea did not stop there, but continued on her revenge, brutally murdering two of her sons, Tisander and Alcimenes. It is probably this act—just one of many heinous deeds—that earns Medea the reputation for being one of literature's most repugnant and reprehensible mothers. As we have noted, she unequivocally declares her hatred for her children early on in the play that bears her name—'You accursed sons of a mother who know nothing but hate, damn you, your father and your whole house.'[10] Be that as it may, she then flew off to Athens in a golden chariot driven by dragons, sent by her grandfather Helios, god of the sun.

According to the poet Eumelus, to whom the fragmentary epic *Korinthiaka* is attributed, Medea's evil filicides were all an accident.[11] The poet Creophylus, however, blamed the murders on the citizens of Corinth, suggesting that Medea's deliberate slaying of her children was a Euripidean invention; however, some scholars believe Neophron created this version.[12] Her murderous behaviour would go on to become the canonical version for later writers.[13] Pausanias records no fewer than five different versions of what happened to Medea's children, reporting that he had actually seen a monument to them while travelling in Corinth.[14]

Medea eventually returned to Colchis, only to find that her father Aeëtes had been deposed by his brother Perses. She killed him and restored Colchis to her father. Diodorus Siculus tells us that it was Hecate who pioneered the use of *pharmaka*, passing down her expertise to Medea, who made excellent use of it: healing the sick; transmogrifying into an old hag; inflicting insanity and dispelling it; rejuvenating Pelias in his boiling cauldron; conjuring up ghostly snakes and a lamb; setting fire to Glauce's wedding gown; and burning down Creon's palace.

Ennius provided an early link between Greek and Latin Medeas, with his adaptation of Euripides' *Medea*. She makes her final appearance in the classical period in the fourth century CE *Orphic Argonautica*; here, Orpheus prepares a sacrifice to Artemis with the help of Medea's *pharmaka*: black poplars and sundry other trees and bushes; barley meal effigies; and black puppies, the stomachs of which were filled with a mixture of their blood and various herbs. A whole cohort of hellish inhabitants are raised forth, including Tisiphone and Hecate; still assisted by Medea and her 'baneful roots', Orpheus charms the snake to sleep with his divine song. The Greek Medeas provided the Romans with a fertile basis on which to found their own Medeas.

Ovid's *Metamorphoses* is rich in infernal and eschatological material; it describes Pythagoreanism, Orpheus' *katabasis*, and Medea. In the *Fasti*, he describes the rites of Tacita, the silent goddess of the dead. In the *Amores*, we meet the witches Circe and Dipsas. Medea takes centre stage in his lost eponymous tragedy.[15] She also features in Ovid's tragic love letters, the *Heroides*, where Hypsipile describes her typical witch-like characteristics: her ability to draw down the moon and meddle with nature; darkening the skies; damming rivers and rolling rocks and trees; frequenting cemeteries, with her hair and clothing in disarray, to snatch the warm bones of the newly buried. She is an expert with *simulacra cerea* (waxen effigies) and the needles she drives into their livers; she perverts the course of true love with *herbae*.[16] Medea reappears in his *Metamorphoses*, in a description which owes much to Apollonius of Rhodes' Medea in the *Argonautica*.[17] In much the same way, Seneca's Medea is spurned in love; she curses Jason, and wishes death on his family and the family of his new wife. In a cauldron of occult materials, tools, and incantations, she unleashes a menagerie of reptiles and dragons, and draws down animals and snakes from the constellations to vent their poison on Earth; she herself mixes toxic herbs and other venoms, invokes Dis and the shades of the dead, and releases the eternally dead and damned (Tantalus, Ixion, and Sisyphus) from their infernal punishments. She can turn the world and nature upside down, or even set it in reverse.[18]

Aesop's *Fable of the Woman Mage* dates to the seventh century BCE. It is the tale of a female magician who claimed to be able to appease the gods with incantations. She was tried in court and found guilty. Afterwards, she was asked how she imagined she could possibly control the gods when she could not even prevent the mere mortals of the court from condemning her. The moral of the fable was that one should not claim extraordinary powers when lacking even modest ones.

Xanthus of Lydia reveals the reputation *mages* had for incest, claiming that they had sexual relations with their mothers, sisters, and daughters; this charge was later echoed by the Roman poet Catullus. Xanthus also tells us that women *mages* were shared by a number of husbands. Xenophon mentions incantations in the *Memorabilia*, where he refers to love potions (*philtra*). He implies that the seductive song of the Sirens is a form of erotic magic that lured sailors to their doom. The unsuccessful efforts to divert Odysseus and his crew is, of course, the most famous example of the Sirens at work. Xenophon's passage also associates rhetorical expertise with magic in the references to Pericles, and to the metaphorical amulet Themistocles placed around Athens to protect it.[19]

Lycophron describes Cassandra's prophecy in his *Alexandra*.[20] Theocritus describes Simaetha's erotic magic, magical dolls, *hippomanes*, and threat to deploy contagious magic (whereby a body part or item of clothing is destroyed, with a view to destroying the whole person). This was later used by Virgil in the Dido episode of the *Aeneid*.[21] Simaetha's dependence on others for magical expertise and her use of erotic magic is notable. The *Pharmakeutria* (*Witch*), and the pharmacopeia it features, influenced Virgil and Horace and, like Theophrastus before, reveals a slice of real life.

Diodorus also tells the story of how Deianeira inadvertently killed her husband Hercules by means of a *philtron*, a love potion. Nessus, a centaur, had tried to rape Deianeira but he was killed with an arrow shot by Heracles. In his dying moments, Nessus gave Deianeira a 'love potion' which he promised would keep Heracles true to her. When Deianeira smeared the philtron on Heracles' tunic, it became apparent that the potion was poisonous. Heracles died in agony: centaur blood and olive oil turned out to be a fatal mixture for Hercules.

Apollodorus describes Hercules' *katabasis* (journey to the underworld) and Medea's sorcery in his *Library of Greek Mythology* in a variant of Apollonius' destruction of Talos; she uses no evil eye, but *pharmaka* to inflict madness.[22] In his *Epitome*, Apollodorus has Circe change Odysseus' crew into lions, donkeys, wolves, and pigs; the lions and wolves may well have been former sailors.

In the Roman era, the Greek writer (and priest) Plutarch deals with superstition in *On Deisidaemonia*. In the *Moralia*, he explains the futility and dangers of *philtra* and other sorceries, as administered by wives on their husbands. Plutarch also gives us a rare insight into the neurological hazards associated with drugs. In *Alexander*, he describes how Arrhidaeus, the healthy son of Philip II of Macedon and stepson of Philip's wife Olympias, suffered mental illness due to the drugs given to him by Olympias, who saw him as a potential obstacle in the succession of her son, Alexander. We know from Plutarch that Olympias was an avid follower of Orphism and a Bacchant, allegedly with a penchant for snakes. Plutarch's *Moralia* also gives us a detailed exposition on the evil eye, and what people believed its properties to be. He describes the amulet that Pericles wore on his death bed as 'stupid'.[23]

The story of Eucrates and his Arab's ring recalls Plato's *Gyges*. Eucrates is assailed by Hecate, a giant of a woman with feet of serpents, armed with a huge sword and a torch, the torso of a Gorgon and snakes for hair, and her hounds, the size of elephants. Manipulation of the ring makes Hecate stamp her feet, exposing Hades and creating a chasm, into which she jumps. Eucrates gets a clear view of the underworld, including Cerberus and the dead, even of his own father dressed in the clothes he wore at his burial. Hesiod described the hellish world of Tartarus and its inhabitants in some detail. He also gives us a biography of Hecate, the witch goddess.[24]

The ghost of Philinnion makes an appearance in the *Mirabilia* by Phlegon of Tralles. She visits Machates, the lodger in her parents' house, in the night to have sex with him. Philinnion is annoyed that her parents seem to begrudge her this physical pleasure, and inflicts on them more grief before she dies again. The grieving Machates commits suicide.[25]

Pasiphae, sister to Circe, was an active sorceress, that is when she was not busy having sex with a bull, or, as Ovid so delicately puts it in his *Ars Amatoria*: '*Pasiphae fieri gaudebat adultera tauri*'—'Pasiphae took pleasure in becoming an adulteress with a bull'. She was an adept practitioner of magical herbal arts, and a goddess no promiscuous man would want to come across. The fidelity charm she inflicted on Minos caused him to ejaculate serpents, scorpions, and centipedes from his penis, with the inevitable result that the concubine on the receiving end died a terrible death; how eye-wateringly painful this was for Minos is not recorded. Cicero records in *De Divinatione* that the Spartan ephors took to sleeping at the shrine of Pasiphae in the hope of dreaming prophetic dreams that might help them govern more wisely.[26] Plutarch adds some detail in *Lives of Agis and Cleomenes*. In one case, one ephor dreamed that some of his colleagues' chairs were removed from the agora, and that a voice called out from nowhere, 'this is better for Sparta'; King Cleomenes was inspired by this to consolidate royal power. During the reign of King Agis, a number of ephors incited the people to revolt, when oracles from Pasiphae's shrine promised remission of debts and redistribution of land.

Other exponents of the dark arts include Andromache; when she was forced into being Neoptomelus' concubine, she gave potions to his wife, Hermione, causing her to miscarry. The well-meaning, if bossy, nurse in Euripides' *Hippolytus* craftily recommends a love potion to a love-stricken Phaedra, yearning for her stepson, Hippolytus. Then there is Simaetha and her erotic magic: a wryneck or *iunx* (a sparrow-sized woodpecker) which was attached to a wheel making a whistling sound as it spins—Simaetha chants an incantation ten times to draw the man she loves to her house. Agamede was a Greek physician, and expert in the healing powers of all the plants on the earth, a noted sorceress. Diotima, as noted above, was a philosopher and priestess who postponed the Plague of Athens; she played a crucial role in developing the notion of Platonic love in the *Symposium*.

Spells, sacrifices, and curses could all be executed individually and personally, but it always helped to invoke a higher agency (or indeed a lower one) for increased effect and efficacy. If any of the classical gods were associated with witches and witchcraft, then it was Pan and through him, the chthonic goddess and divine witch, Hecate. Ghosts, necromancy, herbal medicine, and witchcraft were Hecate's areas of expertise, and quite properly so, if worldly witches (novice and expert alike) were to turn to her for advice and assistance. It was prudent to place shrines in her honour at the doorways of homes and at the entrances to cities, to earn protection from the ghosts of the dead and other spirits. Hecate had specific responsibility for restless and bothersome ghosts: the *aoroi*, who were the phantoms of people who had died prematurely, usually children or babies; *biothanatoi*, people who had died violent deaths; *agamoi*, girls who had died before marriage and motherhood; and a*taphoi*, those denied proper burial. Careful obeisance to Hecate was a prerequisite for success, not just in witchery, but in achieving a quiet life.

It was Hecate who brought aconite to the world and, ever the perfect hostess, used it as a dressing on food given to visitors, even going so far as to poison her own father with it. A predilection for human sacrifice was another essential attribute; sacrificing worshippers in her temple of Artemis was a frequent event. Shrines to Hecate sprang up at three-way crossroads where food offerings were left at a new moon because she was 'the triple goddess'. Crossroads were literally 'nowhere places', liminal points that could be used with impunity by witches or sorcerers because they belonged to no town or city; the bodies of convicts and sorcerers were dumped here when they died.

Veneficia—part of the witch's armamentarium—is derived from Venus, goddess of love. The original meaning of the word *veneficium* was a love potion, a meaning that graduated over time to mean the making of spells, and finally, a poison. The adjective *venificus* describes something poisonous or magical, while the noun is a poisoner or sorcerer and even a chamaeleon; the feminine, *venifica*, can be a witch.

In Pergamon, a third-century magician's kit has been discovered. It has a bronze table and base covered with mystic symbols, a dish also decorated with symbols, a large bronze nail with letters inscribed, two bronze rings, and three black polished stones with the names of supernatural powers etched on them; how these were to be used we do not know.

Legally speaking, there is little evidence of legislation or litigation relating to magic in ancient Greece, although we do learn that in the fifth century BCE, the Teians passed a law against the production of harmful drugs against the state and its citizens; the penalty was execution, including the perpetrator's family. Theoris, allegedly a witch from Lemnos, was executed along with all her family for getting mixed up with incantations and drugs. In the world of ideal laws, Plato recommends life imprisonment and solitary confinement for 'soul charmers' (*psuchagogousi*). In the first century BCE, there is an inscription that tells members of a private cult to shun malicious spells, love charms, abortifacients, and contraceptives just as they should shun rape, robbery, murder, and the seduction of another man's wife.

The Graeae ('old women', 'grey ones', or 'grey witches') also go by the name of Grey Sisters, and the Phorcides ('daughters of Phorcys'); they were ancient sea ghosts who personified the white foam of the sea but, more horribly were three grotesque looking sisters who shared one eye and one tooth between them, which they took in turns to share.

> And to Phorkys (Phorcys) Keto (Ceto) bore the Graiai (Graeae), with fair faces and grey from birth, and these the gods who are immortal and men who walk on the earth call Graiai, the grey sisters, Pemphredo robed in beauty and Enyo robed in saffron.[27]

Their names were Deino, Enyo, and Pemphredo; appropriately enough, they were also sisters to the Gorgons. Etymologically, their credentials were impeccable: Pemphredo (Πεμφρηδώ) means 'alarm', and Enyo (νυώ) means 'horror', 'waster of cities'—a goddess of war; Deino, a third not mentioned by Hesiod, (or Persis according to Hyginus) was 'something terrible'. In poetry, they are euphemistically and ironically described as beautiful, or, according to Aeschylus, siren-shaped monsters with the head and arms of old crones, and the bodies of swans. The sisters formed the chorus of Aeschylus' *The Phorcydes*, one of his trilogy of plays on the life of Perseus, describing his quests for Medusa's head. They were of a prodigious age. Perseus had the measure of them though, in his fight with Medusa; he stole their eye while they were passing it among themselves, and forced them to reveal the whereabouts of the three objects he needed to kill Medusa (or the whereabouts of Medusa herself), by ransoming the eye in return for the information. Aeschylus paints a horrid picture:

> The Gorgonean plains of Kisthene where the daughters of Phorkys dwell, ancient maids (*dênaiai korai*), three in number, shaped like swans (*kyknomorphoi*), possessing one eye amongst them and a single tooth; neither does the sun with his beams look down upon them, nor ever the nightly moon. And near them are their three winged sisters, the snake-haired Gorgons, loathed of mankind, whom no one of mortal kind shall look upon and still draw breath. Such is the peril that I bid you to guard against.[28]

It was not always all sinister though, and the magic was not always black; there is an episode in the *Odyssey* where a *pharmakon* is used to a beneficial, recreational end. Helen gives Menelaus and Telemachus a drug to put in their wine, guaranteed to make them forget their troubles however bad, and to cheer them up.[29] The drug is nepenthe or *polydamna*: a drug that has 'the power of robbing grief and anger of their sting and banishing all painful memories'. Manto, the daughter of the seer Tiresias, is compared to Circe and Medea, but without the evil bits, showing that some witches could be a force for the good, and were not always malevolent. Thrace was the eponymous heroine and witch queen of Thrace. She was the daughter of Oceanus and Parthenope, and sister of Europa.

Theocritus wrote the *Pharmakeutria* (*The Sorceress*), a textbook on medicinal and magical herbs and potions. He describes a love potion in *Idyll* 2; excavated amulets, curse tablets and magical papyri confirm its authenticity. Pliny the Elder tells us that Menander wrote a comedy, the *Thessala*, about the notorious witches of Thessaly, and their fearsome habit of drawing down the moon.[30] Apollodorus describes Hercules' descent to the underworld, his *katabasis,* and Medea's sorcery in his *Library of Greek Mythology.*[31]

Herodotus leaves us an account of Melissa's *nekuomanteion* (an oracle in which the dead prophesy), and Periander's necrophilia. Melissa is initially reticent because the clothes in which she was buried had not been burned, and so she was as cold as hell in hell. Periander had thrown his loaves into a cold oven, as it were, indicating that he had had sex with Melissa's corpse.

Witches were part of the fabric of ancient Greek life. A witch was usually totally unscrupulous, devoid of any morals, and prepared to do whatever it took to get her evil way. They were often liminal people at the margins of society—peripatetic and rootless. In mythology, they are magical, evil, and scheming; in literature, witches are excoriated and ridiculed. Circe, Medea, and their goddess Hecate never existed, of course, but they are indicative of what sorceresses did in the real world. Generations of Greeks (from the time of Homer onwards) would have heard or read about them.

Closely associated with witches, and just as scarily malevolent, was the bogeywoman (witch lite). Plato observed 'of all wild things, the child is most unmanageable ... the most unruly animal there is. That's why he has to be curbed by a great many bridles.' One of these bridles, apparently endorsed by flustered wet nurses, was the terrifying bogeywoman, interjected into the impressionable imaginations of children in their charge. Bogeywomen often turned up as big bad wolves (precursors of the one that later horrified Little Red Riding Hood), who gobbled down naughty boys and girls alive; they were never without a freshly devoured one in her stomach. In ancient Greece, she took the shape of Mormo (a terrible monster with the legs of a woman), either queen of the Lystraegones bereft of her own children and now vengefully murdering the children of others, or a child-eating Corninthian. Another was Empusa who appeared either as a cow, donkey, or beautiful woman; Diodorus Siculus lists Empusa as a beautiful, cannibalistic child-eater.[32] Another example is Gello, a malevolent female spirit and child-snatcher.

Ancient Greek women could set themselves up as amateur witches, practicing a do-it-yourself form of witchcraft in the form of binding spells and curses, and in the deployment of voodoo dolls. These spells were usually perpetrated as acts of malicious, perverted revenge and spite; they were sparked by thwarted love, failed lawsuits, or commercial disputes. As well as often being on the wrong end of them, women handed them out as well, with alacrity.

Many spells that are extant today originated in Egypt in the *Papyri Graecae Magicae* (the *Greek Magical Papyri*). This amazing collection is the last word in how to scare the wits out of a rival or an enemy; it is a mine (and a minefield) of potions and spells, arcane occult knowledge, and recipes for magical concoctions that accumulated over the centuries; it is full of formulae and prayers, magic words often in shorthand or abbreviated. Some may well be the working manuals of travelling magicians. In addition, there are the *voces magicae* and the *Ephesia Grammata*—Greek magic formulae made up of what can only be described as mumbo jumbo chanted to ward off evil. There are also masses of magical *ostraca*, the damning-to-hell *tabellae defixionum*, curse tablets, voodoo dolls, love philtres, amulets, and phylacteries, etched with magical formulae designed to terrify, with the object of maiming and killing, or reducing the decidedly unfortunate recipient to a physically and sexually abused victim.

The popularity and ubiquity of this evil and sinister form of ancient hate mail is illustrated by the fact that 1,600 *defixiones* (curse tablets) or *katadesies* (binding spells) have been found. *Katadesies* reach back as far as the fourth century BCE in Greece. Fittingly, they were traditionally consecrated to the gods of the underworld. Mainly a practice of the lower classes, they allowed the curser to vent their anger, malice, and vindictiveness.

Typically, the victim's name was written on a lead tablet (although gold, silver, and marble are not unknown); blanks have been found, suggesting that there was a steady ongoing trade. The consecration was made, and a nail stuck through the name; this was often followed by the name of the target's mother, to avoid any mistaken identity that would invalidate the curse. Magic words and symbols were added, to enhance the chances of success. Some tablets feature a portrait of the victim, which is also pierced with nails. The texts were anonymous. In tablets inspired by jilted love, a lock of the intended's hair was sometimes attached. By the Hellenistic period, a variant appears; 'vindictive prayers' usually bore the name of the author.

Here is some of the work done through Hecate, as recorded in the *Greek Magical Papyri (PGM)*:

PGM III. 1-164 A spell to deify a cat by drowning it and make it into a charm. Hecate is invoked with Hermes.

PGM IV. 2006-2125 Necromantic spell to bind a spirit of the dead. Hecate is drawn on a flax leaf 'with three heads and six hands, holding torches in her hands, on the right side of her face having the head of a cow; and on the left side the head of a dog; and in the middle the head of a maiden with sandals bound on her feet.'

PGM IV. 2622-2707 This spell 'attracts in the same hour, it sends dreams, it causes sickness, produces dream visions, removes enemies when you reverse the spell, however you wish.' The phylactery for the spell is a heart-shaped magnetite carved with 'Hecate lying about the heart, like a little crescent.'

PGM IV. 2708-2784 A hymn to the full moon to secure the affections of a lover. Hecate is syncretised with Artemis, Persephone and Selene.
PGM IV. 2785-2890 Another hymn with a protective charm: a lodestone carved with 'a three-faced Hekate. And let the middle face be that of a maiden wearing horns, and the left face that of a dog, and the one on the right that of a goat.'

PGM IV. 2943-2966 Love spell to make a lover 'lie awake for me for all eternity'.

Around one quarter of the tablets show erotic magic, deployed to wreak bitter revenge on duplicitous lovers, and bind an object of desire to love and sex with the dedicator for the rest of their days. Here are some examples of papyri with women as targets, and as the curser:

> Charm of Hekate Ereschigal against fear of punishment: If she comes forth, let her say: 'I am Ereschigal', holding her thumbs, and not even one evil can befall her. But if she comes close to you, hold your right heel and say: 'Ereschigal, virgin, dog, serpent, wreath, key, herald's wand, golden is the sandal of the Lady of Tartaros', and you will prevail upon her.
>
> '*Askei kataski erôn oreôn iôr mega semnuêr baui*', (three times), 'Phobantia, remember, I have been initiated, and I went down into the chamber of the Dactyls, and I saw the other things down below, virgin, dog', etc. Say it at the crossroads, and turn around and flee, because it is at those places that she appears. Say it late at night, about what you wish, and it will reveal it in your sleep; and if you are led away to death, say these things while scattering seeds of sesame, and it will save you.
>
> '*Phorba phorba breimô azziebua*'. Take bran of first quality and sandalwood and vinegar of the sharpest sort and mold cakes. And write his name upon them, and so hide them, saying into the light the name of Hekate, and 'Take away his sleep from so-and-so', and he will be sleepless and worried. (PGM LXX)

This was tame when compared with the more typical *defixio* that rains down every kind of disaster on the recipient: 'May burning fever seize all her limbs, kill her soul and her heart; O gods of the underworld, break and smash her bones, choke her, *arourarelyoth*, let her body be twisted and shattered, *phrix, phrox*'.[33]

Curses were not exclusively heterosexual; one from the second century CE describes a 'lesbian' curse, where Heraias brings and binds the heart and soul of Sarapias. In another, Sophia attempts to inflame the heart, liver, and spirit of Gorgonia through a corpse demon in an Egyptian curse.[34]

Tomb raiding was obviously taken very seriously; this stark warning was found at Agios Tychon, Cyprus—'anyone who does anything bad to my tomb, then the crocodile, hippopotamus, and lion will eat him.' Another forbids the thief to urinate, defecate, speak, sleep, or be in good health, unless and until he brings back what he has stolen to the temple of Mercury. This was found in London, and is now in the British Museum, but is probably typical of curses found all over the Greek world.

Physical violence was not always on the agenda; there are some examples of love *defixiones* where a lover will invoke underworld deities in a heartfelt bid to win the love of his life. Successus dedicates his wife in a bid to see his love for her requited—'may Successa burn, let her feel herself aflame with love or desire for Successus'. Plenty of fire but no sign of brimstone here; let us hope that Successus was successful.

However, the depravity evident in the sexually perverted, excessively malevolent, and obsessively perverted curse projected at women is more typical:

> I bind you, Theodotis, daughter of Eus, to the snake's tail, the crocodile's mouth, the ram's horns, the asp's poison, the cat's whiskers, the god's appendage, so that you may never be able to have sex with another man, not be fucked or be sodomised or fellate, nor do anything that brings you pleasure with another man, unless I alone, Ammonion, the son of Hermitaris, am that man … Make this erotic binding-spell work, so that Theodotis, may no longer be penetrated by a man other than me alone, Ammonion, the son of Hermitaris, dragged in slavery, driven crazy, taking to the air in search of Ammonion, the son of Hermitaris, and that she may rub her thigh on my thigh, her genitals to my genitals, for sex with me for the rest of her life. (Suppl. Mag. 38 (second century CE))

For good measure, this obsessive curse is complemented with a series of pictures that depict a god with a sceptre, a snake, a crocodile, a couple kissing, and a penis penetrating a vagina. The wife of Aristocydes curses him and his lovers, so that he will never marry another woman, or a boy, for that matter.

What these curses uniquely and importantly reveal is the inner secrets of the sexual and social lives of women, both as the victims of perverted, paranoid lovers and insecure stalkers, and as the dispensers themselves of malicious and evil intent, driven by wild jealousy and bitterness.

Voodoo dolls were another popular, perverted way of cursing the people that some Greeks loved to hate; thirty-eight have been found. They are made from a variety of materials, including lead, bronze, and clay, as well as wax, wool, and dough. The typical doll demonstrated a number of characteristics: their legs or arms twisted behind the back as if bound; they were impaled with nails; the extremities and upper torso may be contorted back to front; they may be confined in a box or similar (like a coffin); and the doll was inscribed with the name of the victim. They were usually found in a grave or sanctuary.

As we have seen, some men and women were prepared to go to inordinate lengths to bind and restrain, to guarantee the fidelity of their women and men; this voodoo doll curse is one of the most notorious and malevolent. Although it is from fourth century AD Greece, it is surely typical of a practice that had been going on for centuries. It takes a typically prescriptive recipe form—'take wax or clay from a potter's wheel and form it into two figures, a male and a female … her arms should be tied behind her back, and she should kneel.'[35]

This is supported by some sinister instructions to inscribe magical words on her head and other parts of her body, including the genitals; to stick a needle into her brain, and twelve others into other organs; tie a binding spell written on a lead plate to the figures, dedicate it to gods of the underworld and leave it at sunset near to the tomb of someone who has died violently or prematurely; invite them to rise from the dead and bring the object of the charm to him, to make her love him. There then follows a litany of evil instructions to deprive the girl of food and drink, sexual intercourse, sleep and health—all designed to make her have sex with the curser in perpetuity. Dehumanisation and ritual abuse (physical, psychological, and sexual subjugation) were the order of the day. 'Love' is very strange. Osthanes had just the thing for any man looking to wreck a woman's sex life:

> If the genitals of a woman are smeared with the blood of a tick from a wild black bull, she will find sex repellent, as Osthanes says, and love too, if she drinks the urine of the billy-goat, with spikenard [an aromatic plant] mixed in to disguise the disgusting taste.[36]

There is more genital smearing with a lotion that has everything going for it, as far as fourth-century CE Akarnachthas is concerned—a guarantee of everlasting love, and exclusive sex. The spell was excavated in Egypt; the very specific recipe comprises a crow's egg, the juice of a crow's foot plant, and the bile of an electric catfish fished from the Nile, all of which are to be ground up with honey and smeared on his penis while chanting the following spell:

> Vagina of NN, open up and take the semen of NN and the unconquerable seed of ... let NN love me for all of her life...and let her remain chaste for me, as Penelope did for Odysseus. And you vagina, remember me all my life because I am AKARNACHTHAS.' Chant these words as you work the ingredients, and whenever you anoint your genitals, and so have sex with the woman you want. She will love only you, and no one but you will fuck her.[37]

It is clear from these examples that the organs targeted were not coincidental. Those tablets seeking to achieve erotic restraint and binding logically focus on the sexual organs of the target. By the same token, tongues are often the object of binding curses intended to influence the outcomes of law suits. One example is fired at Selinontios whose tongue is to be twisted until it is rendered useless.[38] Examples of literary evidence for this include Aristophanes' *Wasps*.[39] When defending Titinia in Rome, Cicero describes how his adversary, Curio, completely dried up as a result of drugs and incantations (*veneficia*), delivered by a witchy Titinia; Ovid's old hag teaches young girls how to bind tongues with lead, thread, beans and the head of a fish.[40, 41]

Much later, Libanius was the victim of tongue binding by a voodoo doll in the shape of a lizard. On a more mundane level, it is Cicero's tongue that Fulvia gleefully cuts out from his decapitated head, in revenge for his tactless remarks regarding her marriage to Mark Antony; she knew how to inflict most damage on the orator even in death.

Around 114 Greek and Latin litigation curses have been uncovered; these are delivered usually by defendants, who feel they have been slighted or wronged in some unjust way. They are launched either before or during the trial, with the aim to compromise the effectiveness of the opposition's delivery and case. As we have seen, disabling the tongue was a good strategy, particularly if your case was weak. Where there are groups of people being cursed, it is reasonable to assume that whole political factions, which interestingly included some women, were under attack.[42]

Competitive curses were used in a number of different scenarios. In Athens, the choral trainers and under-trainers of Theagenes were damned in a theatrical curse.[43] A well in the Athenian Agora has yielded a curse aimed at the wrestler Eutychian and other athletes.[44]

Trade and commercial competition, then as now, brought out the worst in people; they were not averse to resorting to sinister curses to beat the opposition. The precedent is set by a very early curse in the Hesiodic hexameter poem *Kiln*, in which aptly-named demons are invoked against rival potters; leaving nothing to chance, the angry dedicator invoked these demons as weapons of mass destruction: Crusher, Smasher, Unquenchable, Unbaked Pot Wrecker, and Shatterer. The destruction is utterly total:

> May the entire kiln be throw into and may the potters wail at length. Just as the horse's jaw grinds, may the kiln also grind all the pots within it reducing them to fragments. Come here to me too, daughter of Helios, Circe of the many drugs cast your wild spells and damage these men and their works. Let Chiron also bring here to me all the centaurs, both those who escaped from Heracles and those who were killed. May they smash these works up, and destroy the kiln. May the potters themselves witness these terrible deeds and lament. But I will rejoice as I look upon their ill-fated handicraft. If any of them peer into the kiln, may fire scorch his whole face be scorched, so that they may all learn to treat people fairly.[45]

The trades involved in this magical warfare range across the whole gamut of classical commerce, from innkeepers to net-makers; from brothel-keepers to shield-makers; from bellows-makers to doctors; from painters to seamstresses; and from goldsmiths to flour sellers. There is nothing to suggest that women were not, on occasions, implicated.

Amulets (*periamma, periapton*) were important and pervasive. They were often used in concert with incantations. Plato has Socrates contend that a certain kind of leaf, when used as an amulet, was quite pointless unless accompanied by a healing incantation (*epaiode*); the combination was effective against headache.[46] In the *Republic*, Socrates includes amulets (and incantations) in a list of ways to cure illnesses.[47] Pindar had done likewise in the 470s BCE.[48]

The evil eye caused particular problems for anyone or anything in its range; those who could project it were in a powerful position:

> For we know of people who do severe harm to children by glaring at them, compromising their development at this weak and tender stage, and corrupting. Those with sturdier and full-grown bodies are less susceptible to this. And yet Phylarchus says that the Thibians…were deadly not just to children but also to adults. Those on the receiving end of a look, a breath, or an utterance from them wasted away and fell sick.[49]

The Greeks and Romans ascribed a number of characteristics to the evil eye, including envy; this was thought to be the catalyst for projecting the evil eye, which was interestingly not confined to projection from the eye, but could also be emitted via speech and breath. It was damaging to fertility, thus particularly effective against women, children, and crops. It was associated with people, especially women, who had double pupils, and was often delivered by a sidelong glance. Paradoxically, it could scupper magic, so sorcerers were especially anxious, working as they did in a world full of envy. It could ruin blossoming love affairs, but might be averted by spitting or by wearing a phallus, and in particular phallus amulets; the skin of the hyena was also an effective weapon. The conjunction of spitting and the phallus can be seen together in a Roman mosaic depicting a phallus ejaculating into a disembodied eye.

Voces magicae were magical words with no obvious meaning, yet their very mysteriousness gave them (and the magic people who uttered them) some considerable power. The most common *voces magicae* are the 'Ephesian letters' (*Ephesia grammata*), which look like Greek words, but are not. They are commonly used in curses, to which they added protective qualities, as illustrated by a fragment of Menander's that shows how they were used to ward off spells from newly married couples.[50]

It is, of course, impossible to gauge just how much occult activity went on in ancient Greece. However, the sheer number of curse tablets found would, on its own, suggest that magic, superstition, and cursing were prevalent, with women and men the purveyors and victims in equal measure. The number of women actually, or allegedly, engaging in witchcraft at any one time was, no doubt, minute; the frequent appearance of witches in the literature, however, cannot be accounted for by the exigencies and traditions of genre alone. Greek epic, comedy, and tragedy are populated with witches and other female pedlars of the occult; it seems plausible that audiences will have been familiar with their activities, and would recognise them from everyday experience, from stories or by traditional superstition.

The 'Incomplete' Woman's Medicine and Female Sexuality

We have noted particularly through Aristotle (though not exclusively) that women were incomplete versions of men; this chapter also explores ancient Greek medicine as it applies specifically to women. The centaur, Chiron, took a wound by Hercules. Although immortal, just to be on the safe side, he invented medicine so that he could heal himself. He then taught Asclepius medical science, which became the font of all divine medical knowledge among the Greeks. Chiron also taught Achilles, who had some expertise in medical things.

Much of Greek medicine was preoccupied with obstetrics, gynaecology, breastfeeding, midwifery, and contraception; the content of the *Hippocratic Corpus* reveals this focus, as does the number of textbooks on gynaecology published around the Greek world. The *Corpus* covers eleven gynaecological subjects out of sixty—they include sections on *Semen* or *Generation* or *Intercourse*; *the Nature of the Child or Pregnancy*; *the Diseases of Women*; *Sterile Women*; *the Diseases of Young Women or Girls*; *Superfoetation*; *the Nature of Woman* and *Excision of the Foetus*.

Hippocrates of Kos (*c.* 460–*c.* 370 BCE) is the 'Father of Modern Medicine', and the founder of the Hippocratic School of Medicine. The School revolutionized medicine in ancient Greece, making it a distinct discipline, and establishing medicine as a profession.

Both Diocles of Carystus (*c.* 375–*c.* 295 BCE) and Cleophantus (*c.* 270–250 BCE) wrote a *Gynaecology*. Herophilos (335–280 BCE) produced nine medical books including a Maiotikon—a midwifery text; they are now all lost.

All of this reproductive medicine is a reflection of the importance of biological woman in Greek society; she was a means to that vital end that required the production of babies (preferably male), to produce citizens and soldiers, to preserve the *oikos*, and to replenish the citizenry.

Evidence of how women fared in terms of mental health is particularly thin on the ground, indicative of the fact that psychiatry as we understand it was not routinely practiced or studied in ancient Greece, and did not exist as a speciality until the nineteenth century; the term '*psychiaterie*' was coined in 1808. There was, however, some work on mental illness—Hippocrates ascribed it to an imbalance of the humours; erotic dreams were an indicator of madness; and very ill patients with no pain were deemed to be mad. Melancholia in women was considered a serious condition; it presented with insomnia, withdrawal, paranoia, depression, tearfulness. and suicidal thoughts. Treatments included purgation, bleeding, and vomiting. This all exhibits similarities to what we today call depression; Hippocrates added delusions and hallucinations to the symptoms, thus bringing it closer to what we know today as schizophrenia. According to the Hippocratics, mania (insanity) was common in girls, and presented with hallucinations and fearfulness. Women with mental health problems would have been treated in much the same way as men; they were shunned, taunted, and often spat at in public, as spitting was thought to prevent the spread of disease and madness.

In the first century CE, Pliny the Elder suggests that women were just as capable of prodigious physical endurance as men; he cites that in 514 BCE, Harmodius and Aristogeiton conspired to overthrow the tyrants Hippias and Hipparchus at Athens. Hipparchus was slain, but Hippias survived and seized the conspirators; among them was the *hetaira* Leaena, lover of Aristogeiton, or Harmodius, or perhaps even both. Leaena endured unspeakable torture to divulge information about the conspiracy, but she bravely and stubbornly refused to betray her fellow conspirators. However, that was only half the story:

> And Leaena also has a splendid reward for her self-control … she was questioned and commanded to reveal those who still escaped detection; but she would not do so and continued steadfast, proving that those men had experienced a passion not unworthy of themselves in loving a woman like her. And the Athenians caused a bronze lioness without a tongue to be made and set up in the gates of the Acropolis, representing by the spirited courage of the animal Leaena's invincible character, and by its tonguelessness her power of silence in keeping a holy secret.[1]

Jerome later adds graphic detail:

> Harmodius and Aristogiton killed the tyrant Hipparchus, and the courtesan Leaena their friend, when compelled with torments, lest she betray her companions, she amputated her tongue with her teeth.[2]

The story is reminiscent of Anaxarchus, a philosopher in the court of Alexander the Great who, under torture, bit off his own tongue to prevent it being used as a potential instrument of treachery, and spat it in the face of his torturer, Nicocreon of Salamis in Cyprus.

Much of Greek gynaecology focussed on the womb, *hystera*, and woman's ability to bear children—the essential medical difference between man and woman. Hippocrates puts it succinctly: 'the so-called women's diseases, the womb is the cause of them all.'[3] The Hippocratic authors believed that women's bodies comprised of flesh that was softer and more porous than men's.[4] An example of this is the female breast, in which the woman's nourishment is converted into milk.[5] This porosity was caused by the absorption of moisture in the form of blood, released each month during the woman's period. The concept of porosity is linked to the knowledge that women leak menstrual fluid, sexual lubricant, locheal discharge, and discharges from various infections through the vagina.

Blood clogging up the venous system in the breasts signifies that the woman is going mad—a physiological explanation for the age-old stereotype that women are naturally neurotic, erratic, and unpredictable. Menstruation as a purging agent was, then, a good thing, as indeed was epitaxis (nose-bleed), which performed a similar purging role. Amenorrhœa caused all manner of physical and psychological illness; virgins were particularly susceptible, which explains their tendency to hang themselves or jump down wells to their deaths. In essence, the physiological differences between men and women supported the belief that women were physically and mentally inferior to men.

Empedocles (b. *c.* 493 BCE) believed that men were hotter than women.[6] Aristotle, as we have seen, taught that men were more perfect than women; this was because they were less able to produce the heat that was vital for generation of the species due to the debilitating effect of menstruation. In contrast to his Hippocratic contemporaries, Aristotle believed that menstruation was not a good thing. Aristotle championed the long-standing myth that the womb comprised two separate compartments, often used to explain the birth of twins; males were born from the right (hotter) chamber; females from the left, with all its sinister implications. He rejected the Hippocratic belief that hysteria in women was attributable to the movements of the womb, and made tentative steps towards an understanding of the Fallopian tubes, largely unknown in antiquity. Some 600 or more years later, Galen also subscribed to this temperature-based theory and the notion of the incomplete woman.

In his *Midwifery*, Herophilus (fourth or fifth century CE) also differed from the Hippocratics in that he believed the womb to be no different from other internal organs. However, thanks no doubt to the knowledge acquired through dissection of cadavers whilst in Alexandria, he furthered the understanding of the female and male reproductive systems. Herophilus was able to highlight the analogous relationship between the male testicles and the female ovaries; he   believed that menstruation was the only physiological contribution women made to conception, and considered menstruation to be a cause of illness in women .

Today, hysteria as a diagnosis or disorder is no longer recognised by the medical profession; it has been replaced by 'histrionic personality disorder', which is associated with conditions such as social anxiety and schizophrenia. Up until the late nineteenth century, it was inextricably linked to movements of the womb, the *hystera*, presenting as a lack of self control caused by intense fear or anxiety, often related to the imagined disease of a particular body part. Treatment was, for nearly two centuries, pelvic massage—in which the doctor stimulated the genitals until the patient achieved hysterical paroxysm, or orgasm.[7] The condition was thought to have been first noted around the time of the early Hippocratic writings, and persisted as a diagnosis right through the Roman era. The Hippocratics never used the term *hysteria*; to them, it was *pnix*—suffocation. They taught that the womb became dry if a woman did not have frequent sexual intercourse. Infrequency would cause the womb to gravitate towards moister organs such as the liver, heart, brain, diaphragm, or bladder; at this point, the woman would faint, lose her voice, and become 'hysterical'. The administration of sweet smelling odours often restored the womb to its rightful place. Failing that, increasingly desperate measures involved binding the woman tightly beneath her breasts, palpating the affected organ, or hanging the woman upside down from a ladder.[8]

Plato believed that an animal living inside a woman's womb was responsible for driving the maternal instinct to have children; if deprived of sexual activity, the animal became restless and wandered throughout the body causing apnea (difficulty in breathing) and other conditions and diseases. Sexual activity relieved the symptoms.[9]

Hysteria was especially problematic in virgins and widows. Hippocrates warns that girls who delay marriage suffer nightmares from the time of their first period. This can result in them choking to death; the blood in their womb cannot escape because the cervix is still intact and so it flows back up to the heart and lungs, driving the woman mad. Fever ensues, accompanied by a tendency to suicide caused by the nightmares; these encourage the woman to jump down wells or to hang themselves. Hippocrates' advice is for girls in such a condition to waste no time in losing their virginity; they will be cured if they fall pregnant.[10] Widows, similarly, are cured by sex, or just by climaxing, so that the retained female semen can be released. The inevitable conclusion was that, deprived of sex, a woman would go mad, and the best way for a woman to preserve her sanity was to have sex, and have it often.

Hippocrates gives us some intriguing gynaecological case studies. A woman from Pheres suffered from idiopathic headache that persisted even after her skull was drained; during her period, the headache was less severe. The headaches stopped when she became pregnant, suggesting that the time-honoured excuse for declining sex is not always the best way to a good night's sleep. A woman from Larissa suffered pain during intercourse (dyspareunia); when she reached sixty, she felt what she thought were severe labour pains after eating lots of leeks. She stood up and felt something in her vagina, and fainted; another woman pulled out what appeared to be the whorl of a spindle—perhaps, a case of working the wool a little too enthusiastically.

What was hopefully a last resort in operations for scoliosis involved succession (*katasteisis*)—tying the patient to a ladder by his or her ankles, raising it to the gable or a tower, dropping it repeatedly, and banging it and the patient hard against the ground, in a bid to straighten the spine. To the best knowledge of the Hippocratic author describing this, there was never a successful outcome, but the procedure did attract large, vulgar crowds who applauded every time the ladder hit the ground.

Uterine dropsy—or hydrometra—results in fever, weak periods, swelling in the abdomen, and withered breasts. Hippocrates recommended a laxative and immersion in a vapour bath made from cow dung, followed by pessaries made from cantharid beetle and then bile; after three days, a vinegar douche was to be inserted. If the fever subsided and the stomach softened, then the woman should have intercourse. She should drink samphire bark and eat dark peony berries with as much mercury plant, raw and cooked garlic as possible, and begin a diet of squid. If she gives birth, she is cured.

For uterine prolapse, the *Hippocratic Corpus* advises garlic, undiluted sheep's milk, fumigation, and a laxative, followed by another fumigation of fennel and absinthe and then two pessaries—one of squill, the other of opium poppies. If the woman's periods have stopped, then she should drink four cantharid beetles (legs, wings, and head removed) and eat four dark peony seeds, cuttlefish eggs, parsley, and wine. If her womb nears her liver, she will lose her voice, turn a dark colour and her teeth will chatter; a bandage should then be tied below her ribs and sweet wine poured into her mouth, while bad smelling vapours are burnt beneath her womb. This condition particularly affects old women and widows.[11]

Menstruation caused much anxiety amongst Greek males. The alleged mysterious, and alarming, qualities of menses, named after from the Latin for month, had their origins in civilisations earlier than the Greek. The book of *Leviticus* refers to it as 'the flower that comes before the fruit of the womb', to mean a child. In the *Talmud*, men were advised not to go near a menstruating woman; if one walked between two men, one of the men would surely die. Persian women were banned from speaking to men or even sit in water during menstruation. Hesiod warned that men should never wash in water that women had already used—just in case it was polluted by menstrual blood.

Ancient Egyptians used softened papyrus as tampons. Hippocrates noted that the Greeks used lint wrapped around wood. Aristophanes called the cloth that women used 'a pigpen'. Greek and Roman women, in common with women of other civilisations, used menstrual cloths.

Roman Pliny the Elder describes the astonishing powers of menstruation: 'it would be hard to find anything that produces as many amazing effects (*magis monstrificium*) as menstrual discharge.'

According to him, a period during a solar or lunar eclipse spelled disaster for the woman, and for any man who copulates with her then. If a man with suicidal tendencies had sex with a menstruating woman, he would commit suicide. If a woman, during her period, walked naked through a field that is filled with pests, those pests will die as she walks past; Metrodorus of Scepsis (*c.* 145–70 BCE) is Pliny's source: he says this happened in Cappadocia during a cantharid beetle plague, and accounts for the fact that women there still walk in the fields with their dresses hitched up above their buttocks. Ironically, cantharidin was to become a popular aphrodisiac in the nineteenth century.

It was believed that childbirth caused the body's smaller vessels to break down and promote blood flow; as such, childbirth was encouraged along with the coitus that preceded it. There was, then, no place for celibacy; it was certainly no coincidence that much of this gynaecology chimed nicely with the male Greek anxiety to marry off daughters as soon as possible after puberty in order to produce (male) children and further the family line. Cutting edge medical science seems to have served social convention and expediency as much as the patient.

Multiple births were a contentious issue. Ancient medical writers and scientists came up with different theories to explain the phenomenon: the Hippocratics believed that multiple births were the result of an ideal fecundity, for Aristotle they were regarded as anomalies associated with monstrosity and excess. Aristotle wrote that multiple births were *praeter naturam*— 'outside nature's normal boundaries' or 'unnatural'. He believed that the largest conceivable multiple birth was five in one confinement—astonishing enough until he adds that the woman repeated the feat four times in her life. In fact, the first valid report of a woman exceeding five did not come until 1888 when septuplets were born of an Italian woman; the report was promptly criticised for contradicting Aristotle's teachings.

The Hippocratics give us causes of miscarriage: carrying too heavy a weight, being physically abused, jumping up into the air, lack of food and fainting, fear, loud shouting, flatulence, and drinking too much. There were numerous 'old wives tales' surrounding miscarriage; Aristotle describes women suffering from nausea in the early stages of pregnancy (hyperemesis gravidarum), which he said is worse if the baby was a girl. There were danger signs to watch for: diarrhoea was a bad sign in a pregnant woman; shrinking breasts means she will miscarry; if she is carrying twins and the right breast loses its fullness, she will lose the male child, or if the left, the female; if she is underweight or in poor shape, she is likely to miscarry. Doctors should not bleed a pregnant woman as this can lead to miscarriage, especially if the fetus is a large one. If the inside of the womb is too smooth, a miscarriage may result because there is no traction to prevent the baby from simply falling out.

Like Herophilus, some Greek writers such as Aeschylus and Aristotle minimised or dismissed the vital role played by the woman in pregnancy, relegating her to little more than a vessel temporarily accommodating the baby while it grows. Aristotle believed that pregnancy came about when semen and menstrual blood mixed in the womb. Most physicians, however, did acknowledge that a baby developed characteristics from both its mother and its father. However, when a woman failed to conceive, it was invariably the woman's fault with never any suggestion that it might be the man who was infertile. Infertility in a woman was thought to be caused by a blockage of some sort; the standard fertility test involved wrapping the woman in a cloak and burning incense beneath her vagina. If the smell could then be detected in the woman's mouth, she was fertile, indicating that she was, quite properly, hollow inside and ready to conceive. If there was no oral smell, then there was a blockage, indicating infertility due to the inability of the semen to penetrate the inside of the womb. One treatment for this required the woman to sit all day in the sunshine outside her house while fumigations of myrrh, wormwood, and garlic 'softened and opened the mouth of the womb', encouraging the flow of semen. It was probably one of the few times the wife got to relax and do nothing. An alternative treatment entailed going to the sanctuary of Asclepius at Epidaurus where patients would spend the night so that their dreams would cure them and lead to conception.

Overweight or obese women were thought to have difficulty conceiving because their fat blocked the entrance to the womb. Another medical myth said that a pregnant woman with a blooming complexion will deliver a male baby; poor colour brought with it the threat of a girl.

Contraception was decidedly makeshift. Aristotle advocated smearing cedar oil, white lead or frankincense on the female genitals while the *Hippocratic Corpus* swore by drinking *misy*, dilute copper sulphate. The Hippocratics vowed not to use pessaries to effect an abortion, but some Hippocratic writings, in contradiction, prescribe them for that very purpose. Herbs were commonly used to prevent conception or to abort. The Pythagoreans were alone in opposing abortion on ethical grounds.

The ancient Greeks would have been exposed to the methods of other cultures. The Egyptian *Kahun Papyrus* (1850 BCE) recommends crocodile faeces either for preventing conception or as an abortifacient. In Arabic medicine, elephant faeces were frequently recommended. The *Ebers Papyrus* (1550 BCE) contains several recipes that 'cause a woman to stop pregnancy in the first, second, or third period'. One recipe for a vaginal suppository comprised of the unripe fruit of Acacia, colocynth, dates, and 6/7 pints of honey being poured onto a moistened plant fibre. Modern Arabic women still take colocynth as an abortifacient.

Probably the most effective contraceptive was silphium, or giant fennel, which had both contraceptive and abortifacient properties. Demand for silphium drove prices so high in the fifth century BCE enabling Aristophanes to write nostalgically in *The Knights*: 'Don't you remember when a stalk of silphium sold so cheap?' It was cultivated in a limited coastal area of North Africa and eventually became extinct from over harvesting; the Greeks then turned to asafoetida. Other contraceptives were Queen Anne's lace or wild carrot, pennyroyal, rue, artemisia, myrrh and pomegranate. Most have both contraceptive and abortifacient properties.

The ancient Greeks had some other interesting methods of birth control. In the empire, Soranus prescribed water that had been used by blacksmiths to cool iron. Dioscorides was something of a birth control specialist; he knew of twenty-four contraceptive potions, three of which were magic, including an amulet made of asparagus. Others involved applying peppermint, honey, cedar gum, axe weed, and alum in various concoctions to the genitals. Soranus is equally unromantic: his contraception of choice is stale olive oil, honey or the sap from a balsam or cedar tree applied to the entrance of the vagina—on its own or (alarmingly) mixed with white lead and bunged up with wool. This has a coagulating and cooling effect that causes the vagina to close before sex, and acts as a barrier to the sperm. An alternative method, just as undignified, involved the woman holding her breath when her partner ejaculates, pulling away so that his semen does not penetrate too deeply, then getting up straight away and squatting and sneezing before wiping her vulva clean. Dioscorides also recommends using vinegar, olive oil, ground pomegranate peel, and ground flesh of dried figs as vaginal suppositories. Olive oil was still being advocated by the Marie Stopes Clinic as recently as 1931, along with other effective spermicides like lemon, alum and vinegar. Douches made from vinegar, alum, or lemon juice were used by the working classes in New York in 1947, and lemons were still in use in 1970s Glasgow.

The Greeks also deployed *prostheta* or pesos. They were made from linen, sponge, or wool and rolled into a finger-like shape and coated with various drugs that could induce an abortion. Others were shaped like a small egg, nipple, or a tiny pencil or acorn. Hippocrates prescribed a pumpkin pessary, described as 'the inside of a pumpkin well crushed in cedar resin, wrapped into a cloth leaving its end bare, then inserted as deep as possible; after it is stained with blood, it is pulled out'.

The Egyptians developed the first diagnostic pregnancy test based on the detection of a unique substance in the urine of both women and domesticated animals. The best known Egyptian pregnancy test is the germination test: this requires the woman to urinate onto bags of wheat and barley. According to the *Berlin Medical Papyrus* 'if the barley grows, it means a male child. If the wheat grows, it means a female child. If both do not grow, she will not give birth at all'. The *Berlin Medical Papyrus* also recommended that a woman should have her nipples and skin examined for unusual pigmentation, or that she should drink milk from a woman who has had a son—if she vomits, she is pregnant. The *Kahun Medical Papyrus* suggests placing a woman in the daylight where pregnancy can be confirmed or not by the colour of her skin. Another test was grasping a woman's fingers and gripping her arm—if the veins in her arms pound against your hand, she is pregnant. Several of these rudimentary pregnancy tests resurface in the Hippocratic Corpus under *About the Barren Woman*.

One of the most innovative forms of contraception involved the application of a potato; a patient presented to a gynaecologist complaining that vines were sprouting from her vagina. The doctor examined her and found that vines were indeed sprouting. On removing the object, the doctor found that it was a potato that had sprouted vines. When asked why she had a potato in her vagina the patient confessed that her mother told her to put a potato in her vagina to stop her getting pregnant.

The debate over when life is thought to begin are ancient and enduring; there has never been complete agreement about when a fetus becomes a person, but the main view in ancient Hebrew, Greek, and Roman thought was that there could be no living soul in an 'unformed' and 'unquickened' body; hence, for example, the law of murder could not apply if a foetus was aborted before that time. Aristotle suggests that the foetus had a 'soul' after forty days from conception if a male, and ninety if female. There was no legislation against abortion in ancient Greece. Plato believed that the state should decree that all pregnancies in women over the age of forty should be terminated. For the ancients Greeks, life did not exist until birth, and thus no stigma or ethics were attached to abortion.

Ancient abortion technique included applying ointments and creams topically on the abdomen, or bruised corn boiled with vinegar and boiled cypress leaves. Physicians, such as Galen, recommended hot baths, blood letting, strenuous exercise, leaping, riding in a shaky carriage, carrying heavy weights, emotional shock, body massages with hot oil, or being vigorously shaken by two strong men.

Surgical abortion was known in the ancient world; due to lack of anesthetics and antibiotics, it was highly dangerous and exceedingly painful. Celsus (*c.* 25 BCE–50 CE) provides the most complete account of the dilatation and curettage operation, which required placing one, sometimes two, hands into the uterus to straighten the fetus and then extracting the fetus with a hook. Hippocratic texts such as *Diseases of Women, Superfetation,* and *On the Excision of the Foetus* refer to a surgical tool called an *embruosphaktes,* 'embryo-slayer'; it was deployed when manipulation failed to effect an embryotomy to evacuate the foetus as soon it was presumed dead, in order to save the mother. Hooked knives were used to dismember the foetus, and thus ease delivery; likewise, decapitating instruments enabled the head to delivered first.[12] Soranus recommended amputating parts of the foetus as they presented, rather than internally, to avoid cutting the vagina with the blade.[13] Unusually, large foetal heads were crushed with a cranioclast (a bowed forceps with teeth) or split with an embryotome; both instruments are still in use today. Traction hooks were also part of the instrumentation; samples have been found in Pompeii. Their use is described in Hippocrates, and by Celsus and Soranus.[14]

Naturally, in attempts to influence the sex of a baby, all the hard work went on trying to ensure a baby boy. Pliny the Elder describes the ancient theory whereby linozostis or parthenion was discovered by the god Mercury, and that many Greeks call it 'Hermes' grass'—the male plant produces male babies and the female plant females. The woman should drink the juice of the plant in raisin wine, or eat the leaves decocted in oil and salt, or raw in vinegar. Some again decoct it in a new earthen vessel with heliotropium and two or three ears of corn until the contents become thick. This decoction should be given to women in food, with the plant itself, on the second day of menstruation for three successive days; on the fourth day, after a bath, the woman should have intercourse.

Hippocrates also recommends linozostis for uterine disorders, adding honey, or oil of roses or of iris or of lilies, also as an emmenagogue and to evacuate the after-birth. Emmenagogues are herbs that stimulate blood flow in the pelvic region and uterus; some stimulate menstruation. He applied the leaves to fluxes from the eyes and prescribed a decoction of it with myrrh and frankincense for strangury—a blockage or irritation at the base of the bladder, resulting in severe pain and a strong desire to urinate—and other bladder troubles. For loosening the bowels, however, or for fever, a handful of the plant should be reduced down and drunk with salt and honey; it is even more powerful if the decoction has been made with a pig's foot or a chicken.

Sexually transmitted infections would have plagued both men and women alike, particularly in a society which freely endorsed their men consorting with male and female prostitutes. Discharges and ulcers are recorded, but there is little on infection or contagion . The Hippocratics, using findings from a dissected inflamed urethra, and Celsus and Galen all describe the symptoms of gonorrhoea, referring to it as 'strangury' (painful urination) caused by the 'pleasures of Venus'. Martial and Galen mention anal warts and piles (*ficus*); Celsus and Galen talk about genital warts; and the Hippocratics and Galen mention oral sores that present during menstruation—possibly *herpes zoster*. All of these conditions would have been common in ancient Greece.[15]

Ancient Greek sexual medicine began with Hesiod in the eighth century BCE when, borrowing heavily from contemporary folk medicine, he repeated the belief that the effects of heat afflicted men more than women, diminishing men's performance and the production of semen from its sources—the head and knees: 'in the draining heat, when goats are plumpest and wine is finest, and women are on heat but men are weak'[16]

Aristotle cautioned against having sex barefoot because bare feet made the body cold and dry, and it needed to be warm and moist during sex. He also taught that the eyelashes of people with a high sex drive drop out; this is because lust makes the upper body cold, thus depriving it of nourishment, causing hair loss.[17]

Men and women have been masturbating, alone and together, since the dawn of time. Our earliest evidence is a clay figurine of the fourth millennium BCE from Malta, showing a woman masturbating. In ancient Sumer, masturbation was a good thing—it was thought to enhance potency, either solitary or with a partner. In ancient Egypt, male masturbation performed by a god was a world changing event—it was considered an elemental or magical act; Atum created the universe by masturbating, and the ebb and flow of the Nile was dictated by the frequency of his ejaculations. Egyptian Pharaohs were required to masturbate ceremonially into the Nile.

To the ancient Greeks, masturbation was a normal and healthy standby for other sexual activity—a handy safety valve against destructive sexual frustration. This may explain why there are so few references to it in the literature; it was quite normal and did not merit much attention.

Miletus was the manufacturing and exporting centre of the *olisbos,* from ὀλισθεῖν (*olistheîn,* to slip, glide) and known to us as the dildo. Our oldest example is a twenty centimeter phallus from the Upper Palaeolithic period, some 30,000 years ago, found in Hohle Fels Cave near Ulm in Germany. As for ancient Greece, what can only be described as dildo-like breadsticks, known as *olisbokollikes* (singular *olisbokollix*), were known before the fifth century BCE. More often, dildos were made either of wood or pressed leather and, obviously, were liberally lubricated with olive oil before use.

A third century BCE mime by Herodas—*A Quiet Chat*—features a conversation between two young women, Metro and Coritto. Metro wants to borrow Coritto's dildo but Coritto says that Nossis has it, and she got it from Euboula:

> That woman wore me down; she begged me so much that I weakened and gave it to her, Metro, before I had even used it myself. After seizing it like a godsend, she gives it away [to Nossis]! ... If I had a thousand I would not have given her one, even if it were all worn out.

Coritto then explains that she bought it from Kerdon, the maker of the dildo, who covers up his black market trade by pretending to be a cobbler who 'works at his house and sells secretly'. Metro then vividly describes Kerdon's expertise:

But the things he makes, all of them, are worthy of Athena; you would believe you could see her hand, instead of Kerdo's. He came here with two, Metro! When I saw them, my eyes nearly popped out with desire. The men certainly have no rams like those!—we are alone—that's for sure! And that's not all: their smoothness—a dream; and the stitches—of down, not of thread! Hunt as you might, you could not find another cobbler so kindly disposed toward.[18]

She then leaves to seek him out. In *Mime* 7, Metro takes some friends to Kerdon's shoe shop and the sexual innuendo continues with footware a metaphor for sex toys.

The *olisbos* is also mentoned in Aristophanes' *Lysistrata* when Calonice, bewailing the absence of the men at war, says:

And so, girls, when fucking time comes… not the faintest whiff of it anywhere, right? From the time those Milesians betrayed us, we can't even find our eight-fingered leather dildos. At least they'd serve as a sort of flesh-replacement for our poor cunts… So, then! Would you like me to find some mechanism by which we could end this war?[19]

The gold standard on dream interpretation in antiquity is the eighty-two section *Oneirocritica*, researched and compiled by Artemidorus of Ephesus in the second century CE; it was based on his own work and that of sixteen predecessors, now all lost.

Women and their sexuality feature prominently in the book. Dreams about legal, consensual intercourse with a wife bodes well, while coercive sex has the opposite effect. On the other hand, dreaming about sex with brothel-based prostitutes indicates a bit of a scandal in the offing, and a small financial outlay in the future. Going into a brothel and getting out again is a good thing; Artemidorus describes an acquaintance who dreamt that he went into a brothel and could not get out; in real life, he died a few days later—a brothel, like a cemetery, is a place 'common to all and the destruction of many human seeds takes place there'.[20] Prostitutes sitting in their stalls, plying their trade, receiving their fee or visibly copulating are a good dream, but streetwalkers in a dream are better still.

Familiarity is important—if a man dreams he is having sex with a woman he does not know, if she is attractive and elegant, wears fine and expensive clothes and gold necklaces, and gives herself willingly, this augurs very well for the dreamer and forecasts future success. That woman will also benefit the man in that she would very likely also give him 'her investments. Often a dream of this kind has helped the dreamer when coping with the mystery of woman, since the woman in such a dream also allows him to touch her secret parts' (Artemidorus : *On the Interpretation of Dreams (Oneirocritica)* 1, 78).

However if the man dreams he has sex with a woman who is 'an ugly, shapeless, shabbily dressed old hag dragging out a life of pain, and she does not consent to sex' it is a bad dream with portents of future bad luck. It is a bad thing to dream of having sex with a legally married woman other than your wife, because that dream delivers the same punishment for a man caught in adultery in real life—death. Dreams relating to female homoeroticism were all about secrets. All will be revealed to the partner when a woman dreams she is pleasuring another woman. Likewise, when a woman dreams she is the object of pleasure, she will either be separated from her husband. or she will be widowed.[21]

The interpretation of dreams about having sex with one's mother then things are not so very straightforward; 'the case of one's mother is both complex and manifold and admits of many different interpretations ... the manner of the embraces and the various positions of the bodies indicate different outcomes.'

It is not good to have sex with a mother who is looking away; it is also unlucky to dream of having intercourse with one's mother while she is standing up 'for men use this position only when they have neither bed nor mattress. Therefore it signifies coercion and oppression. It is also bad to have intercourse with one's mother while she is kneeling and worse while she is prostrate. For it signifies great poverty because of the mother's immobility'. Woe betide anyone who has a dream in which he takes his mother 'from underneath while she is in the 'rider' position'; this means death to the dreamer'.

In conclusion, Artemidorus helpfully teaches:

> It is not auspicious to use many different positions on one's mother. For it is not right to insult one's mother ... the worst dream by far is one in which the dreamer practices fellatio with his mother. For this signifies to the dreamer the death of children, the loss of property, and serious illness. I know of a man who, after this dream, lost his penis. For it was understandable that he was punished in the part of the body with which he had sinned.[22]

The Hippocratic case history of Phaethousa of Abdera is interesting. Phaethousa had a baby after her husband was sent into exile. Phaethousa eventually stopped menstruating, grew a beard and died. Some have argued that the story exemplifies the role of lust—her husband was not around to to satisfy her needs and she missed him so much that she came to resemble him. Others emphasize the fact that otherwise she was *oikouros*, a stay-at-home wife and *epitokos*, highly fertile; in other words, she satisfied the criteria as the model wife who was so good a person she simply had to become a man.[23] No woman could ever be that good.

Epilogue

In my introduction, I explained that the aim of this book was to reveal manifestations of the role of women in ancient Greek society, to reanimate the ancient Greek woman, to rescue her from relative obscurity for the twenty-first century. Despite the welcome explosion of scholarship related to women in antiquity that has taken place in the last forty or so years, and a long overdue reappraisal of women's role in ancient Greek society, there remains a tendency still to write off women as being secluded and excluded, denuded of their very real and significant contribution to ancient Greek life right across the civilisation. The mantra goes that women were not party or privy to the important things in Greek life—politics and war—and that is the end of it. I have shown through various forms of evidence that this generalistion is, to some extent, illusory.

However, women were undoubtedly, for the most part, debarred from any involvement in public, political and military life; I say 'for the most part' because in Minoan Crete, Sparta, and Macedon, all the evidence shows that there were varying degrees of female involvement in politics, power and the military. In Greece in general, quite naturally, women are prominent in the polytheistic pantheon and extensive mythology as forces for good and evil; this of course percolates down into the literature—epic, tragic, and comedic.

Thanks to the demonisation of Pandora and the vivid depiction of other troublesome female characters, there is much misogyny, stereotyping, and generalisation, although some of this can be put down to male posturing, pandering to audiences, and the demands required of various genres. Furthermore, the bad women are balanced by good women, like Penelope and Andromache. In real life, women are said to have been disregarded and unappreciated, condemned to a life of drudgery, making the clothes, balancing the budget, raising the children, and producing babies with no appreciation, love, or affection. Women did indeed do all these things, but the epigraphical evidence and New Comedy shows that love did exist in marriages, and that women took pride in husbands and children, pride, and love that was reciprocated.

Often, the assumption is that women were confined not only to the home, but within certain rooms inside it too. Some undoubtedly were, but the evidence for the whole population being segregated and imprisoned is weak, and we know for sure that many women went out to socialise or work, even if it was just fetching the water or as a *hetaira*. Women also played an important, high profile, and responsible role in state religion, and in organising family funerals; they may well have attended the theatre. They were undoubtedly poorly educated but, nevertheless, some overcame this to become capable poets, doctors, scientists, and philosophers. Male philosophers were ambivalent about the role of women, with some schools of thought welcoming them and championing their potential contribution to society, and others condemning them to more of that domestic drudgery; in the end though, the thoughts of a philosopher and his dialectic are based as much on opinion as reality.

The idea that women were excluded and secluded is then something of a convenient illusion, a generalisation. Women in ancient Greece were denied involvement in political public life, they had a hugely important and demanding domestic role, and they were a lot more active, obtrusive, and 'out there' than they are often given credit for.

Endnotes

Introduction

1. Aristotle, *Politics* 4 (1254b 13–14).
2. Demosthenes, *Apollodorus Against Neaera*, 3, 122.
3. A school exercise attributed to the Athenian fourth Century BCE playwright Menander. *Synkrisis* 1, 209–10 Jakel.
4. Phaedra, in *Hippolytus.*
5. Andromache, in *Andromache,* 108.
6. *Iphigenia in Aulis,* 1394.
7. Euripides, *Andromache.* Aristophanes, *Lysistrata* 8-11; 42–5.
8. Hipponax, Fr. 68 (West).
9. Hyperides, Fr. 204.
10. Thucydides, 2, 45, 2.
11. Semonides, 7, 115–118.
12. Xenophon, *Oeconomicus* 7, 6.
13. *Ibid.* 7, 22.
14. *Ibid* 7, 35–7.
15. Gomme, *The Position of Women in Athens in the Fifth and Fourth Centuries*
16. Kitto, H. D. F. *The Greeks,* especially pp. 219-36.
17. Seltman, C. *The Status of Women in Athens* and *Women in Antiquity,* especially Chapter IX—'The New Woman'.
18. Aristotle, *Politics*, 1245b 13–14.
19. Soranus, *Gynaecology* 34.
20. Xenophon, *op. cit.* 7, 42–3.

Chapter One

1. Hesiod, *Works and Days*, 42-105. Trans. adapted from H. G. Evelyn-White. *Works and Days* 55ff, Cambridge, MA., Harvard University Press London, 1914.
2. *Poetics* 9, 1451b5–8.
3. Euripides fragment 484 Nauck.
4. Hesiod, *Cat.* fr. 1, 1–5.
5. Fragment 19: Europa. Scholiast on Homer, Iliad. 12, 292; translations all H. G. Evelyn White.
6. Fragment 8 Endymion. Scholiast on Apollonius Rhodes, Arg. 4, 5.
7. Fragment 53 Aeacus. Scholiast on Pindar, Nem. 2, 21.
8. We need not go as far as Seltman, *Women in Antiquity* p. 10 in his note to his Second Edition where he describes Hesiod's views as 'crude like any other peasant's views on peasant women'.
9. *Metamorphoses* 6, 1-145.

10. Apollodorus, 1, 9, 17.
11. Apollonius of Rhodes, *The Voyage of the Argo* 1, 625 ff.
12. *Libation Bearers* 594 ff.
13. St Augustine, *On the City of God*, 18, 9.
14. Hesiod, *Theogeny*, 221-5.
15. Plato, *Republic*, 617c.
16. *Lycidas*, l. 75.
17. Fragmenta Chorica Adespota, 5. Diehl.
18. *Description of Greece* 8, 21, 3.
19. *Biblioteca* 1, 65.
20. Songwriters J. Whitney and R. Chapman.
21. Homer, *Iliad* 3, 278ff; 19, 260ff.
22. Hesiod, *Theogeny* 187.
23. Aeschylus, *Eumenides* 321 ff; Lycophron, *Alexandra* 432; Ovid, *Metamorphoses* 4, 451; Virgil, *Aeneid 6,* 250; 12. 848 ff.
24. Aeschylus, *Libation Bearers* 1048 ff ; Euripides , *Orestes* 317, *Iphigenia in Tauris*, 290; *Virgil Aeneid* 12, 848; *Orphic Hymn* 68, 5.
25. Plato, *Phaedo* 107d ff; 112e; see aslo Quintus Smyrnaeus, *Fall of Troy* 5, 520 ff; Hyginus, *Fabulae* 79.
26. Bacchylides (Frag. 52), *Orphic Hymn* (69,) Apollodorus (1, 3); Virgil, *Aeneid* 6, 572ff.
27. Euripides, *Melanippe Captive* Fr 499 Nauck.
28. Pausanias, *op.cit.* 2, 21, 7.
29. Ovid, *Ibis* 459–460.
30. Aeschylus, *Eumenides*, 50.
31. Virgil, *op. cit.* 3, 209 ff.
32. Homer, *Odyssey* 12, 45–6; Robert Fagles' translation.
33. Pliny, *Natural History* 10, 70
34. Homer, *op.cit.* 1, 241; 14, 371
35. *Ibid.* 20, 78

Chapter Two

1. Gomme, *Position of Women*, p.4.
2. Seltman, *Status of Women*, p.120.
3. See Cartledge (1993), page 101 and Syropoulos (2012), p.1.
4. Homer, *Odyssey* 1, 330-359; 360–364; 21, 56, 330
5. Homer, *Iliad*, 19, 261-3.
6. Homer, *Odyssey*, 354–361.
7. *Ibid.* 7, 14–20; 6, 303–315.
8. *Ibid.* 23, 254-5, 299–373.
9. *Vera Historia*, 2, 35.
10. *Fabulae*, 243.
11. Homer, *Odyssey*, 7, 311f; 8, 457-68.
12. Homer, *Iliad*, 6, 425, 470–72; 6, 450–465.
13. *Ibid.* 6, 485ff.
14. *Ibid.* 6, 370–373; 6, 433–439.
15. *Ibid.* 22, 440–6.
16. *Ibid.* 6, 466–483.
17. *Ibid.* 22, 477–514.
18. *Ibid.* 6, 390–470; 22, 437–515.
19. Trans. Anne Carson, *If Not, Winter: Fragments of Sappho* (New York, 2002).

20. Euripides, *Andromache*, 643-58. Apollodorus *Bibliotheca* 3, 12, 6, and *Epitome* 5, 23; 6, 12; Euripides' *Andromache* and *The Trojan Women*; Virgil, *Aeneid* 3, 294–355; Ovid, *Ars Amatoria* 3, 777–778, and Seneca, *The Trojan Women*.

21. Calypso: Homer, *Odyssey* 1, 11-19; 5, 151–158; 7, 259. Diogenes Laërtius 2, 26.

22. Euripides, *Alcestis* 177

23. *Idem. Hippolytus* 373–430

24. Aeschylus, *Agamemnon* 351, 606–9.

25. Euripides, *Medea* 112

26. *Ibid.* 251.

27. Euripides, Fr 13 GLP=Fr 499 Nauck; *Idem. Ion* 843

28. Eubulus, Fr. 77 PCG; *Chrysilla* Fr. 115 PCG. Sophocles, *Tereus*, Fr. 583; translation by Lloyd Jones

29. *Imagines*, 2, 29.

30. Apollodorus, *Epitome of the Library*, 3, 21

31. The *Hesiodic Catalogue of Women* 1, 43, 1

32. Aristophanes *Ecclesiazusae* 1015.

33. *Ibid.* 220ff.

34. *Thesmophoriazusae*, 785ff. Trans, adapted from *Aristophanes: Women at the Thesmophoria. The Complete Greek Drama, vol. 2*. Eugene O'Neill, Jr. (New York, 1938)

35. *Ibid.* 520ff.

36. *Ibid.* 380ff.

37. *Idem.* 735–6. See also *Lysistrata* 113–4; 195–239; 395; *Thesmophoriazusae* 447–8; 556–7.

38. Aristophanes, *Lysistrata* 507–20; 160–2; 516; 519–20. Divorce: *op. cit.* 157. See also the coverage of domestic abuse in Chrystal, *In Bed with the Ancient Greeks*.

39. Aristophanes, *Clouds* 46ff. Trans. adapted from *The Comedies of Aristophanes*, William James Hickie. (London, 1853).

40. Aristophanes, *Peace* 1127–58.

41. Aristophanes, *Ecclesiazusae* 311; 323-6; 335–8.

42. Eg. *Lysistrata* 72; *Thesmophoriazusae* 478-89; *Ecclesiazusae* 33–51. See Ireland, S. (1992), *Menander Dyskolos, Samia and Other Plays*

43. *Lysistrata*, 258–61.

44. www.usu.edu/markdamen/ClasDram/chapters/101latergkcomedy.htm III. New comedy

45. Anaxandrides 53, 4–7 K.–A. For women in Greek theatre generally and how they were marginalised, see this National Theatre film at www.nationaltheatre.org.uk/video/women-in-greek-theatre-1: 'This film explores the role of women in Ancient Greek society and the representation of female identity in Antigone, Women of Troy and Medea. Dr Lucy Jackson, Teaching Fellow at King's College London & Knowledge Exchange Fellow at the Oxford Research Centre in the Humanities (TORCH) looks back over these recent Greek productions at the National Theatre, featuring Helen McCrory and Jodie Whittaker'.

Chapter Three

1. *Theogeny*, 590-59

2. *Women*, by Semonides of Amorgos 7, 1-5

3. *Women*, by Semonides of Amorgos 7, 50-55

4. *Women*, by Semonides of Amorgos 7, 84-94

5. See Osborne, *The Use of Abuse: Semonides 7*; Morgan, *The Wisdom of Semonides, Fragment 7*.

6. Phokylides of Miletus, *Satire on Women*

7. Euripides, Hippolytus 616-55.

8. Carcinus II, *Semele*, TGrF Fr. 70 F3.

9. Alexis, fr. 36 *PCG*.

10. Amphis, Fr 1 PCG.

11. Menander, Fr 333, Koerte.
12. *The Fragments of 'Attic Comedy'* After Meineke, Bergk, and Kock; edited by John Maxwell Edmonds page 295; #253

Chapter Four

1. Herodotus 2, 111
2. Herodotus 1, 173–4; trans G. C. Macaulay.
3. *Idem.* 4, 180.
4. *Ibid.*
5. *Idem,* 4, 176.
6. *Idem,* 4, 172, 2; 1, 216, 1.
7. Found on Oxyrhynchus Papyri 1358 fr. 2.
8. *Herodotus,* 4, 168.
9. *Idem.* 4, 205
10. Jordanes, *De Origine Actibusque Getarum.*
11. Herodotus 1, 214; trans. George Rawlinson.
12. *Idem.* 1, 216.
13. Telesilla: Plutarch, *On The Bravery of Women* 4, *Moralia* 245c-f; Pausanias 2, 20, 8; Marpessa, Pausanias 8, 48, 4–5; *Tractatus de Mulieribus* 11; Polyaenus, *Strategems* 8, 53, 4. The role of ancient Greek women in war is comprehensively dealt with in Chrystal, *Women at War in Ancient Greece and Rome.*
14. Polyaenus, *Strategems.* 8, 53.
15. *Idem.* 7, 99.
16. *Idem.* 8, 68.
17. *Idem.* 8, 88.
18. Herodotus, 8, 93.
19. Polyaenus, *Strategems* 8, 53, 4
20. Herodotus, 8, 102.
21. Diodorus Siculus, 16, 14; Xenophon, *Hellenica* 6, 4, 37; Cicero, *De Officiis* 7; *Idem. De Inventione* 2, 49; Aristotle. *ap. Cicero de Div.* 1. 25; *The Dream of Eudemus.*
22. Herodotus, 1, 7, 2; 1, 7–13.
23. *Idem.* 1, 8, 2; 1, 10, 3.
24. *Idem.* 7, 61, 114, 9, 108–113. See also Ctesias, *Persica* c. 20. 30; Plutarch, *Alcibiades* p. 123, c.
25. *Idem.* 7, 114.
26. Xenophon, *Anabasis* 7, 8.
27. *Ibid, Hellenica* 3, 1, 10-14.
28. *Xenophon in Seven Volumes, 1 and 2.* Trans. C. L. Brownson. (Harvard University Press, 1918 and 1921).
29. Polyaenus, *op. cit* 8, 26-71; 54.
30. Xenophon, *Cyropaedia* 1, 3; 6, 1, 31; 4, 2; 7, 3, 2.
31. See Chrystal, *Women in Ancient Rome,* Chapter 3.
32. Plutarch, *Cimon* 4, 14, *Pericles* 10; Nepos, *Cimon* 1.
33. The line is from Archilocus. See O'Higgins, *Women and Humor in Classical Greece* p. 113.

Chapter Five

1. Isaeus 10.10. A *medimnos* was a measure of dry grain. In Attica, it was approximately equal to 51.84 litres, although it was very much subject to regional variations: the Spartan *medimnos* was approximately equal to 71.16 litres. The *medimnos* was divided into smaller units: the

tritaios (one third), the *hekteus* (one sixth), the *hemiektos* (one twelfth), the *choinix* (one forty-eighth) and the *kotyle* (0.27-l).

2. Apollodorus, *Against Neaera*.
3. Quoted in *The Persian Empire and the West*. Frank E. Adcock, Cambridge, 1953 p. 492
4. Isaeus, 3.64.
5. Golden '*Donatus* and Athenian Phratries' *Classical Quarterly* p. 10; Roy '*Polis* and *Oikos* in Classical Athens', *Greece & Rome* p. 12; Patterson *Family in Greek History* p. 93.
6. According to Plutarch, *Agis, Cleomenes, Aratus* and Pausanias, *Description of Greece* 8, 7, 2.
7. Herodotus 6, 127; 129-130.

Chapter Six

1. *Palatine Anthology* 7, 351, cited and translated by Douglas E. Gerber, Greek Iambic Poetry, Loeb (1999) page 49.
2. Athenaeus: *The Deipnosophistae* 13.
3. *Ibid*. 35.
4. Papaspiridi: *Guide du Musée Nationale d'Athènes* (1927), 132 *c*.340-320 BCE.
5. CEG 530.
6. CEG 2.
7. CEG 135
8. CEG 526
9. Menander, *Epitrepontes*.
10. Plato, *Phaedo*, 60a-b, 116b; Xanthippe is also mentioned in two short, apocryphal pieces ascribed to Plato: *Halcyon* and the *Epigrams*; Xenophon, *Memorabilia*, 2, 2, 7-9
11. Xenophon, *Symposium* 2, 11.
12. Aelian, *Varia Hist* 11, 12; Xenophon, *Moralia, On the Control of Anger* II, 2, 1-14; Diogenes Laërtius 2, 36-7.
13. Athenaeus, 13, 555D–556A; Diogenes Laërtius, 2, 26.
14. Plutarch, *Aristides*, 27, 3–4.
15. Diogenes Laërtius, *ibid*.
16. Plato, *Theaetetus* 149a.
17. *Aristotle, The Politics & Economics of Aristotle*, trans.Edward English Walford & John Gillies, (London: G. Bell & Sons), 1908.
18. *Politics*, 1, 1, 5; 125b 5.
19. *Trans. Anne Carson, If Not, Winter: Fragments of Sappho* (*New York, 2002*).
20. Anonymous, *Greek Anthology* Book 6 H41
21. *Lysistrata*, 574ff.

Chapter Seven

1. Seltman: *Life in Ancient Crete II*.
2. Blegen, C. W. (2001), *A Guide to the Palace of Nestor, Mycenaean Sites in its Environs and the Chora Museum* (2 ed.), ASCSA; Blegen, C W(1966–1973), *The Palace of Nestor at Pylos in Western Messenia*, Princeton University Press
    v. 1. The buildings and their contents, by C. W. Blegen pt. 1. Text. pt. 2. Illustrations.
    v. 2. The frescoes, by M. L. Lang.
    v. 3. Acropolis and lower town: tholoi, grave circle, and chamber tombs; discoveries outside the citadel, by C. W. Blegen and others.
3. See S. Wagner-Hasel, *Women's Life in Oriental Seclusion? On the History and Use of a Topos*.
4. Homer, *Odyssey* 3, 183.

5. Demosthenes, Apollodorus *Against Neaera*.
6. Xenophon, *Oikonomikos* 9.5.
7. Lysias I, 9–10.
8. Aristophanes, *Thesmophoriazusae*, 481f. Antiphon, *Prosecution for Poisoning*, 14.
9. *History of Animals* 775a4-17 and *op. cit*. 608all-608b18.
10. Hippocrates, *Epidemics* V, 50
11. Adapted from translation by Jack Lindsay.
12. *Thesmophoriazusae* 395–7; see also 479–89
13. *Ecclesiazusa* 225; 499-501.
14. Pausanias, *Description of Greece* 5, 6.
15. *Idem*. 5, 15, 1–6.
16. *Idem*. 5, 16, 5.
17. Aristophanes, *Frogs*, 1049ff.
18. Aristophanes, *Birds*, 793-6; *Peace* 962-7; 50-2.
19. Aristophanes, *Thesmophoriazusae* 446ff.
20. Aristophanes, *Plutus* 959-1094.

Chapter Eight

1. *FH*, 177m.
2. Gravestones: *IG* II, 1561, 22–7; 1570, 73; 1576, 15f; 1578, 5f.
3. Euripides, *Helen* 171.
4. Euripides *Electra*, 51.
5. Homer, *Odyssey*, 20, 105.
6. Aristophanes, *Lysistrata*, 327ff.
7. *Wasps* 1387ff; *Lysistrata* 357; *Frogs* 858; in *Wasps*, the breadwoman serves a writ on Philicleon for damage done to her buns, taking Chaerephon as her witness.
8. *Ecclesiazusae* 841.
9. *Thesmophoriazusae* 446—ruined by Euripides' heresy.
10. *Lys*. 457; 562; *Plutus* 427.
11. *Wasps* 497; *Thesm*. 387; *Lys*. 456.
12. *Lys*. 457.
13. *Pl*. 435; 1120; *Thesm*. 347.
14. *Clouds* 41.
15. *Lys*. 746.
16. *Knights* 715 ff.; *Thesm*. 609; *Lys*. 958.
17. *Thesm*. 558; cf. II72 ff.
18. *Pl*. 426; *Frogs* 114; *Lys*. 458.
19. Euripides, *The Trojan Women*, 491.
20. Aristophanes, *Plutus*, 644-770.
21. Hesiod, *Works and Days*, 405.
22. Pausanias, *Description of Greece*, 3, 8, 1–3.
23. Oxhrynchus, 268/7.
24. *IG* 9, 2, 526, 19–20.
25. *IG* 2, 23 13 9–5; 23 13 60; 23 14.50–1.

Chapter Nine

1. Plutarch, *Moralia* 241.
2. See Plutarch; trans. Scott-Kilvert, Ian (1973). *Life of Pyrrhus,* 16-28.

3. Plutarch, *op. cit*, 16-28.
4. See Llewelyn-Jones, *Veiling the Spartan Woman.*
5. *Protagoras*, 342d.
6. Trans. Benjamin Jowett (London, 1900)
7. Fr. 1, vv. 64–7; Fr 3, vv. 79–81.
8. Athenaeus 13, 566.
9. *Ibid.* 555–6.
10. Homer, *Iliad*, 24, 496.
11. Herodotus, 4, 51
12. *Ibid.* 7, 239.
13. See Polybius 12, 6b, 8; Xenophon, *Constitution* 1.7–9; Plutarch, *Lycurgus* 15, 6–9. Caesar, *De Bello Gallico* 5, 2; Theopompus, *Histories* 43.
14. Justin, v. 2; Plutarch, *Alcibiades* 23.
15. Thucydides 8, 12, 45; Plutarch, *Lysander* 22; *Agesilaus.* 3.
16. See Qviller, *Reconstructing the Spartan Partheniai.*
17. Herodotus 6, 7; *AP* 13, 16.
18. Xenophon, *Minor Works, Agesilaus* 9, 1, 6; *Idem.* 20, 1.
19. Pausanias, *Description of Greece* 3, 8, 1-3.
20. Plutarch, *op. cit.* 14.2, 14.4.
21. In 'Sparta: A Modern Woman Imagines'. *Classical Review*, 54 (2): 465–467

Chapter Ten

1. See, for example, Llewellyn-Jones, *Veiling the Spartan Woman.*
2. Alexis, ap. Athen. XIII p.568C; Xenophon. *Oecon.* 10, 2; Aristophanes. *Eccl.* 878, 929.
3. Alexis, ap. Athen. l.c.; Eubulus, ap. Athen. XIII p557F.
4. Sappho Fragment 98, translated by Barbara Hughes Fowler.
5. From www.rwaag.org/hair; accessed 31.01.16: Aristophanes, *Lysistrata* 47; *Ibid.* 79; *Ibid.* 149; Aristophanes, *Ecclesiazusae* 117; Euripides, *Hippolytus* 1426; *Idem. Electra* 1070ff; Homer *Iliad* 14, 175 (of Hera).
6. Aristophanes, *Lysistrata* 47.
7. Aristophanes, *op. cit.* 79.
8. Aristophanes, *op. cit.* 149.
9. Aristophanes, *Ecclesiazusae*, 117.
10. Euripides, *Hippolytus*, 1426.
11. Euripides, *Electra*, 1070ff.
12. Homer, *Iliad* 14, 175 (of Hera).
13. Theophrastus *De Odoribus* 5, 25.
14. Hippias Fr. 14.
15. Plutarch :*Moralia* 141C; Athenaeus, *Deipnosophistae* 13.609 b-c.
16. Quoted by Athenaeus, *Deipnosophistae* 13, 609. Strabo, *Geographia*, 13, 46: 'Tenedos itself, which is not more than forty stadia distant from the mainland'.
17. Diodorus Siculus 1, 47, 1.
18. Sophocles, *op. cit.* 1- 2; Athenaeus: *The Deipnosophistae* 13, 42.

Chapter Eleven

1. Fr. 258 K.
2. Fr. 94G.
3. Fr. 384.

4. www.poetryfoundation.org/bio/sappho accessed 16 December 2016.

5. Athenaeus, *Deipnosophistae*, 7, 297 a- b. Translation by Charles Burton Gulick.

6. Diogenes Laërtius, *Lives of Eminent Philosophers* 8, 7; Porphyry, *Life of Pythagoras* 41.

7. Stobaeus, 1, 49, 27.

8. Lucian, *In Praise of a Fly*, 11.

9. Clement of Alexandria, *Stromata*, 5, 19; Suda, *Myia, Theano*; Iamblichus, *Life of Pythagoras*, 30, 36; Porphyry, *op. cit.* 4.

10. Stobaeus, 4, 23, 11.

11. Athenaeus, *op.cit.* 13, 596e

12. Diogenes Laërtius 2, 114.

13. Diogenes Laërtius, 10, 23; Athenaeus, *op. cit.* 13. 588, 593.

14. Diogenes Laërtius, 10, 5.

15. Pliny, *Nat. Hist.*, 35.99

16. Cicero, *De Natura Deorum* i. 33/93

17. Pliny, *op. cit.*, praefatio, 29.

18. Cicero, *De Finibus*, 2, 21, 68.

19. Diogenes Laërtius, 10, 25, 26.

20. *Suda*, 'Arignote'; *Idem. Pythagoras; Idem. Theano*; Clement of Alexandria, *Stromata*, 6, 19; Porphyry, *Life of Pythagoras*, 4. Plutarch, *Moralia* 1A—14C; see Mary Ellen Waithe, (1987), *A History of Women Philosophers. Volume 1, 600 BC-500 AD*, Stuttgart, p. 12

21. Diogenes Laërtius, 3, 46. This cross-dressing may apply to Axiothea of Phlius who also studied in the Academy. Diogenes Laërtius 4, 2.

22. Athenaeus 7, 279; 12, 546.

23. *P. Oxy* 3656.

24. Diogenes Laërtius, 6, 96; 97.

25. *Suda*, 'Krates'.

26. Diogenes Laërtius 6, 91; Musonius Rufus, 14, 4.

27. Apuleius, *Florida* 2, 49.

28. Long, *The Socratic Tradition*, p. 42; see Diogenes Laërtius 6, 69, 6, 46, and 6, 72.

29. *Suda*, 'Hipparchia'. Diogenes Laërtius 6, 97. Cf Euripides, *Bacchae* 1236. In the play the line is spoken by Agave when she boasts of her prowess as a hunter, before realizing that her prey is her own son.

30. Cf. Diogenes Laërtius 6, 46. See also Diogenes Laërtius 2, 116; Theophrastus, *Characters* 11, 1, 2, Diodorus Siculus 1, 83

31. Diogenes Laërtius, 6, 93; 6, 98; 6, 88. *AP* 7, 413.

32. *Greek Anthology*, 7,413. Translation by William R. Paton (1918).

33. Plutarch, *Pericles* 24.

34. Plato, *Menexenus* 263a.

35. *The Staff of Odysseus* p. 62.

36. Xenophon, *Memorabiia* 2, 6, 36; *Oeconomicus* 3, 14.

37. Cicero, *De Inventione* 1, 51–53.

38. Lucian, *A Portrait Study*, 27.

39. C. Glenn, *Locating Aspasia on the Rhetorical Map*, 23; See also Jarratt-Onq, *Aspasia: Rhetoric, Gender, and Colonial Ideology*, 9–24.

40. D. Kagan, *Pericles of Athens and the Birth of Democracy,* 182

41. R. Just, *Women in Athenian Law and Life,* 144

42. P. Allen, *The Concept of Woman*, 29–30

43. Plato, *Symposium* 201d. Xenephon *Memorabilia* 2, 36; *Oeconomicus* 3, 15.

44. Pliny the Elder, *NH* 35, 11, 40; 40, 140, 147.

45. See Virginia Brown's translation of Boccaccio's *Famous Women*, pp 123–124; Harvard University Press, 2001.

46. Pliny, *op. cit.* 35, 12.

47. Pliny, *op.cit.* 35, 35, 59; 40, 147.
48. Homer *Iliad*, 11, 668.
49. Propertius 2, 4; Theocritus *Idylls*, 2, 10.
50. See Bicknell: *The Witch Aglaonice and Dark Lunar Eclipses*. Plutarch *Coniugalia Praecepta* 48 = 145c; *De Defectu Oraculorum* 13 = 417a; *Scholion to Argonautica* 4, 59.
51. Plutarch, *Moralia* 14b-c.
52. Plutarch, *Conjugalia Praecepta*.
53. Xenophon, *Symposium* 2, 8-9.
54. Athenaeus, *op.cit.* 13, 46.
55. Plutarch, *Demetrius* 16, 4 and 27,4. Plutarch confirms that Demetrius was partial to older women.
56. Athenaeus 13, 577c.
57. Diodorus Siculus, 17, 72.
58. Ovid, *Remedia Amoris* 383.
59. Dante, *Inferno*, 18, 133–136.
60. Pliny *op. cit.* 36, 12, 17.
61. See P. Chrystal, *In Bed with the Ancient Greeks*

Chapter Twelve

1. Seltman, *Status of Women* p. 121.
2. For a full discussion see Chrystal, *In Bed with the Ancient Greeks* chapter five, from which this is condensed.
3. *Scientific American,* Scobie and Taylor on 8 August 2013; blogs.scientificamerican.com/bering-in-mind/hearts-of-stone-sexual-deviants-in-antiquity/
4. Athenaeus: *Deipnosophistae* 13, 601-606: 'But the statue spoken of is the work of Ctesicles; as Adaeus of Mytilene tells us in his treatise On Sculptors. And Polemon, or whoever the author of the book called Helladicus is, says…'

Chapter Thirteen

1. Euripides Fr 13 GLP = Fr 499 Nauck Pausanias, *Description of Greece* 1, 27, 3.
2. Farnell, The *Cults of the Greek States* vol. IV, p.189.
3. *Lysistrata*, 641–7.
4. Homer, *Iliad* 11. 427.
5. Aristophanes , *Lysistrata*, 63-4; 700-3.
6. *Idem, Plutus*, 768ff; 1197-1207.
7. Aristophanes *Frogs*, 444-6; 409-13.
8. Pausanias 10,5, 7, 10,6., 7; Strabo, 9; Pliny the Elder *HN*. 7, 57; Clement of Alexandria, *Stromata* i. pp. 323, 334; Schol. ad Eurip. Orest. 1094; Eustathius Prol. ad Iliad.; Fabricius *Bibl Graec*. vol. i.
9. Plutarch *Moralia* 414b.
10. Plutarch, *De Defectu Oraculorum* and *De Pythiae Oraculis* in *Moralia*, vol. 5.
11. Pausanias, 10, 13.
12. See Sophocles, *Trachiniae*, 69.
13. See James Prendeville, *Photographic Facsimiles of the Antique Gems Formerly Possessed by the Late Prince Poniatowski, accompanied by a description and poetical illustrations of each subject, Vol. 2* (London, 1859), p. 189: No 340: 'Hercules seizing the tripod of the Priestess of Delphi'.
14. Thucydides, *Peloponnesian War* 4, 133, 2.
15. Thucydides, 2, 2, 1.

16. Pausanias, 2, 17, 7; 3, 5, 6.
17. Plato, *Republic* 5, 451c–457b; trans. Grube, revised by Reeve.
18. *Laws*, 7.805d.
19. Plato, *Republic* 5, 457b–466d.
20. See CCW Taylor, *The Role Of Women In Plato's Republic*.
21. Plato, *op. cit.* 5, 459d-e.
22. Diogenes Laërtius 3, 46.
23. Plato, *Laws* 8, 805 c-d; see also 7, 788a-8, 842a; 7, 904d-806c.
24. Plato, *Timaeus* 90e.
25. Aristotle, *Poetics* 6, 1254b12
26. Aristotle, *Generation of Animals*. See Smith, Nicholas D. "Plato and Aristotle on the Nature of Women". *Journal of the History of Philosophy*. 21 (4): 467–478. 1983
27. Aristotle, *Generation of Animals* 775a 13-21
28. Aristotle, *Politics* 2, 1269h, 32
29. Aristotle, *Politics* 2, 1254b 16-25. This so impressed Thomas Aquinas in the thirteenth century that he used it as the basis for his argument against women being priests, an argument that continues to impress the Catholic Church into the twenty-first century. See, for example, *Summa Theologiae*, q.92, a.1, Reply to Objection 2: 'Subjection is twofold. One is servile, by virtue of which a superior makes use of a subject for his own benefit; and this kind of subjection began after sin. There is another kind of subjection which is called economic or civil, whereby the superior makes use of his subjects for their own benefit and good; and this kind of subjection existed even before sin. For good order would have been wanting in the human family if some were not governed by others wiser than themselves. So by such a kind of subjection woman is naturally subject to man, because in man the discretion of reason predominates'. Translation at http://www.aquinasonline.com/Questions/women.html
30. Aristotle, *History of Animals* 9, 1
31. See Aristotle, *Politics* 1259a41; 1245b1; 1260a11; *Generation of Animals* 737a. 28; *Politics,* 1259b. 1, 1260a. 24.
32. Aristotle, *History of Animals*, 608b. 1–14.
33. Garland, *Deformity and Disfigurement*.
34. Aristotle, *Generation of Animals* 6, 728a.
35. Aristotle, *Politics* 1277b

Chapter Fourteen

1. Homer, *Odyssey*, 11. 489–91. Aeaea: Hesiod, *Catalogues of Women* Fragment 46 (from Scholiast on Apollonius Rhodius 3. 311); Apollonius after Hesiod, says that Circe came to Tyrrhenia on the chariot of Helios. And he called it Hesperian, because it lies towards the west. Apollonius Rhodius, *Argonautica* 3. 311 ff : 'I myself was whirled along it in the chariot of my father Helios (the Sun), when he took my sister Circe to the Western Land and we reached the coast of Tyrrhenia, where she lives, far, far indeed from Colchis." (Trans Rieu). Valerius Flaccus, *Argonautica* 7. 120 ff (trans. Mozley): 'Circe was borne away (from the land of Colchis) by winged Dragons.'
2. Pausanias 10, 28, 71; 9, 5, 8; 4, 33, 7.
3. *Aeneid*, 6, 119–123.
4. *Odyssey*, 19, 562–9; 10, 504ff; 19, 562–9; 9, 62–66; 24,1ff; for Circe generally see 10, 133–405 and 569–74 as well.
5. *Iliad*, 23, 62–76; *Odyssey* 4. 560 ff.
6. *Works & Days*, 121ff; *Theogony*, 720ff.
7. *Olympian* 2, 56-80; *Fragment* 114 OCT; *Fragment* 127 OCT
8. F534-6 *TrGF; Oedipus* 530-526; *Persae*, 607-99.

9. Herodotus, *Histories*, 5.92

10. Empedocles F101 Wright (1981); F111 DK (Diogenes Laërtius 8.59).

11. *Phaedo* 81B-D; 111C ff; *Gorgias* 493A; 526C; *Cratylus* 400C; *Phaedrus* 250C. See also *Timaeus* 30ff.

12. *Republic* 613E-621D, For the *katabasis* discovered on papyrus with its classification of sinners probably dating from Hellenistic times see Merkelbach (1951) 2ff and Treu (1954) 24ff.

13. Pythagoreanism: Ovid, *Metamorphoses* 15, 75ff; Orpheus *katabasis*, *Ibid*. 10.

14. Homer, *Iliad*, 23, 71.

15. Aristophanes, *Ecclesiazusae* 1030ff; 536–8; *Lysistrata* 612–3.

16. Sophocles, *Electra*, 792.

17. Ioulis on Keos, late fifth century BCE, Ditt. Syll. 1218.

18. Homer, *op. cit.* 22, 405ff.

19. Homer, *op. cit.* 24, 714f.

Chapter Fifteen

1. Hesiod, *Catalogue of Women* Fragment 46 (from *Scholiast on Apollonius Rhodius* 3. 311); Apollonius Rhodius, *Argonautica* 3, 311 ff; Valerius Flaccus, *Argonautica* 7, 120 ff.

2. Homer, *Odyssey* 10, 133-405; 569-574. See also Hesiod, *Theogony* 956 ff; Pseudo-Apollodorus, *Bibliotheca* 1, 80; Apollonius Rhodius, *Argonautica* 4. 584 ff; Diodorus Siculus, *Library of History* 4, 45, 1.

3. Homer, *Odyssey* 8, 447 ff: *ibid* 9, 23 ff.

4. Ptolemy Hephaestion, *New History* Book 4 (summary from Photius, *Myriobiblon* 190) (trans. Pearse) (Greek mythographer first to second CE); Pseudo-Hyginus, *Fabulae* 127.

5. According to Lycophron's *Alexandra* (808) and John Tzetzes' scholia on the poem (795–808).

6. Parthenius, a Greek mythographer from the first century BCE tells us about Calchos in his *Love Romances* 12 (trans. Gaselee).

7. Ovid, *Metamorphoses* 14. 308 ff; Virgil, *Aeneid* 7, 187 ff.

8. Apollonius Rhodius 3, 475-80; 533; 1026-62; 1191-1224; 1246-67; 4, 123-66; 445-81; 1636-91.

9. Diodorus Siculus, 4, 50, 6 ; see also Diodorus 4, 45, 1; 4, 54, 5; Statius, *Thebaid* 4, 536 ff.

10. Euripides, *Medea* 112f.

11. As noted in a scholium to Pindar's Olympian Ode 13, 74; cf. Pausanias 23, 10-11.

12. As noted in the scholium to *Medea* 264.

13. Hyginus *Fabulae* 25; Ovid *Metamorphoses* 7, 391ff; Seneca *Medea*; *Bibliotheca* 1, 9, 28 favours Euripides' version of events, but also records the variant that the Corinthians killed Medea's children in retaliation for her crimes.

14. Pausanias 2, 3, 6–11

15. Pythagoreanism *Metamorphoses* 15, 75ff; Orpheus' *katabasis*, *ibid* 10; Medea's witchcraft *ibid* 7.159-351 and *Heroides* 6, 83-94; *Fasti* 2, 572-583: the rites of Tacita; *Amores* 3,7, 27-36, 73-84: Circean witchcraft; Dipsas the witch *ibid* 1,8, 1-20, 105-14. Quintilian (10, 1, 98) praises his lost tragedy, *Medea*; see also Tacitus *Dialogus* 12.

16. Ovid *Heroides* 6, 83–94.

17. *Idem. Metamorphoses* 7, 1–351. For Ovid's *Medea* see Quintilian 10, 1, 98; Quintilian found it rather indulgent.

18. Seneca, *Medea* 6-23; 670–843.

19. Xenophon, *Memorabilia* 2, 6, 10–13.

20. For this see Horsfall (1991) 206. For the *katabasis* discovered on papyrus with its classification of sinners probably dating from Hellenistic times see Merkelbach (1951) 2ff and Treu (1954) 24ff.

21. *Idyll* 2; Virgil *Aeneid* 4, 300ff.

22. *Bibliotheca* 2, 5, 1; 1, 9, 26.

23. Hesiod, *op. cit.* 270 ff (trans. Evelyn-White).

24. Plutarch, *On Deisidaemonia; Moralia* 139a; *Alexander* 77; 2; *Moralia* 109b-d. *Cimon* 6; *Moralia* 555c. See also *Moralia* 560e-f. Evil eye: *op. cit* 680c-683b. Pericles: *idem, Pericles* 38.
25. Phlegon of Tralles, *Mirabilia* 1. The story forms the basis of Goethe's *Bride of Corinth*.
26. Cicero *De Divinatione* 1.96.
27. See Lycophron, *Alexandra* 840; Pseudo-Hyginus, *Preface*; Pseudo-Hyginus, *Astronomica* 2, 12; Ovid, *Metamorphoses* 4. 770 ff; Nonnus, *Dionysiaca* 24, 270 ff.
28. Aeschylus, *Prometheus Bound* 788 ff (trans. Weir Smyth).
29. Helen: Homer, *op. cit.* 4, 219-439.
30. Antiphon 1, 14-20. For Lycophron see Horsfall, *Virgil and the Poetry of Explanations* p. 206. Theocritus *Idyll* 2. Diodorus Siculus 4.36, 38.
31. Apollodorus *Bibliotheca* 2, 5, 1; 1, 9, 26.
32. Plutarch, *Moralia* 138a-146a; *idem, de Superstitione*. Pliny, *NH* 28, 47 and 104; Plato *Laws* 7, 808d. Translation is by T.J. Saunders. Mormo: Plato, *Crito* 46c; Lucian, *Vera Historia* 139; Empusa: Aristophanes, *Frogs* 285-295; Gello: Sappho *frag* 178; Diodorus Siculus 20, 41.
33. *CIL* 8, 12507; *PGM* 36, 283-294; 1, 83-87; 1, 167-168; 32. Sophia and Gorgonia *SGD* # 151
34. Ziebarth 24, 1-4, pp. 1042ff.
35. *PGM* 4, 296-466.
36. *SGD* 161.
37. Pliny *NH* 28, 256.
38. *SGD* 99.
39. Aristophanes, *Wasps* 946-8.
40. Cicero, *Brutus* 217.
41. Ovid, *Fasti* 2, 57182.
42. *SGD* 48.
43. *DTA* 34.
44. *SGD* 24-9.
45. Homer Epigram 14 at Life of Homer 32 = Hesiod F302 MW.
46. Plato, *Charmides* 155e5-8.
47. *Republic* 426b 1-2
48. Pindar, *Pythian Ode* 3, 47-53
49. Plutarch *Moralia* 680c–683b (Table Talk 7).
50. Menander F313 Korte.

Chapter Sixteen

1. Plutarch, *On Talkativeness, Moralia* 505E. See also Pausanias, *Description of Greece* 1, 23, 1–2 and Athenaeus, *Deipnosophistae* 13, 596f.
2. Jerome, *Beginning of the Consuls of the Romans*. For a fuller description of women's medicine see Chrystal, *In Bed with the Ancient Greeks* chapter 13 from which much of this chapter is adapted.
3. Hippocrates, *Places in Man* 47. This section adapted from chapter seven of my *Women in Ancient Rome*.
4. Hippocrates, *Diseases of Women* 1, 1.
5. Hippocrates, *Glands* 16.
6. *Frag.* A81, B65, B67.
7. See King, *Once upon a Text*.
8. See *Maines, The Technology of Orgasm*.
9. *Timaeus* 91a-c.
10. Hippocrates, *On Virgins* 8, 466-70
11. See Jackson, *Doctors and Diseases in the Roman Empire* pp. 89-94 for uterine disorders.
12. Celsus, *De Medicina* 7, 29, 7

13. Soranus *Gynaecology* 4, 2.
14. Celsus, *op cit* 7, 29, 4-5; Soranus, *Gynaecology* 4, 12
15. Celsus, *op.cit.* 4, 28; Galen *Natura Mulierum* 109; *Epidemics* 3, 7; Martial 1, 65, 4; 7, 71
16. Hesiod, *Works and Days* 582-588
17. Aristotle, *Problems* 877a-877b
18. Herodas, *A Quiet Chat, Mime* 6, 86
19. Aristophanes *Lysistrata* 107ff; translated by George Theodoridis.
20. Artemidorus, *Oneirocritica* 1, 78
21. *Op. cit.* 1, 80.
22. *Op. cit.* 1, 79.
23. Hippocrates, *Epidemics* 6, 8, 32

Glossary of Greek terms

agoge—junior military school in Sparta
andron—men's quarters in an Athenian house
archon—the chief magistrate in various Greek city states
dodekatheon (Δωδεκάθεον)—the top twelve Olympian gods
ékthesis—exposure of abnormal babies or unwanted girls
epikleros—heiress
gynaikon or *gynaikonitis*—women's quarters in an Athenian house
hetaira—high class, educated and socially sophisticated prostitute
katedeseis—binding spell
kolossoi—voodoo dolls
kyrios—a woman's legal guardian
medimnos—a measure of dry grain
oikos—the household, the house, the family unit
periamma—amulet
periapton—amulet
pharmaka—pharmaceutical drugs; spell; poison
pharmakis—witch, sorceress
philtrum—love potion
polis—a city state; the basic ancient Greek political entity
rhizotomos—root-cutter; quack
thiasos—school where girls received education and attention from female teachers
venefica—witch, sorceress
veneficium—poisoning

Primary Sources Cited

Aelian (*c.* 175–*c.* 235 CE), *Varia Historia*
Aeschylus (*c.* 525–*c.* 456/455 BCE), *Agamemnon; Prometheus Bound; Libation Bearers; Eumenides*
Aeschines (389–314 BCE), *On the Embassy*
Alexis, ap. Athen. (*c.* 375–*c.* 275 BCE)
Amphis (fourth century BCE)
Anaxandrides, an Athenian middle comic poet. *Fl.* 376 BCE
Anonymous, (second century BCE), *Tractatus De Mulieribus Claris In Bello*
Antipater of Thessaloniki (first century BCE)
Antiphon (480–411 BCE), *Against the Grandmother for Poisoning*
Antoninus Liberalis (*fl.* between 100 and 300 CE), *Metamorphoses*
Apollodorus (first or second century CE), *Bibliotheca; Epitome; Against Neaera*
Apollonius Rhodius (b. 295 CE), *Argonautica*
Apuleius (late second century CE), *Florida*
Archilochus *(c. 680 – c. 645* BCE*)* Greek lyric poet
Aristophanes (*c.* 446–*c.* 386 BCE), *Thesmophoriazusae; Lysistrata; Ecclesiazusae; Frogs; Clouds; Peace; Birds; Plutus*
Aristotle (385–322 BCE), *Politics, Historia Animalium;The Dream of Eudemus; Poetics; Generation of Animals*
Arrian, *Indica* (*c.* 95–175 CE), *Anabasis Alexandri; De Rebus Successorum Alexandri*
Artemidorus, *Oneirocritica*
Athenaeus of Naucratis (*fl.* late second century CE), *Deipnosophistae*
Augustine (354–430 CE), *City of God*
Bacchylides (*fl.* fifth century BCE)
Boccaccio, *Famous Women*
Caesar, Julius (100–44 BCE), *De Bello Gallico*
Carcinus II (fourth century BCE tragic poet), *Semele*
Celsus (*c.* 25 BCE–*c.* 50 CE), *De Medicina*
Cicero (106–43 BC), *De Divitatione; De Officiis; De Inventione; De Finibus; De Natura Deorum; Brutus*
CIL—*Corpus Inscriptionum Latinarum,* Berlin 1863
Clement of Alexandria (*c.* 150–*c.* 215 CE), *Stromata*
Ctesias (fifth century BCE), *Persica*
Curtius Rufus (first century CE), *Historiae Alexandri Magni*
Dante, *Inferno*
Demosthenes, *Apollodorus Against Neaera*
Diodorus Siculus (*fl.* 60–30 BCE), *Bibliotheca Historica*
Diogenes Laërtius (*fl.* third century CE), *Lives and Opinions of Eminent Philosophers*
Eubulus, ap. Athen. (*fl.* 370 BCE), *Chrysilla*
Euripides (*c.* 480–406 BCE), *Hippolytus; Andromache; Alcestis; Medea; Electra; Bacchae; Ion;*

Iphigenia in Tauris; Trojan Women; Hippolytus; Iphigenia in Aulis; Heracleidae; Orestes; Helen
Greek Anthology

Galen (*c.* 130 CE–*c.* 210 CE) *Natura Mulierum.; Commentaries on Hippocrates'* Epidemics

Herodas, *A Quiet Chat; the author of short mimes in verse; third century BC.*

Herodotus (484–425 BCE), *Histories*

Hesiod (*fl.* 750–650 BCE, *Works and Days; Catalogue of Women* or *Ehoiai; Theogeny*

Hippias of Elis (late fifth century BC), a Greek sophist

Hippocrates, (460–370 BCE) *On Virgins; Epidemics; Glands; Places in Man; Diseases of Women*

Hipponax (541–487 BCE), iambic poet

Homer (*c.* 850 BCE), *Odyssey; Iliad*

Hyginus (*c.* 64 BCE–17 CE), *Fabulae*

Hyperides (390–322 BCE), Athenian speechwriter

Iamblichus (*c.* 245–*c.* 325 CE) *Life of Pythagoras*

Isaeus (*fl.* early fourth century BCE), Attic orator

Jordanes (sixth century CE), *De Origine Actibusque Getarum*

Jerome (*c.* 347–420 CE), *Beginning of the Consuls of the Romans*

Josephus (37–*c.* 100 CE), *Against Apion*

Justin (second century CE), Philippic History of Pompeius Trogus

Lucian (*c.* 125–*c.* 180 CE), *In Praise of a Fly; Vera Historia; A Portrait Study*

Lycophron (third century BCE), *Alexandra*

Lysias, (445–380 BCE) Attic orator, *On the Murder of Eratosthenes*

Menander (*c.* 342/41–*c.* 290 BCE), *Epitrepontes; Synkrisis*

Metz Epitome, Liber de Morte Alexandri Magni Testamentumque

Milton, John, *Lycidas*

Musonius Rufus (first century CE), Stoic philosopher

Nepos, Cornelius (*c.* 110–*c.* 25 BCE), *Cimon*

Nonnus, (fifth century CE), *Dionysiaca*

Orphic Hymn

Ovid (43 BCE–17 CE), *Metamorphoses; Remedia Amoris; Ibis; Heroides; Fasti; Amores; Ars Amatoria*

Palatine Anthology—the collection of Greek poems and epigrams discovered in 1606 in the Palatine Library in Heidelberg. It comprises material from the seventh century BCE to 600 CE, and later formed the main part of the *Greek Anthology.*

Panathenaic Victor Lists (second century BCE)

Parthenius (first century BCE; d. 14 CE), *Erotica Pathemata*

Pausanias (*c.* 110–*c.* 180 CE), *Description of Greece*

PGM = K. Preisendanz, *Papyri Graecae Magicae,* Leipzig 1928

Philostratus *Imagines*

Phlegon of Tralles (second century CE), *Mirabilia*

Photius, *Bibliotheca/ Myriobiblon* ninth century work of Byzantine Patriarch of Constantinople

Pindar (*c.* 522–*c.* 443 BCE), *Pythian Ode; Hymn to Fates* ; *Olympian Ode*

Plato (428–348 BCE), *Phaedo; Halcyon; Epigrams; Theaetetus; Laws; Crito, Republic; Charmides; Menexenus; Phaedrus; Cratylus; Timaeus; Gorgias*

Pliny the Elder (23–79 CE), *Historia Naturalis*

Plutarch (*c.* 45-125 CE), *Moralia; Cimon; Agis, Cleomenes, Aratus; Aristides; Pyrrhus; Lycurgus; Alcibiades, Lysander; Agesilaus; Alexander; Eumenes; Pyrrhus; Demetrius; Coniugalia Praecepta; De Defectu Oraculorum; De Superstitione; On Deisidaemonia; Pericles; On the Bravery of Women; On Talkativeness*

Polyaenus (second century CE), *Strategems*

Polybius (*c.* 200–*c.* 118 BCE) Greek historian, *The Histories*

Porphyry (*c.* 234–*c.* 305 CE), *Life of Pythagoras*

Propertius (50–45 BC-15 BCE), *Elegies*

Pseudo-Apollodorus (first or second century CE), *Bibliotheca*

Pseudo-Diogenes (died after 1095), *Epistles*

Pseudo-Hyginus (first century CE), *Fabulae*

Ptolemy Hephaestion (356–324 BCE), *New History*

Quintilian (*c.* 35–*c.* 100 CE), *Institutio Oratoria*

Quintus Smyrnaeus (fourth century CE), *Fall of Troy*

Sappho (630–612–*c.* 570 BCE)

Scholiast on Homer, *Iliad*

Scholiast on Pindar

Scholion to *Argonautica*

Semonides (seventh century BCE), *Types of Women*

Seneca (*c.* 4 BCE–65 CE), *Medea*; *Trojan Women*

Sophocles (*c.* 497–406 BCE), *Ajax*, *Antigone*; *Tereus*; *Trachiniae*

Soranus (*fl.* 100 CE) *Gynaecology*

Statius (*c.* 45–*c.* 96 CE), *Thebaid*

Stobaeus: Joannes Stobaeus (*fl.* fifth century CE), from Stobi in Macedonia

Strabo (64 BCE–*c.* 24 CE), *Geography*

Suda, a huge tenth century Byzantine encyclopedia of the ancient Mediterranean world

Tacitus (*c.* 56–117 CE), *Dialogus*

Theocritus (*fl. c.* 270 BCE), *Idylls*

Theognis (550 BCE), *On Marriage*

Theophrastus, (*c.* 371–*c.* 287 BCE), *Characters*; *De Odoribus*

Theopompus of Chios (*c.* 380–*c.* 315 BCE), *Histories*

Thucydides (460–395 BCE), *History of the Peloponnesian War*

Tractatus de Mulieribus

Valerius Flaccus (d. 90 CE), *Argonautica*

Virgil (70–19 BCE), *Aeneid*

Xenophon (*fl.* 371 BCE). *Oeconomicus; Memorabilia; Hellenica; Anabasis; Symposium; Cyropaedia; Moralia: On the Control of Anger; Constitution of the Spartans; Minor Works*

Abbreviations

AJP—American Jnl of Philology
Anc Soc—Ancient Society (Louvain)
BHM—Bulletin of the History of Medicine
BICS—Bulletin of the Institute of Classical Studies
C&M—Classica et Mediaevalia
CB—Classical Bulletin
CEG—P. A. Hansen, Carmina Epigraphica Graeca, Berlin 1983
CJ—Classical Journal
CIL—Corpus Inscriptionum Latinarum, Berlin 1863
CA News—Classical Association News
CP—Classical Philology
CQ—Classical Quarterly
CR—Classical Review
CW—Classical World
EMC—Echos du Monde Classique
G&R—Greece and Rome
GRBS—Greek, Roman and Byzantine Studies
HN—Historia Naturalis, Pliny the Elder
HSCP—Harvard Studies in Classical Philology
JHS—Journal of Hellenic Studies
JRS—Journal of Roman Studies
JWAG—Journal of the Walters Art Gallery
NH - Pliny the Elder, *Natural History*
PBSR—Papers of the British School at Rome
PCPS—Proceedings of the Cambridge Philosophical Society
PGM—K. Preisendanz, Papyri Graecae Magicae, Leipzig 1928.
P. Oxy—The Oxyrhynchus Papyrus
PSI—Papyri Greci e latini: Societa italiana per la Ricerca dei Papiri Greci e Latini in Egitto
RBPH—La Revue Belge de Philologie et d'Histoire
SO—Symbolae Osloensis
SHPBBS—Studies in History & Philosophy of Biological & Biomedical Sciences
TAPA—Transactions of the Proceedings of the American Philological Asscn
WHO—ICD: International Classification of Diseases (10 version, Geneva 2010)
WS—Wiener Studien

Bibliography

Aguirre, C. M., 'Expressions of Love and Sexual Union in Hesiod's Catalogue of Women', *CFC (G):
Estudios griegos e indoeuropeos 192, 15 19-25* (2005), 19–25

Alden, M., Ancient Greek Dress, *Costume* 37 (2003)

Alexiou, M., *The Ritual Lament in Greek Tradition* (New York, 2002)

Allen, (Sister) P., *The Concept of Woman: the Aristotelian Revolution, 750 BC–AD 1250* (Montreal, 1985)

American Psychiatric Association, *Diagnostic and Statistical Manual of Mental Disorders IV* (Arlington,
1994)

Amunsden, D. W., The Age of Menarche in Classical Greece and Rome, *Human Biology* 42, (1970), 79–86

Anderson, J. E. A., Two Sides to Every Story: A Tale of Love and Hate on a Lakonian Stele, *ΣPARTA:
Journal of Ancient Spartan and Greek History* 3

Anderson, Ø., The Widows, the City, and Thucydides, *SO* 62 (1987), 33–50

Androutsos, G., Hermaphroditism in Greek and Roman Antiquity, *Hormones* 5 (2006),214–217

Angel, J. L., 'The Length of Life in Ancient Greece', *Journal of Gerontology* 2 (1947), 18–24

Ankerloo, B., *Witchcraft and Magic in Europe Vol 2: Ancient Greece and Rome* (London, 1998)

Annas, J., 'Plato's Republic and Feminism', in Osborne (ed), *Woman in Western Thought*, 24–33.

Archer, L. J., (ed.) *Women in Ancient Societies: An Illusion of the Night* (London, 1994);
Aristophanes and Menander: *Women in Power; Wealth; The Malcontent; The Woman from Samos*
(London, 1994)

Arkins, B., 'Sexuality in Fifth-Century Athens', *Classics Ireland* 1 (1994)

Arnott, W. G., *Menander, Plautus and Terence* (Oxford, 1975)

Arthur, M. B., 'Early Greece: The Origins of the Western Attitude toward Women', in Peradotto, J.,
Women in the Ancient World: The Arethusa Papers, (Albany, 1984), 7–58

Ashari, D., 'Laws of Inheritance, Distribution of Land and Political Constitutions in Ancient Greece',
Historia: Zeitschrift für Alte Geschichte 12 (1963), 1–21

Augoustakis, A., *Motherhood and the Other: Fashioning Female Power in Flavian Epic* (Oxford, 2010)

Ault, B. A., *Ancient Greek Houses and Households: Chronological, Regional, and Social Diversity*
(Philadelphia, 2005)

Austin, N., *Helen of Troy and Her Shameless Phantom* (Ithaca NY, 1994)

Badian, E., 'ROXANE,' Encyclopædia Iranica, online edition, 2015, www.iranicaonline.org/articles/
roxane (accessed on 31 January 2016)

Bahn, P. G., *Ancient Obscenities: Or Things You Shouldn't Know About the History of Mankind* (London,
2003)

Bahrani, Z., *Women of Babylon: Gender and Representation in Ancient Mesopotamia* (London, 2001)

Baird, J., *Ancient Graffiti in Context* (London, 2010)

Barber, E. W., *Women's Work: The First 20,000 Years—Women, Cloth and Society in Early Times*
(London, 1996)

Bardis, P. D., 'Selected Aspects of Sex Life in Ancient Greece', *Indian Journal of Social Research* 7 (1966), 57–63

Barras, V., Galen's Psychiatry in *Hamanaka*, pp. 3–8

Beard, M., *Pompeii: The Life of a Roman Town* (London, 2008)
"With this body I thee worship': Sacred Prostitution in Antiquity' in Wyke, M. *Gender and the Body
in the Ancient Mediterranean*, 56–79 (Oxford)

Beard M. R., *Woman as Force in History: a Study in Traditions and Realities* (1946)
  On Understanding Women (1931)
Bell, L. A., *Visions of Women: Being A Fascinating Anthology With Analysis Of Philosophers' Views Of Women From Ancient To Modern Times* (London, 2003)
Bell, R., *The Oxford Handbook of Childhood and Education in the Classical World* (Oxford, 2014)
Bell, R. E., *Women of Classical Mythology: A Biographical Dictionary* (Oxford, 1993)
  'Cassandra in the Classical World' in Bell, *Women in Classical Mythology*
Bertman, S., *The Conflict of Generations in Ancient Greece and Rome* (Amsterdam, 1976)
Betz, H. D., *Greek Magical Papyri in Translation 2/e* (Chicago 1997)
Bicknell, P., 'The Witch Aglaonice and Dark Lunar Eclipses in the Second and First Centuries BC', *Journal of the British Astronomical Association* 93, 160–163
Blair, E., *Plato's Dialectic on Woman: Equal, Therefore Inferior* (London, 2012)
Blake-Reed, J. S., *Manchester Guardian*, 23 February 1922
Blanshard, A. J. L., (2010) 'Roman Vice', in *Sex: Vice and Love from Antiquity to Modernity* (Oxford), 1-88.
Bloch, E., 'Sex Between Men and Boys in Classical Greece: Was it Education for Citizenship or Child Abuse?', *Journal of Men's Studies* (2001)
Blok, J., 'Virtual Voices: Towards a Choreography of Women's Speech in Classical Athens' in André Lardinois (ed) *Making Silence Speak: Women's Speech in Ancient Greece* (Princeton, 2001), 95–116
  The Appointment of Priests in Attic Gene. *Zeitschrift für Papyrologie und Epigraphik* 169 (2008), 95–121
  (ed) *Sexual Asymmetry: Studies in Ancient Society* (Amsterdam, 1987)
Blondell, R., *Ancient Sexuality: New Essays* (Columbus OH forthcoming) (ed.) *Women on the Edge: Four Plays by Euripides* (New York, 1999)
Bluestone, N. H., *Women and the Ideal Society: Plato's Republic and Modern Myths of Gender* (Massachusetts, 1988)
Blundell, S., *The Sacred and the Feminine in Ancient Greece* (London, 1998)
  Women in Ancient Greece, (Cambridge MA, 1995)
Blyth, J. M., 'Women in the Military: Scholastic Argument and Medieval Images of Female Warriors', *History of Political Thought* 22 (2001), also at www.imprint.co.uk/hpt/179.pdf
Bodel, J., *Epigraphic Evidence: Ancient History from Inscriptions* (London, 2001)
Boehringer, S., *L'Homosexualite Feminine dans l'Antiquite Greque et Romain* (Paris, 2007)
  Homosexualite: Aimer en Grece et Rome (Paris, 2010)
  'Sex, Lies and (Video) Trap: The Illusion of Sexual Identity in Lucian's Dialogues of the Courtesans' in Blondell, *Ancient Sex Des Femmes en Action: L'individu et la Fonction en Grèce Antique* (Athens, 2013)
  'Female Homoeroticism', in Hubbard, T.K. *A Companion to Greek and Roman Sexualities* (Chichester, 2014), 150-163
Bosman, P., (ed) *Mania: Madness in the Greco-Roman World* (Pretoria, 2009)
Boswell, J., *The Kindness of Strangers: The Abandonment of Children in Western Europe from Antiquity to the Renaissance*, (New York, 1998)
Bouvrie, S., des *Women in Greek Tragedy* (Oslo, 1990)
Bowden, H., *Classical Athens and the Delphic Oracle: Divination and Democracy* (Cambridge, 2005)
Bowman, L., 'Nossis, Sappho and Hellenistic Poetry', *Ramus* 27 (1998), 39–59
Boys-Stones, G., *The Oxford Handbook of Hellenic Studies* (Oxford, 2009)
Brashear, W. M., 'The Greek Magical Papyri: 'Voces Magicae', *Aufstieg und Niedergang der Römischen Welt* II, 18 (1995), 34–35
Bremmer, J., 'Greek Pederasty and Modern Homosexuality', in Bremmer, *From Sappho to De Sade*, 1–14
  From Sappho to De Sade: Moments in the History of Sexuality (London, 1991)
Brisson, C., *Sexual Ambivalence: Androgyny and Hermaphroditism in Graeco-Roman Antiquity* (Berkeley, 2002)
Brisson, L., 'Women in Plato's Republic', *Etudes Platoniciennes* 9 (2012), 129-136
Brooten, B. J., *Love between Women: Early Christian Responses to Female Homoeroticism* (Chicago, 1996)
  'Lesbian Historiography before the Name?' *GLQ: A Jnl of Lesbian and Gay Studies* 4 (1998), 606-630
Brosius, M., *Women in Ancient Persia, 559–331 BC* (Oxford, 1996)
Brown, P. G. M., 'Love and Marriage in Greek New Comedy', *CQ* 43 (1993) 189-205
Brule, P., *Women of Ancient Greece* (Edinburgh, 2003)
Brumfeld, A., 'Aporetta: Verbal and Ritual Obscenity in the Cults of Ancient Women', in Hagg, R. (ed), *The Role of Religion in the Early Greek polis*, 67-74 (Stockholm, 1996)

Budin, S., *The Myth of Sacred Prostitution in Antiquity* (Cambridge, 2008)

Buis, E. J., 'Mythology' in *Encyclopedia of Rape*, (ed) Merril D. Smith. (Westport, 2004), 132–134

Bunchan, B., *Women in Plato's Political Theory* (New York, 1999)

Bushnell, R. W., (ed), *A Companion to Tragedy*, (Chichester, 2005)

Butrica, J. L., 'Some Myths and Anomalies in the Study of Roman Sexuality', in *Same-Sex Desire and Love in Greco-Roman Antiquity*, 218, 224

Bryk, F., *Circumcision in Man and Woman: Its History, Psychology and Ethnology* (Honolulu, 2001)

Cahill, J., *Her Kind: Stories of Women from Greek Mythology* (Peterborough, Ont., 1995)

Calame, C., *The Poetics of Eros in Ancient Greece* (Princeton, 2013)

Caldwell, J. M., *Religion and Sexual Violence in Late Greco-Roman Antiquity*. (PhD thesis, Syracuse University, 2003)

Calimach, A., *Lovers' Legends: The Gay Greek Myths* (New Rochelle, 2002)

Cameron, A., (ed) *Images of Women in Antiquity* (London, 1983)

    'Love (and Marriage) Between Women', *GRBS* 39 (1998), 137-156

Cantarella, E., 'Gender, Sexuality, and Law' in Gagarin, M. *The Cambridge Companion to Ancient Greek Law* (Cambridge, 2011) 236–253

    Bisexuality in the Ancient World (London, 2002)

    Pandora's Daughters: The Role and Status of Women in Greek and Roman Antiquity (London, 1987)

Carey, C., 'Apollodoros' Mother: The Wives of Enfranchised Aliens' in Athens *CQ*41 (1991), 84–89

Carney, E. D., *Olympias: Mother of Alexander the Great* (London, 2006)

    'Women and Dunasteia in Caria', *AJP* 126 (2005), 65–91

    Women and Monarchy in Macedonia, (Norman OK, 2000)

Carpenter, T. A., (ed) *Masks of Dionysus* (Ithaca NY, 1993)

Carroll, M., *Woman in All Ages and in All Countries* Vol. 1 1907. (Reprint. London: Forgotten Books, 2013)

Carson, A., 'Putting Her in Her Place: Woman, Dirt, and Desire', in Halperin, (ed.), *Before Sexuality: The Construction of Erotic Experience in the Ancient Greek World* (Princeton, 1990), 135–69

Cartledge, P., 'Alexandria the Great', *History Today* 59 (2009)

    The Spartans: An Epic History, 2nd edition (2003)

    The Greeks. A Portrait of Self and Others (Oxford, 1993)

    'Engendering History: Men *v.* Women' in Cartledge, *The Greeks: A Portrait of Self and Others* (Oxford, 1993)

    'Spartan Wives: Liberation or License?', *CQ* 31 (1981)

Chandezon, C., 'Dream Interpretation, Physiognomy, Body Divination', in Hubbard (2014), 297–313

Chrystal, P., *In Bed with the Ancient Greeks: Sex and Sexuality in Ancient Greece* (Stroud, 2016)

    Ancient Greece in 100 Facts (Stroud, 2017)

    Record Keeping and Communication in Ancient Rome (Stroud, 2017)

    Women at War in Ancient Greece and Rome (Barnsley, 2017)

    Roman Women: The Women Who Infuenced the History of Rome (Stroud, 2015)

    In Bed with the Romans: Sex and Sexuality in Ancient Rome (Stroud, 2015)

    Women in Ancient Rome (Stroud, 2014)

    Differences in Attitude to Women as Reflected in the Work of Catullus, Propertius, the Corpus Tibullianum, Horace and Ovid (MPhil thesis, University of Southampton, 1982)

Chugg, A. M., *Alexander's Lovers*, 2nd edition (2012)

Cilliers, L., *Mental Illness in the Greco-Roman Era* in Bosman (2009), 130–140

Clark, G., *Women in the Ancient World* (Oxford, 1989)

Clauss, J. J., (ed), *Medea: Essays on Medea in Myth, Literature, Philosophy and Art* (Princeton, 1997)

Cohen, B., 'Exposing the Female Breast of Clothes in Classical Sculpture' in A. G. Koloski-Ostrow (ed), *Naked Truths. Women, Sexuality and Gender in Classical Art and Archaeology*, (London, 1997), 66–92

    (ed) *The Distaff Side: Representing the Female in* Homer's *Odyssey* (Oxford, 1995)

Cohen, D., *Law, Sexuality, and Society: The Enforcement of Morals in Classical Athens* (Cambridge, 1991)

    'Seclusion, Separation and the Status of Women' in McAuslan, I., *Women in Antiquity*, 134–145

    'Law, Society and Homosexuality in Classical Athens' in Golden (ed) *Sex and Difference in Ancient Greece and Rome*

    'Consent and Sexual Relations in Classical Athens', in Laiou, A. E. (ed), *Consent and Coercion to Sex and Marriage inAncient Societies*, (Washington DC 1993), 5–16

Cohen, E. E., 'Sexual Abuse and Sexual Rights: Slaves' Erotic Experience at Athens and Rome' in Hubbard (2014), 184f

'Whoring Under Contract: The Legal Context of Prostitution in Fourth-Century Athens', in Hunter, V., (ed.) *Law and Social Status in Classical Athens* (Oxford, 2000) 113–47

'Written Contracts of Prostitution in Fourth-century Athens', in Triantaphyllopoulos, M.I (Komotini, 2000) 109-22

Cohen, I. M., 'The Hesiodic Catalogue of Women and Megalai Ehoiai', *Phoenix* 40 (1986), 127–42

'Traditional Language and the Women in the Hesiodic Catalogue of Women', *Studia Classica Israelica* 10 (1989), 12–27

Colin, G., *Rome et la Grece de 200 a 146 BC avant JC* (Paris, 1905).

'Luxe Oriental et Parfums Masculins dans la Rome Alexandrine', *RBPH 33* (1935), 5–19

Collins, D., (ed) *Magic in the Ancient Greek World* (Oxford, 2008)

Colton, R. E., Juvenal and Martial on Women who Ape Greek Ways, *CB* 50 (1973), 42–44

Connelly, J. B., *Portrait of a Priestess: Women and Ritual in Ancient Greece* (Princeton, 2009)

Cooper, K., *The Virgin and the Bride: Idealized Womanhood in Late Antiquity* (Cambridge MA, 1996)

Corbeil, A., *Sexing the World: Grammatical Gender and Biological Sex in Ancient Rome* (Princeton NJ, 2015)

Corbier, M., 'Male Power and Legitimacy through Women', in Hawley, (1995), 178–93

'Child Exposure and Abandonment', in Dixon ed., *Childhood, Class and Kin in the Roman World* (London, 2001) 52–73

Cox, C. A., *Household Interests: Property, Marriage Strategies, and Family Dynamics in Ancient Athens* (Princeton NJ, 2014)

Cyrino, M. S., *Screening Love and Sex in the Ancient World* (London, 2013)

Dalby, A., *Empires of Pleasures: Luxury and Indulgence in the Roman World* (London, 2000)

Dasen, V., 'Multiple Births in Graeco-Roman Antiquity', *Oxford Journal of Archaeology* 16, 1 (1997), p. 61

Dauphin, C. M., 'Brothels, Baths and Babes: Prostitution in the Byzantine Holy Land', *Classics Ireland* 3 (1996), 47–72

Davidson, J., *Courtesans and Fishcakes: The Consuming Passions of Classical Athens* (London, 1997)

Dayton, L., 'The Fat, Hairy Women of Pompeii', *New Scientist* 1944, 24 September 1994

Deacy, S., (ed) *Rape in Antiquity* (London, 1997)

DeBrohun, J., Fashion and Dress: Power Dressing in Ancient Greece and Rome. *History Today* 51 (2001)

Dean-Jones, L., 'The Politics of Pleasure: Female Sexual Appetite in the Hippocratic Corpus', in Stanton 1992, *Discourses* 48–77

Medicine: The 'Proof' of Anatomy, in Fantham, *Women in the Classical World* 183-215: 1994

Women's Bodies in Classical Greek Science (Oxford, 1994)

DeBois, P., *Centaurs and Amazons: Women and the Pre-history of the Great Chain of Being* (Ann Arbor, 1993)

Demand, N., *Birth, Death, and Motherhood in Classical Greece* (Baltimore, 2004)

Women and Slaves as Hippocratic Patients in Joshel, *Women* (1998), 69–84

Deslauriers, M., 'Women, Education and Philosophy', in James, *Companion* (2012), 343–353

Detel, W., *Foucault and Classical Antiquity Power: Ethics and Knowledge.* (Cambridge, 2005)

Detienne, M., 'The Violence of Well-born Ladies: Women in the Thesmophoria', in Detienne, M. (ed), *The Cuisine of Sacrifice among the Greeks*, (London, 1989)

Dewald, C., 'Biology and Politics: Women in Herodotus' 'Histories', *Pacific Coast Philology* 15 (1980), 11–18

'Women and Culture in Herodotus' *Histories'*, *Women's Studies* 8 (1981), 93–127

Dickason, A., 'Anatomy and Destiny: The Role of Biology in Plato's Views of Women', in Gould (ed), *Women and Philosophy: Toward a Theory of Liberation*, (New York, 1976)

Dickie, M. W., 'Who Practised Love-magic in Classical Antiquity and in the Late Roman World?' *CQ* 50 (2000), 563–583

Magic and Magicians in the Graeco-Roman World (London, 2001)

Dickison, S., 'Abortion in Antiquity', *Arethusa* 6 (1973), 158-166

Dillon, M., 'Were Spartan Women Who Died in Childbirth Honoured with Grave Inscriptions?', *Hermes* 135 (2007)

Girls and Women in Classical Greek Religion (London, 2002)

Doherty, L. E., Putting the Women Back into the Hesiodic Catalogue of Women, in M. Leonard, *Laughing at Medusa: Classical Myth and Feminist Thought*, (Oxford, 2006), 297–325

Siren's Songs: Gender, Audiences, and Narrators in the Odyssey (Ann Arbor TX, 1995)

Donahue, J., *The Study of Women and Gender in the Ancient World* (Portland OH, 1997)

Doniger, W., *Splitting the Difference: Gender and Myth in Ancient Greece and India 2nd ed.* (Chicago, 1999)

Dossey, L., Wife-beating and Manliness in Late Antiquity, *Past & Present* 199 (2008), 3–40

Doumanis, M., *Mothering in Greece: From Collectivism to Individualism* (New York, 1983)

Dover, K. J., *Greek Homosexuality* (London, 1978)

   'Greek Homosexuality and Initiation' in *Que(e)rying Religion: A Critical Anthology* (London, 1997), 19–38

   'Classical Greek Attitudes to Sexual Behavior', in Golden, *Sex and Difference* p.114–125

Du Bois, P., *Sowing the Body: Psychoanalysis and Ancient Representations of Women* (Chicago, 1988)

Ducat, J., *Spartan Education: Youth and Society in the Classical Period*, (Swansea, 2006)

Duff, T., *Plutarch's Lives: Exploring Virtue and Vice* (Oxford, 1999), 17-25

Dutsch, D., (ed) *Ancient Obscenities: Their Nature and Use in the Ancient Greek and Roman Worlds* (Ann Arbor, 2015)

Easterling, P. E., 'The Infanticide in Euripides' Medea" in Mossman, J. (ed) *Euripides* (Oxford, 2003), 187–200

   (ed), *Greek and Roman Actors* (Cambridge, 2002)

   'Women in Tragic Space', *BICS* 34 (1988), 15–26.

Edmonds, R. G., 'Bewitched, Bothered, Bewildered: Erotic Magic in the Greco-Roman World', in Hubbard T. K., (ed) *A Companion to Greek and Roman Sexualities* (Chichester, 2014), 282–296

Elia J. P., History, Etymology, and Fallacy: Attitudes Toward Male Masturbation in the Ancient Western World. *Journal of Homosexuality* (1987) 14, 1–19

Elia, O., *Pitture Murali e Mosaici nel Musea Nazionale di Napoli* (Rome, 1932)

Ellinger, T. H., *Hippocrates on Intercourse and Pregnancy* (New York, 1952)

Ellis, H., *Studies in the Psychology of Sex*, vol. 2: Sexual Inversion. Project Gutenberg text

El Nahas, A., 'Legal Status of Women In Menander', *Bulletin of the Faculty of Arts Cairo University* 63 (2003) 305–348

Elsom, H. E., 'Callirhoe: Displaying the Phallic Woman', in Richlin, *Pornography* (1992)

Engel, D. M., 'Women's Role in the Home and the State', *History of Political Thought* 101 (2003), 267–288

Engels, D., 'The Problem of Female Infanticide in the Greco-Roman World', *CP* 75 1980), 112–120

Eyben, E., 'Antiquity's View of Puberty', *Latomus* 31 (1972), 677-697

   'Family Planning in Graeco-Roman Antiquity', *Anc.Soc* 11-12 (1980), 5–82

Fabre-Serris, J., (ed) *Women and War in Antiquity* (Baltimore, 2015)

Famin, S. M. C., *Musée Royal de Naples; Peintures, Bronzes et Statues Erotiques du Cabinet Secret, avec leur Explication (Paris, 1861)*

Fantham, E., *Women in the Classical World: Image and Text* (New York, 1994)

Faraone, C., 'Magical and Medical Approaches to the Wandering Womb in the Ancient Greek World', *Cl Ant* 30 (2011), 1–31

   Prostitutes and Courtesans in the Ancient World (Madison WI, 2006)

   Ancient Greek Love Magic (Harvard, 2001)

   'Agents and Victims: Constructions of Gender and Desire in Ancient Greek Love Magic', in *The Sleep of Reason*, p. 410

Farnell, L., *The Cults of the Greek States Vol. IV* (1907)

Faulkner, T. M., (ed) *Contextualizing Classics: Ideology, Performance, Dialogue* (Lanham, MD 1999)

Felson-Rubin, N., *Regarding Penelope: From Character to Poetics* (Princeton, NJ, 1993)

Filbee, M., *A Woman's Place* (London, 1980)

Fildes, V., *Breasts, Bottles and Babies: A History of Infant Feeding* (Edinburgh, 1987)

   Wet Nursing: A History from Antiquity to the Present (Oxford, 1998)

Finley, M. I., *Aspects of Antiquity* (Harmondsworth, 1972)

   Studies in Ancient Society (London, 1974)

Firebaugh W. C., *The Inns of Greece and Rome: And a History of Hospitality from the Dawn of Time to the Middle Ages* (2012)

Fisher, N., Athletics and Sexuality, in Hubbard (2014), 244-264

Fitzpatrick, D., Reconstructing a Fragmentary Tragedy 2: Sophocles' *Tereus, Practitioners' Voices in Classical Reception Studies* 1 (2007)

Flacelliere, R., *Love in Ancient Greece* (Westport CT, 1973)

Flemming, R., *Medicine and the Making of Roman Women* (Oxford, 2000)

   'Women, Writing and Medicine in the Classical World', *CQ* 57 (2007), 257–279

Florence, M., 'The Body Politic: Sexuality in Greek and Roman Comedy and Mime', in Hubbard (2014), 366–380

Fogen, T., *Bodies and Boundaries in Graeco-Roman Antiquity* (Amsterdam, 2009)

Foley, H. P., *The Homeric Hymn to Demeter: Translation, Commentary, and Interpretive Essays* (Princeton NJ, 1994)

'Reverse Similes and Sex Roles in the Odyssey' in Peradotto (ed) *Women in the Ancient World, The Arethusa Papers*, 59- 78 (New York, 1984)

(ed) *Reflections of Women in Antiquity* (London, 1981)

'Women in Ancient Epic' in Foley, J. M. (ed) *A Companion to Ancient Epic*, 105–118 (Chichester, 2008)

'The Conception of Women in Athenian Drama', in Foley, H., (ed), *Reflections of Women In Antiquity* (New York, 1981), 127–68

'The Politics of Tragic Lamentation' in Sommerstein, A., (ed), *Tragedy Comedy and the Polis* (Bari, 1992), 102–4.

'Tragedy and Democratic Ideology' in B. Goff, (ed.), *History, Tragedy, Theory* (Austin TX, 1995), 131–50.

'Antigone as Moral Agent' in Silk, M. S., (ed), *Tragedy and the Tragic* (London, 1996), 49–73

'The 'Female Intruder' Reconsidered in Women in Aristophanes' *Lysistrata* and *Ecclesiazusae*,' *CP*, 77 (1982), 1–21.

Forberg, F. K., (1824). *De figuris Veneris* (trans. into English as *Manual of Classical Erotology* by Viscount Julian Smithson, and printed privately in 1884 in Manchester; repr. in 1966 ed.), New York

Foucault, M., *The History of Sexuality: The Care of the Self* (New York, 1988)

Foxhall, L., *Studying Gender in Classical Antiquity* (Cambridge, 2013)

(ed) *Thinking Men: Masculinity and Self-presentation in the Classical Tradition* (London 1998)

Freisenbruch. A., *The First Ladies of Rome* (London, 2010)

French, R., (ed) *Science in the Early Roman Empire* (London, 1986)

Furst, L. R., (ed) *Women Physicians and Healers* (Lexington, 1997)

Gaca, K. L., *The Making of Fornication: Eros, Ethics and Political Reform in Greek Philosophy and Early Christianity* (Berkeley, 2003)

'Girls, Women, and the Significance of Sexual Violence in Ancient Warfare' in Heineman, E. D., *Sexual Violence in Conflict Zones: From the Ancient World to the Era of Human Rights* (Philadelphia 2011), 73–88.

Ancient Warfare and the Ravaging Martial Rape of Girls and Women: Evidence from Homeric Epic and Greek Drama in Masterson, M. *Sex in Antiquity: Exploring Gender and Sexuality in the Ancient World* (New Yorkm 2015)

Gage, J., 'Matronalia', *Latomus* 60 (1963)

Gager, J., *Curse Tablets and Binding Spells from the Ancient World* (New York, 1992)

Gaimster, D., 'Sex and Sensibility at the Art Museum', *History Today*, 50 (2000), 10–15

Gardner, H. H., 'Ventriloquizing Rape in Menander's *Epitrepontes*', *Helios* 39 (2012) 121–143

Garland, R., *Celebrity in Antiquity* (London, 2006)

'Deformity and Disfigurement in the Graeco-Roman World', *History Today* 42 (1992)

The Eye of the Beholder: Deformity and Disability in the Graeco-Roman World (Bristol, 2010)

Garlick, B., (ed.) *Stereotypes of Women in Power* (New York, 1992)

Garrison, D. H., *A Cultural History of the Human Body in Antiquity* (London, 2014)

Sexual Culture in Ancient Greece (Norman OK, 2000)

Gibbs-Wichrowska, L., 'The Witch and the Wife: A Comparative Study of Theocritus Idyll 2, Simonides Idyll 15 and Fatal Attraction' in Archer, *Women in Ancient Societies* (1994), 252–68

Gilbert, A. N., 'Conceptions of Homosexuality and Sodomy in Western History', in Golden (ed) *A Cultural History of Sexuality Volume I In The Classical World*. p. 57–68

Gilman, S., *Hysteria Beyond Freud* (Berkeley, 1993)

Glazebrook, A., G'reek Prostitutes in the Ancient Mediterranean 800 BCE–200 CE', www.academia.edu/6518282/Greek_Prostitutes_in_the_Ancient_Mediterranean_800_BCE-_200_CE (2016)

'Greek and Roman Marriage' in Hubbard (2014), 69–82

'Sexual Rhetoric from Athens to Rome' in Hubbard (2014), 431–445

'Cosmetics and Sôphrosunê: Ischomachos' Wife in Xenophon's *Oikonomikos*', *CW* 102 (2009), pp. 233–248

'The Making of a Prostitute: Apollodoros's Portrait of Neaira', *Arethusa* 38,2 (2005) 161–87

(ed) *Greek Prostitutes in the Ancient Mediterranean, 800 BCE–200 CE* (Wisconsin, 2011)

Glendinning, E., 'Reinventing Lucretia: Rape, Suicide and Redemption from Classical Antiquity to the Medieval Era', *International Journal of the Classical Tradition* (2013)

Glenn, C., *Locating Aspasia on the Rhetorical Map. Listening to Their Voices* (Columbia SC, 1997)
    'Sex, Lies, and Manuscript: Refiguring Aspasia in the History of Rhetoric', *Composition and Communication* 45, 180–199
Glotz, G., *Ancient Greece at Work: An Economic History of Greece* (London, 1926)
Goebel, G. A., 'Andromache 192–204: The Pattern of Argument', *CP* 84, (1989) 32–35
Goff, B., *Citizen Bacchae: Women's Ritual Practice in Ancient Greece* (Berkeley, 2004)
    'The Priestess of Athena Grows a Beard: Latent Citizenship in Ancient Greek Women's Ritual Practice: in G. Polock, *The Sacred and the Feminine', Imagination and Sexual Difference*, (London 2007) 49–60
Goldberg, S., Comedy and Society from Menander to Terence in McDonald, M. (ed) *Cambridge Companion to Greek and Roman Theatre* (Cambridge, 2007), 124–138
Golden, M., ;Did the Ancients Care When their Children Died?' *G&R* 35, 1988, 152–163
    Sex and Difference in Ancient Greece and Rome (Edinburgh, 2008)
    'Donatus and Athenian Phratries', *CQ* 35 (1985), 9–13
    (ed) *A Cultural History of Sexuality Volume I In The Classical World* (Oxford, 2011)
    Demography and the Exposure of Girls at Athens, Phoenix 35, (1981) 316–31
    Children And Childhood In Classical Athens (Baltimore, 1990)
Goldhill, S., *Foucault's Virginity: Ancient Erotic Fiction and the History of Sexuality*, (Cambridge, 1995)
Gomme, A., 'The Position of Women in Athens in the Fifth and Fourth Centuries', *CP* 1925, 1–25
Gonzalez-Reigosa, F., 'Greek Homosexuality, Greek Narcissism, Greek Culture: the Invention of Apollo', *Psychohistory Review* 17 (1989) 149–181
Gould, J., 'Law, Custom and Myth: Aspects of the Social Position of Women in Classical Athens', *Journal of Hellenic Studies* 100 (1980), 38–59
Gordon, R. L., 'Aelian's Peony: The Location of Magic in Graeco-Roman Tradition', *Comparative Criticism* 9 (1987), 59–95
    'Imagining Greek and Roman Magic', in Ankerloo, B. (ed) *Magic and Witchcraft in Europe: Greece and Rome* (Philadelphia PA, 1999)
    'Innovation and Authority in Graeco-Egyptian Magic', in *Kykeon Studies in Honour of H. S. Versnel* (Leiden, 2002)
Gourevitch, D., *Women Who Suffer from a Man's Disease* in Hawley, Women (1995), 149–165
Graf, F., *Magic in the Ancient World* (Cambridge MA, 1999)
Grant, M., *Eros in Pompeii: The Erotic Art Collection of the Museum of Naples* (New York, 1997)
Graves, F. P., *The Burial Customs of the Ancient Greeks* (repr. 2015)
Green, M. H., *Making Women's Medicine Masculine: The Rise of Male Authority in Pre-Modern Gynaecology* (Oxford 2008)
Griffith, M., *Sophocles' Antigone* (Oxford, 1998)
Grmek, M., *Les Maladies a l'Aube de la Civilisation Occidentale* (Paris 1983)
    Diseases in the Ancient Greek World (Baltimore 1989)
Grubbs, J. E., 'The Dynamics of Infant Abandonment: Motives, Attitudes and (unintended) Consequences', in K. Mustakallio (ed.)
    The Dark Side of Childhood in Late Antiquity and the Middle Ages. Unwanted, Disabled and Lost (Oxford, 2011), 21-37
Gusman, P., *Pompeii: The City, It's Life and Art* (London, 1910)
Haas, N., Hairstyles in the Art of Greek and Roman Antiquity, *Jnl of Investigative Dermatology Proceedings* 10 (2005), 298-300
Habinek, T., The Invention of Sexuality in the World-City of Rome, in Habinek, T., *The Roman Cultural Revolution,* (Cambridge, 2004)
Hackworth Petersen, L., *Mothering And Motherhood In Ancient Greece And Rome* (Austin TX, 2013)
Haley, H. W., *The Social and Domestic Position of Women in Aristophanes, HSCP* 1 (1890), 159–186
Halperin, D. M., *One Hundred Years of Homosexuality and Other Essays on Greek Love* (New York, 1990)
Hame, K. J., 'All in the Family: Funeral Rites and the Health of the oikos in Aeschylus' *Oresteia', AJP* 125, (2004), 513–538
Hamel, D., *Trying Neaira: The True Story of a Courtesan's Scandalous Life in Ancient Greece* (Yale, 2005)
Hamilton, G., 'Society Women Before Christ', *North American Review* 151 (1896)
Hanson, A. E., 'The Restructuring of Female Physiology at Rome', in *Les Ecoles Médicales à Rome* (Nantes, 1991), 267ff.
    'The Medical Writers' Woman, in Halperin', *Before Sexuality* (1990), 309–338

'The Eight Months' Child and the Etiquette of Birth: *obsit omen!*', *BHM* 61 (1987), 589–602

Harris, E.M. 'Did Rape Exist in Classical Athens? Further Thoughts on the Laws about Sexual Violence', *Dike* 4 (2004) 41–83. [Reprinted in *id., Democracy and the Rule of Law in Classical Athens: Essays on Law, Society, and Politics* (Cambridge 2006) 297–332]

Harris, W. V., 'The Theoretical Possibility of Extensive Female Infanticide in the Graeco-Roman World', *CQ* 32 (1982), 114–116

Ancient Literacy (Cambridge Mass., 1989)

Hart, G. D., *Asclepius: the God of Medicine* (London, 2001)

Harvey, F. D., 'The Wicked Wife of Ischomachus', *EMC* 3 (1984)

Hasan, A., 'Plato's Antifeminism: A New Dualistic Approach', *E-Logos Electronic Journal for Philosophy* 22 (2012) nb.vse.cz/kfil/elogos/ethics/hasan12.pdf

Havelock, C. M., *The Aphrodite of Knidos and Her Successors: A Historical Review of the Female Nude in Greek Art* (Ann Arbor TX, 2010)

Haward, A., *Penelope to Poppaea* (Bristol, 1990)

Hawley, R., 'The Problem of Women Philosophers in Ancient Greece' in Archer, *Women in Ancient Societies: An Illusion of the Night* (1994), 70–87

(ed) *Women in Antiquity: New Assessments* (London, 1995)

'Ancient Collections of Women's Sayings', *BICS* 50 (2007), 161–169

"Give Me a Thousand Kisses': The Kiss, Identity, and Power in Greek and Roman Antiquity', Leeds International Classical Studies 6 (2007)

Hays, M., *Female Biography or Memoirs of Illustrious and Celebrated Women of all Ages and Countries 6 volumes* (London, 1803)

Heckel, W. *Who's Who in the Age of Alexander the Great: Prosopography of Alexander's Empire,* (Chichester, 2006)

Henderson, J., *The Maculate Muse: Obscene Language in Attic Comedy 2nd Edition* (Oxford, 1991)

'Women in the Athenian Dramatic Festivals': *TAPA*, 121 (1991), 133–47

Henry, M. M., *Prisoner of History: Aspasia of Miletus and Her Biographical Tradition* (Oxford, 1997)

Heyob, S. K., *The Cult of Isis Amongst Women of the Graeco-Roman World* (Leiden, 1975)

Hodges, F. M., 'The Ideal Prepuce in Ancient Greece and Rome: Male Genital Aesthetics and their Relationship to Lipodermos, Circumcision, Foreskin Restoration, and the *Kynodesme*', *BHM* 75 (2001), 375-405

Hodkinson, O., 'Epistolography', in Hubbard, T.K. (ed) *Companion to Greek and Roman Sexualities,* Chichester 2014), 463-478

Hodkinson, S., *Property and Wealth in Classical Sparta,* (Swansea, 2000)

Holland, L. B., 'The Mantic Mechanism at Delphi', *American Journal of Archaeology* 37, 201–214 (1933)

Holmberg, I. E., 'Sex in Ancient Greek and Roman Epic', in Hubbard, (2014), 314–334

Holst-Warhaft, G. *Dangerous Voices: Women's Laments and Greek Literature* (New York, 1992)

Holt, F. L. 'Alexander the Great's Little Star', *History Today* 38 (1988)

Hong, Y., 'Talking About Rape in the Classics Classroom', *CW* 106 (2013), 669–675

Hornblower, S., (ed) *The Oxford Classical Dictionary, third edition.* (Oxford, 1996)

Hubbard, T. K., (ed) *Companion to Greek and Roman Sexualities* (Chichester, 2014)

(ed) *Homosexuality in Greece and Rome: A Sourcebook of Basic Documents* (Berkeley, 2003)

Hufnagel, G. L., *A History of Women's Menstruation from Ancient Greece to the Twenty-first-century: Psychological, Social, Medical, Religious, and Educational Issues* (New York, 2012)

Hughes, B., *Helen of Troy: Goddess, Princess, Whore,* (London, 2005)

Hunter, V. J., *Gossip and the Politics of Reputation in Classical Athens, Phoenix* 44 (1990), 299–325.

Hyde, H. M., *A History of Pornography* (London, 1969)

ICD: *International Classification of Diseases* (10 version, Geneva 2010), see WHO

Ireland, S., *Menander: Dyskolos, Samia and Other Plays* (Bristol, 1992)

Isager, S., *Gynaikonitis—The Women Quarters, Museum Tusculanum* 33 (1978), 39ff.

Jackson, R., *Doctors and Diseases in the Roman Empire* (London, 1988)

James, S.L., *Companion to Women in the Ancient World* (Chichester, 2012)

Johansson, L., 'The Roman Wedding and the Household Gods' in Loven, L.L. (ed), *Ancient Marriage in Myth and Reality* (Newcastle, 2010), 136–149

Johns, C., *Sex or Symbol: Erotic Images of Greece and Rome* (London, 1982)

Johnson, M., *Sexuality in Greek and Roman Society and Literature: A Sourcebook* (London, 2005)

Johnson, M., *Ancient Greek Dress* (Chicago, 1964)

Johnson, S. I., *Restless Dead: Encounters Between the Living and the Dead in Ancient Greece* (Berkeley, 2013)

Jones, R., 'Ariadne's Threads: the Construction and Significance of Clothes in the Aegean Bronze Age', *Aegaeum: Annales liégeoises et PASPiennes d'archéologie égéenne* 38. (Liège, 2015)

Jones, C. P., 'Stigma: Tattooing and Branding in Graeco-Roman Antiquity', *JRS* 77 (1987), 139–155

Jope, J., 'Stoic and Epicurean Sexual Ethics', in Hubbard, (2014), 417–430

Joplin, P. K., 'The Voice of the Shuttle Is Ours' in Higgins, L. A. *Rape and Representation* (New York, 1991), 35–64

Joshel, S. R., *Women and Slaves in Graeco-Roman Culture* (London, 1998)

Joy, M., *Women and the Gift: Beyond the Given and All-Giving* (Bloomington IN, 2013)

Joyce, R. A., *Ancient Bodies, Ancient Lives: Sex, Gender and Archaeology* (London, 2008)

Just, R., *Women in Athenian Law and Life* (London, 1989)

Kallet-Marx, L. *Thucydides 2.45.2 and the Status of War Widows in Periclean Athens*, in Nomodeiktes: *Greek Studies in Honor of Martin Ostwald* (ed.) Ralph M. Rosen (1993), 133–143

Kampen, N., (ed) *Sexuality in Ancient Art: Near East, Egypt, Greece, and Italy*, (Cambridge, 1996)

Kapparis, K. A., *Abortion in Antiquity* (London, 2002)

Karanika, A., *Voices at Work: Women, Performance, and Labor in Ancient Greece* (Baltimore, 2014)

Karnezis, J. E., *The Epikleros* (Athens, 1972)

Karras, R. M., 'Active/Passive, Acts/Passions: Greek and Roman Sexualities', *American Historical Review* 105 (2000), 1250–1265

Katz, M., 'Women and Democracy in Ancient Greece', in Faulkner T. M., *Contextualizing Classics* I'deology and 'The Status of Women' In Ancient Greece', *History & Theory* 31 (1992) *Penelope's Renown: Meaning and Indeterminacy in the Odyssey* (Princeton NJ, 1991)

Keesling, C., 'Heavenly Bodies: Monuments to Prostitutes in Greek Sanctuaries' in Faraone, C. A., *Prostitutes and Courtesans in the Ancient World* (Madison WI, 2006)

Kennedy, R., Herodotus, Nitocris, and Harmonizing Extraordinary Ancient Women Into History, www.pointloma.edu/sites/default/files/filemanager/History__Political_Science/Herodotus_Nitocris.pdf and *Historically Speaking*, 6 (2005), 9–10

Kennell, N. M., *The Gymnasium of Virtue: Education and Culture in Ancient Sparta* (Chapel Hill NC, 1995)

Kersey, E. M., *Women Philosophers: A Bio-critical Source Book* (New York, 1989)

Keuls, E. C., *The Reign of the Phallus: Sexual Politics in Ancient Athens* (Berkeley, 1993)

King, H., 'Sowing the Field: Greek and Roman Sexology', in Porter, R., *Sexual Knowledge, Sexual Science: The History of Attitudes to Sexuality* (Cambridge, 1994), 38ff
'Producing Woman: Hippocratic Gynecology', in Archer, *Women in Ancient Societies* (1994), 102–114
Once upon a Text: Hysteria from Hippocrates in Gilman, S. *Hysteria Beyond Freud* (1993), 3–90
Self-help, Self-knowledge: in Search of the Patient in Hippocratic Gynaecology in Hawley, (1995), 135–148
Women and Goddess Traditions, (Minneapolis MN, 1997)
Hippocrates' Woman: Reading the Female Body in Ancient Greece (London, 1998)
Greek and Roman Medicine (London, 2003)
The Disease of Virgins: Green Sickness, Chlorosis and the Problems of Puberty (New York, 2004)
'Healthy, Wealthy and—Dead?', *Ad Familiares* 33 (2007), 3–4

Kitto, H. D. F., *The Greeks* (London, 1951)

Knight, R. P., *A Discourse on the Worship of Priapus* (London, 1786)

Konstan, D., 'Between Courtesan and Wife: Menander's *Perikeiromene*', *Phoenix* 41 (1987) 122–39. [Reprinted in *id.*, *Greek Comedy and Ideology* (New York, 1995).]

Koortbojian, M., 'In Commemorationem Mortuorum', *Text and Image Along the Street of Tombs* in Elsner, 210-233

Kraemer, R. S., *Maenads, Martyrs, Matrons, Monastics* (Philadelphia PA 1988)
Women's Religions in the Greco-Roman World: A Sourcebook (New York, 2004)

Krenkel, W. A., *Fellatio* and *Irrumatio*, *W.Z. Rostock* 29 (1980), 77–88
'Tonguing', *W.Z. Rostock* 30 (1981), 37–54

Kruger, K. S., *Weaving the Word: the Metaphorics of Weaving and Female Textual Production* (Selinsgrove: Susquehanna University Press, 2001)

Kudlien, F., Medical Education in Classical Antiquity in O'Malley, *The History of Medical Education* (1970), 3–37

Kuhrt, A., Non-Royal Women in the Late Babylonian Period: A Survey in *Women's Earliest Records: From Ancient Egypt and Western Asia*, Barbara S. Lesko, (ed) (Atlanta, GA, 1989)

Kurke, L., 'Inventing the 'Hetaira': Sex, Politics, and Discursive Conflict in Archaic Greece', *Classical Antiquity* 16 (1997: 107–108)

Kuttner, A. L., 'Culture and History at Pompey's Museum', *TAPA* 129 (1999), p. 343

Lacey, W. K., *The Family in Classical Greece* (Ithaca NY, 1968)

Laes, C., (ed) *Children and Family in Late Antiquity: Life, Death and Interaction* (Leuven, 2015)

Laiou, A. E., *Consent and Coercion to Sex and Marriage in Ancient and Medieval Societies* (Washington DC, 1993)

Lambert, R., *Beloved and God: The Story of Hadrian and Antinous* (London, 1984)

Lambropoulou, V., 'Some Pythagorean Female Virtues', in Hawley, R. (1995), *Women in Antiquity* (London, 1995)

Lape, S., *Reproducing Athens: Menander's Comedy, Democratic Culture, and the Hellenistic City* (Princeton, 2003)
  'Solon and the Institution of the 'Democratic' Family Form', *Classical Journal* 98 (2002), 117–139
  'Democratic Ideology and the Poetics of Rape in Menandrian Comedy', *Classical Antiquity* 20 (2001) 79–119

Lardinois, A., (ed) *Making Silence Speak: Women's Voices in Greek Literature and Society*, (Princeton, 2001)

Larson, J., *Greek and Roman Sexualities: A Sourcebook* (London, 2012)
  'Sexuality in Greek and Roman Religion', in Hubbard (2014), 214–229

Larsson, L. L., (ed) *Aspects of Women in Antiquity* (1997)
  '*Lanam fecit*: Woolmaking and Female Virtue', in Larsson, *Aspects* (1997), 85–95

Laurence, R., (ed) *Families in the Greco-Roman World* (London, 2011)
  Roman Passions (London, 2009)

Lawler, L. B., *The Dance in Ancient Greece* (1964)

Lear, A., 'Ancient Pederasty: An Introduction' in Hubbard (2014), 102–127
  Images of Ancient Greek Pederasty: Boys Were Their Gods (London, 2008)

Lee, M. M., *Body, Dress, and Identity in Ancient Greece* (Cambridge, 2015)

Lefkowitz, M. R., *Women in Greek Myth* (London, 2007)
  Heroines and Hysterics (London, 1981)
  Women's Life in Greece & Rome Third Ed. (London, 2005)
  'Wives and husbands' in McAuslan, I., (ed), *Women in Antiquity* (Oxford 1996) 67–82

Leigh, M., 'Funny Clones: 'Greek' Comedies on the Roman Stage', *Omnibus* 54 (2007), 26–28

Leisner-Jensen, M., '*Vis comica*. Consummated Rape in Greek and Roman New Comedy', *C&M* 53 (2002), 173–196

Leitao, D. D., 'Sexuality in Greek and Roman Military Contexts' in Hubbard (2014), 230–243

Leshem, D., 'What Did the Ancient Greeks Mean by Oikonomia?' *Journal of Economic Perspectives* 30 (2016), 225–231

Leunissen, M., 'Physiognomy in Ancient Science and Medicine', mleunissen.files.wordpress.com/.../leunissen-physiognomy (2012)

Licht, H., *Sexual Life in Ancient Greece* (London, 1994)

LiDonnici, L., 'Burning for It: Erotic Spells for Fever and Compulsion in the Ancient Mediterranean World', *GRBS* 39 (1998), 63–98

Lidov, J. B., 'Sappho, Herodotus, and the Hetaira', *CP* 97 (2002), p. 21.

Lightman, M., *A to Z of Ancient Greek and Roman Women* (New York, 2008)

Lipking, D., *Abandoned Women and Poetic Tradition* (Chicago, 1988)

Lloyd-Jones, H., *Females of the Species: Semonides on Women* (London, 1975)

Llewellyn-Jones, L., 'Veiling the Spartan Woman' in Harlow, M., (ed), Dress and Identity (Oxford, 2011), 19–38
  'Dress, Textiles, Hair and Hairstyles' in *Homer Encyclopedia*, (ed.) M. Inkelberg, (Oxford, 2011)
  'Domestic Violence in Ancient Greece' in *Socialable Man. Essays in Greek Social Behaviour in Honour of Nick Fisher*, (ed.) S. Lambert, (Swansea, 2011), 231–266
  'The Big and Beautiful Women of Asia: Picturing Female Sexuality in Greco-Persian Seals' in *The World of Achaemenid Persia*, (ed) Simpson, S. (London, 2010), 165–176
  'Prostitution' in *Oxford Encyclopedia of Greece and Rome*, ed. M. Gargarin, (Oxford, 2010)
  'Orietalism in Western Dress and Stage Costume in Berg Encyclopedia of World Dress—The Middle East and Central Asia' (ed), Vogelsang-Eastwood, G., (2010) 321–22
  'House and Veil in Ancient Greece' in (ed) Fisher, N., *Building Communities: House, Settlement and Society in the Aegean and Beyond* (Athens, 2007)

'Athens' Lady Boys? Gesture and the Male Performance of Women in Athenian tragedy', in D.L. Cairns (ed), *Gesture and Non-Verbal Communication in Classical Antiquity* (London, 2005)

'A woman's view? Dress, Eroticism, and the Ideal Female Body in Athenian Art', in Llewellyn-Jones, L., (ed), *Women's Dress in the Ancient Greek World* (Swansea, 2002), 171–202

'Sexy Athena: the Dress and Erotic Representation of a Virgin War Goddess', in Deacy, S., (ed), *Athena in the Classical World* (Leiden, 2001), 233–57

Greek and Roman Dress from A to Z (The Ancient World from A To Z) (London, 2007)

Aphrodite's Tortoise: The Veiled Woman of Ancient Greece (London, 2003)

Eunuchs in Antiquity and Beyond (Swansea, 2002)

Lloyd, G. E. R., (ed) *Hippocratic Writings* (Harmondsworth, 1978)

Magic, Reason and Experience (Cambridge, 1979)

Long, A. A., 'The Socratic Tradition: Diogenes, Crates, and Hellenistic Ethics', in Bracht Branham, R., *The Cynics: The Cynic Movement in Antiquity and Its Legacy*, (Berkeley CA, 1996)

Longrigg, J., *Greek Rational Medicine* (London, 1993)

Greek Medicine: From the Heroic to the Hellenistic Age A Source Book (London, 1998)

Loraux, N., *Aspasie, l'étrangère, l'intellectuelle. La Grèce au Féminin* (Paris, 2003)

The Children of Athena: Athenian Ideas about Citizenship and the Division Between the Sexes (Princeton NJ, 1994)

Tragic Ways of Killing a Woman (Cambridge MA, 1987)

Lovibond, S., 'An Ancient Theory of Gender: Plato and the Pythagorean Table' in Archer, *Women in Ancient Societies* (1994) 88–101

Lowe, J. E., *Magic in Greek and Latin Literature* (Oxford, 1929)

Luck, G., *Arcana Mundi: Magic and the Occult in the Greek and Roman Worlds* (Baltimore, 1985)

Latin Love Elegy 2/e (London, 1969)

Luntz L. L., 'History of Forensic Dentistry', *Dent Clin. North Am.* 21: 7–17, (1977)

Luschnig, C., *Granddaughter of the Sun A Study of Euripides' Medea* (Leiden, 2007)

Lyons, D., 'Dangerous Gifts: Ideologies of Marriage and Exchange in Ancient Greece', *Classical Antiquity* 22, (2003) 93–134

Macdowell, D. M., 'Love versus the Law: An Essay on Menander's Aspis', *G&R* 29 (1982), 42–5

Maclachlan, B., *Women in Ancient Greece: A Sourcebook* (New York, 2012)

McLeod, G., *Virtue and Venom: Catalogs of Women from Antiquity to the Renaissance* (Ann Arbor TX, 1991)

Maines, R. P., *The Technology of Orgasm: 'Hysteria', the Vibrator, and Women's Sexual Satisfaction* (Baltimore, 1998)

Maiuri, A., *Pompeii* (Rome, 1934)

Maloney, L. M., 'The Arguments for Women's Difference in Classical Philosophy and Early Christianity', *Concilium: International Journal for Theology* (1991)

Mantle, I., *Violentissimae et Singulares Mortes*, *CA News* 39 (2008), 1–2

Women of the Bardo, *Omnibus* 65, January 2013, 4–6

Mantos, K., 'Women and Athletics in the Roman East', *Nikephoros* 8 (1995), 125–144

Marquardt, P. A., 'Hesiod's Ambiguous View of Women', *CP* 77, (1982) 283–91

Marshall, A. J., 'Roman Women and the Provinces', *Anc Soc* 6 (1975), 109–129

Martin, M., *Magie et Magiciens dans le Monde Gréco-romain* (Paris, 2005)

Sois maudit !: Malédictions et Envoûtements dans l'Antiquité (Paris, 2010)

La Magie dans l'Antiquité (Paris, 2012)

Mason, M. K., *Ancient Athenian Women of the Classical Period*, www.moyak.com/papers/athenian-women.html

Annotated Bibliography of Women in Classical Mythology, www.moyak.com/papers/women-classical-mythology.html

Massey, M., *Women in Ancient Greece and Rome* (Cambridge, 1988)

Masterson, M., *Sex in Antiquity* (London, 2015)

'Studies in Ancient Masculinity' in Hubbard, (2014) 17–30

Exploring Gender and Sexuality in the Ancient World (2014)

Matz, D., *Voices of Ancient Greece and Rome: Contemporary Accounts of Daily Life* (New York, 2012)

Maurizio, L., 'The Voice at the Centre of the World: The Pythia's Ambiguity and Authority' in Lardinois, A., (ed.) *Making Silence Speak: Women's Voices in Greek Literature and Society*, (Princeton NJ, 2001)

Mayor, A., *Greek Fire, Poison Arrows, and Scorpion Bombs: Biological and Chemical Warfare in the Ancient World* (New York, 2003)

McAuslan, I., (ed) *Women in Antiquity* (Oxford, 1996)

McC. Brown, P. G., 'Love and Marriage in Greek New Comedy', *CQ* 43, (1993), 189–205

McLaren, A., *History of Contraception: From Antiquity to the Present Day* (Chichester, 1992)

McLees, H. *A Study of Women in Attic Inscriptions* (New York, 1920)

McClure, L. K., *Courtesans at Table: Gender and Greek Literary Culture in Athenaeus*, (New York, 2003)
   'Subversive Laughter: The Sayings of Courtesans in Book 13 of Athenaeus' *Deipnosophistae*', *AJP* 124 (2003), 268f
   Sexuality and Gender in the Classical World (Chichester, 2002)
   Spoken Like a Woman: Speech and Gender in Athenian Drama (Princeton NJ, 1993)

McDermott, E., *Euripides' Medea: The Incarnation of Disorder* (University Park, PA 1985)

McHardy, F., (ed) *Women's Influence on Classical Civilisation* (London, 2004)

McManus, B., *Classics and Feminism: Gendering the* Classics (New York, 1997)

Meyer, J. C., *Women in Classical Athens in the Shadow of North-West Europe or in the Light from Istanbul*
   www.hist.uib.no/antikk/antres/womens%20life.htm

Miner, J., 'Courtesan, Concubine, Whore: Apollodorus' Deliberate Use of Terms for Prostitutes', *AJP* 124 (2003) 19–37

Minois, G., *History of Old Age* (Chichester, 2012)

Montserrat, D., *Changing Bodies, Changing Meanings: Studies on the Human Body in Antiquity* (London, 2011)

Moog, F. P., 'Between Horror and Hope: Gladiator's Blood as a Cure for Epileptics in Ancient Medicine', *Journal of the History of the Neurosciences* 12 (2003), 137–43

Morales, H., 'Fantasising Phryne: The Psychology and Ethics of Ekphrasis', *Cambridge Classical Journal* 57 (2011), 71–104

Morgan, T., 'The Wisdom of Semonides Fragment 7', *Cambridge Classical Journal* 51 (2005), 72–85

Morton, R. S., 'Sexual Attitudes, Preferences and Infections in Ancient Greece: Has Antiquity Anything Useful For Us Today?', *Genitourinary Medicine* 67 (1991), 59–66

Murnaghan, S., 'Women in Tragedy' in Bushnell R., (ed) *A Companion to Tragedy*, (Oxford, 2005), 234–251.

Mustakallio, K., *Hoping for Continuity: Childhood Education and Death in Antiquity* (Helsinki, 2005)

Nais, D., 'The Shrewish Wife of Socrates', *EMC* 4 (1985), 97–9

Nardo, D., *Women of Ancient Greece* (San Diego, 2000)

National Theatre: www.nationaltheatre.org.uk/video/women-in-greek-theatre-1

Neils, J., *Women in the Ancient World* (London, 2011)

Neuburg, M., 'How Like A Woman: Antigone's 'Inconsistency'', *CQ* 40, (1990): 54–76

Nevett, L. C., *House and Society in the Ancient Greek World* (Cambridge, 2001)

Nikolaidis, A. G., 'Plutarch on Women and Marriage', *WS* 110 (1997), 27–88

Nikoloutsos, K. P., 'Beyond Sex: The Poetics and Politics of Pederasty in Tibullus 1.4', *Phoenix* 61 (2007), 55–82
   (ed) *Ancient Greek Women in Film* (Oxford, 2013)

North, H. 'The Mare, the Vixen, and the Bee: Sophrosyne as the Virtue of Women in Antiquity', *Illinois Classical Studies* 2 (1977)

Nussbaum, M. C., 'The Incomplete Feminism of Musonius Rufus, Platonist, Stoic, and Roman' in Nussbaum *The Sleep of Reason: Erotic Experience and Sexual Ethics in Ancient Greece and Rome* (2002), p. 305f
   Same-Sex Desire and Love in Greco-Roman Antiquity and in the Classical Tradition of the West (Binghamton NY, 2005)

Nutton, V., *Ancient Medicine 2/e* (London, 2013)
   'Galen and Medical Autobiography', *PCPS* 18 (1972), 50f.
   'The Drug Trade in Antiquity', *Jnl of the Royal Society of Medicine* 78 (1985), 138–145
   'Murders and Miracles: Lay Attitudes to Medicine in Antiquity' (1985) in Porter: *Patients and Practitioners* 25–53
   'The Seeds of Disease: An Explanation of Contagion and Infection from the Greeks to the Renaissance', *Medical History* 27 (1983), 1–34

Oakley, J. H., *The Wedding in Ancient Athens* (Madison WI, 1993)

Ogden, D., *Magic, Witchcraft and Ghosts in the Greek and Roman Worlds* (Oxford, 2002)
   Greek and Roman Necromancy (Princeton NJ, 2004)
   Night's Black Agents: Witches Wizards and the Dead in the Ancient World (London, 2008)
   Polygamy, Prostitutes and Death: The Hellenistic Dynasties (Swansea, 2010)
   'Homosexuality and Warfare in Ancient Greece', in *Battle in Antiquity* (Swansea, 2009)

'Gendering Magic', *CR* 50 (2000), 476–78

'Rape, Adultery and the Protection of Bloodlines in Classical Athens' in Deacy, S., (ed.), *Rape in Antiquity: Sexual Violence in the Greek and Roman Worlds*, (Swansea 1997), 25–41.

Ogilvie, M., (ed) *Biographical Dictionary of Women in Science: Pioneering Lives From Ancient Times to the Mid-20th Century* (New York, 2000)

Women in Science: A Biographical Dictionary with Annotated Bibliography (Cambridge MA, 1990)

O'Higgins, L., *Women and Humor in Classical Greece* (Cambridge, 2003)

Olsen, B. A., *Women in Mycenaean Greece: The Linear B Tablets from Pylos and Knossos* (Hoboken, NJ 2004)

'Women, Children and the Family in the Late Aegean Bronze Age: Differences in Minoan and Mycenaean Constructions of Gender', *World Archaeology* 29, *Intimate Relations* (1998), 380–392

O'Malley, C. D., (ed) *The History of Medical Education* (Berkeley CA, 1970)

Omitowoju, R., *Rape and the Politics of Consent in Classical Athens* (Cambridge, 2002)

O'Neal, W. J., 'The Status of Women in Ancient Athens', *International Social Science Review* 68 (1993)

Onq, R., 'Aspasia: Rhetoric, Gender, and Colonial Ideology' in Lunsford, A. A., *Reclaiming Rhetorica* (Pittsburgh PA, 1995)

O'Pry, K., 'Social and Political Roles of Women in Athens and Sparta', *Saber and Scroll*, 1 (2012), 7–14

Ormand, K., *Controlling Desires: Sexuality in Ancient Greece and Rome* (New York, 2008)

'Marriage, Identity, and the Tale of Mestra in the Hesiodic Catalogue of Women', *AJP* 125 (2004) 303–338

Orrells, D., *Sex: Antiquity and its Legacy* (London, 2015)

Osborne, M. L., (ed) *Woman in Western Thought* (New York, 1979)

Osborne, R., 'The Use of Abuse: Semonides 7', *Cambridge Classical Journal* 47 (2001), 47–64

Padel, R., 'Women: Model for Possession by Greek Daemons' in Cameron A., *Images of Women in Antiquity* (Canberra, 1986), 3–19.

Palmer, L. R., 'Homer and Mycenae, Part II: The Last Days of Pylos', *History Today* 7 (1957)

Pantel, P. S., *A History of Women from Ancient Goddesses to Christian Saints* (Cambridge MA, 1992)

Papadopoulos I., 'Priapus and Priapism: From Mythology to Medicine', *Urology* 32 (1988), 385–386

Papadopoulou, M., 'The Woman in Ancient Sparta: The Dialogue between the Divine and Human', *Sparta*, 6, 2 (2010), 5–10

Alcman, *Sparta*, 6, 1 (2010), 1–11

Papagrigorakisa, M. J., 'Facial Reconstruction of an 11-year-old Female Resident of 430 BC Athens', *Angle Orthodontist* 81, (2011)

Parca, M., *Finding Persephone: Women's Rituals in the Ancient Mediterranean* (Urbana-Champaign IL, 2007)

Parke, H. W., *Sibylls and Sibylline Prophecy in Classical Antiquity* (London 1998)

Parker, D., 'The Congresswomen of Aristophanes', *Arion* 6, (1967), 23–37

Parker, H. N., 'Love's Body Anatomized: The Ancient Erotic Handbooks and the Rhetoric of Sexuality', in Richlin, *Pornography* (1992)

'The Myth of the Heterosexual: Anthropology and Sexuality for Classicists', *Arethusa* 34 (2001), 313–362

'Women Physicians in Greece, Rome and the Byzantine Empire', in Furst (2004), 134–150

'Women and Medicine' in James, *Companion* (2012), 107–124

Parsons, B. A., 'Aristotle On Women' in *Women's Studies Encyclopedia*, ed. Tierney, H., (Greenwood Press, 2002)

Patterson, C. B., 'Not Worth the Rearing: The Causes of Infant Exposure in Ancient Greece', *TAPA* 115 (1985) 103–23

The Family in Greek History (Cambridge, MA 1998)

Pellauer, M., 'Augustine on Rape' in Adams, C. J. *Violence Against Women and Children: A Christian Theological Sourcebook* (New York 1998), 207-241

Peradotto, J., (ed) *Women in the Ancient World: The Arethusa Papers* (Albany NY, 1984)

Percy, W. A., *Pederasty and Pedagogy in Archaic Greece* (Chicago, 1996)

Petersen, L. H., *Mothering and Motherhood in Ancient Greece and Rome* (Austin TX, 2013)

Phillips, E. D., Doctor and Patient in Classical Greece, *G&R* (1953), 70–81

Phillips, K. M., *Sex Before Sexuality: A Premodern History* (Cambridge, 2011)

Pierce, K. F., 'The Portrayal of Rape in New Comedy' in Deacy, S., *Rape in Antiquity* (London, 1997), 163–184

Pinault, J. R., 'The Medical Case for Virginity in the Early 2nd Century CE: Soranus', *Helios* 19, 123–39

Plant, I. M., *Women Writers of Ancient Greece and Rome: An Anthology*, (Norman OK, 2004)

Pomeroy, S. B., *Ancient Greece: A Political, Social, and Cultural History* (New York, 2011)

'Selected Bibliography on Women in Antiquity', *Arethusa* 6 (1973), 125–157

Women in Roman Egypt: A Preliminary Study Based on Papyri in Foley, pp. 301–322

(ed) *Women's History and Ancient History* (Chapel Hill, 1991),

Goddesses, Whores, Wives and Slaves (New York, 1995)

Spartan Women (Oxford, 2002)

The Murder of Regilla: A Case of Domestic Violence in Antiquity (Cambridge, 2007)

Families in Classical and Hellenistic Greece (Oxford, 1997)

Porter, R., (ed) *Sexual Knowledge, Sexual Science: The History of the Attitudes to Sexuality* (Cambridge, 1994)

(ed) *Patients and Practitioners* (Cambridge, 1985)

Post, L. A., 'Woman's Place in Menander's Athens', *TAPA* 71 (1940), 420–459

Powell, A., 'Sparta: A Modern Woman Imagines', CR 54 (2004): 465–467

Athens and Sparta: Constructing Greek Political and Social History from 478 BC Second edition (London, 2016)

'Athens' Pretty Face: Anti-feminine Rhetoric and Fifth-century Controversy over the Parthenon' in *The Greek World* (London 1995)

Euripides, Women, and Sexuality. (London 1990)

Prince, M., 'Medea and the Inefficacy of Love Magic', *CB* 79 (20030, 205-218)

Puschmann, T., (ed.) *Alexander of Tralles, Twelve Books on Medicine* (1878)

Queenan, E., 'Patron Goddesses of Sparta: Athena's and Artemis' Significance to Ancient Spartan Society', *Sparta* 7 (2011), 12–17

'Entertainment: Spartan Style', *Sparta*, 5(2009), 4–10

Qviller, B., *Reconstructing the Spartan Partheniai* (1996)

Rabinowitz, N. S., *Among Women: From the Homosocial to the Homoerotic in the Ancient World* (Austin TX, 2002)

(ed.) *Feminist Theory and the Classics* (New York, 1993)

Rawles, R., 'Erotic Lyric', in Hubbard, (2014), 335–351

Redfield, J., 'The Women of Sparta', *CJ* 73 (1978)

Reeder, E., (ed.) *Pandora: Women in Classical Greece* (Princeton, NJ, 1996)

Rees, O., 'Musings on Sparta's Muses', *Sparta* 5, 2 (2009), 24–26

Rehm, R., *Marriage to Death: the Conflation of Wedding and Funeral Rituals in Greek Tragedy* (Princeton NJ 1994)

Reinhold, M., 'The Generation Gap in Antiquity', in Bertman, pp. 15–54

Ricci, J.V., *The Development of Gynaecological Surgery and Instruments* (Philadelphia, 1949)

Richlin, A., (ed) *Pornography and Representation in Greece and Rome* (Oxford, 1992)

'Reading boy-love and Child-love in the Greco-Roman World' in Masterson, M., *Sex in Antiquity* (New York, 2015)

Riddle, J. M., *Contraception and Abortion from the Ancient World to the Renaissance* (Cambridge MA, 1992)

Rinaldo, M., 'Women, Culture and Society', in Blok, J., *Sexual Assymetry* 17–42 (Amsterdam, 1987)

Rist, J. M., 'Hypatia', *Phoenix* 19 (1965), 214–225

Robb, J., *The Body in History: Europe from the Palaeolithic to the Future* (Cambridge, 2015)

Roberts, J. T., *Athens on Trial: The Antidemocratic Tradition in Western Thought* (Princeton, 1994)

Roice, P., *Ancient Greek Education* (Portland OH, 1997)

Roisman, H. M., 'Greek and Roman Ethnosexuality', in Hubbard, 2014), 398–416

Rose, M. L., 'Demosthenes' Stutter: Overcoming Impairment' in *The Staff of Oedipus* (Michigan, 2003)

Rosen, R. M., 'Greco-roman Satirical Poetry', in Hubbard (2014), 381–397

Rosivach, V. J., *When a Young Man Falls in Love: The Sexual Exploitation of Women in New Comedy* (London, 1998)

Rouselle, A., *Porneia: On Desire and the Body In Antiquity* (Oxford, 1993)

Rowlandson, J.,*Women and Society in Greek and Roman Egypt: A Sourcebook* (Cambridge, 1998)

Roy, J., 'Polis and Oikos in Classical Athens', *G&R* 46 (1999), 1–18

'An Alternative Sexual Morality for Classical Athenians', *G&R* 44 (1997), 11–22

Rudd, N., 'Romantic Love in Classical Times?', *Ramus* 10 (1981), 140-158

Sancisi-Weerdenburg, H., 'Exit Atossa: Images of Women in Greek Historiography on Persia' in Cameron, A., (ed): *Images of Women in Antiquity* (Detroit, 1983), 23ff

Saxonhouse, A. W., 'Another Antigone: the Emergence of the Female Political actor in Euripides'
Phoenician Women', *Political Theory*, 33, (2005), 472–94

Scanlon, T. F., *Eros and Greek Athletics* (Oxford, 2002)

Schapira, L. L., *The Cassandra Complex: Living with Disbelief—A Modern Perspective on Hysteria*
(Toronto, 1988)

Schaps, D. M., 'What was Free about a Free Athenian Woman?', *TAPA* 128 (1998), 161–188
'Women in Greek Inheritance Law', *CQ* 25 (1975), 53–57
Economic Rights of Women in Ancient Greece (Edinburgh 1979)

Scheid, J., *The Craft of Zeus: Myths of Weaving and Fabric* (tr. Carol Volk) (Cambridge, MA 1996)

Scheidel, W., 'The Most Silent Women of Greece and Rome: Rural Labour and Women's Life', *G&R* 42
and 43 (1995–1996), 202–17, 1–10
'Libitina's Bitter Gains: Seasonal Mortality and Endemic Disease', *Ancient Society* 25 (1994), 151–175
The Cambridge Economic History of the Greco-Roman World (Cambridge, 2007)

Schmitt, J-Cl., 'Prostituées, Lépreux, Hérétiques: les Rayures de l'infamie", *L'Histoire* 148 (1991), 89

Schrader, H. P., Sons and Mothers, *Sparta: Journal of Ancient Sparta and Greek
History* 7, (2011), 24-26
Scenes from a Spartan Marriage, *Sparta* 6 (2010), 46-9

Scurlock, J. A., Baby-snatching Demons, Restless Souls and the Dangers of
Childbirth, *Incognita* 2 (1991), 135-183

Sealey, R., *The Justice of the Greeks* (Ann Arbor, MI 1994)
Women and Law in Classical Greece (Chapel Hill NC, 1990)

Seidensticker, B., 'Women on the Tragic Stage' in Goff, B. (ed), *History, Tragedy, Theory* (Austin, TX
1995), 151-73.

Seller, R., *The Family and Society* in Bodel (2001), 95-117

Seltman, C., 'The Status of Women in Athens', *G&R* Vol. 2, (1955), 119–124
Women in Antiquity (London, 1956)
'Life in Ancient Crete II: Atlantis', *History Today* 2 (1952)

Sharrock, A. R., 'Womanufacture', *JRS* 81 (1991), 36–49

Shaw, M., 'The Female Intruder: Women in Fifth-century Drama', *CP* 70 (1975) 255–66

Shepherd, G., 'Women in Magna Graecia' in James, *Companion* (2012), 215–228

Simon, B., *Mind and Madness in Ancient Greece* (Ithaca NY, 1978)

Sissa, J., *Sex and Sensuality in the Ancient World* (London, 2008)

Skinner, M. B., *Sexuality in Greek and Roman Culture, 2nd Edition* (Chichester, 2014)
'Aphrodite Garlanded: Erôs and Poetic Creativity in Sappho and Nossi' in Rabinowitz, *Among
Women: From the Homosocial to the Homoerotic in the Ancient World
Corinna of Tanagra and Her Audience* (Tulsa OK, 1983)

Slater, P., *The Glory of Hera: Greek Mythology and the Greek Family* (Princeton NJ, 1992)

Smith, N. D., 'Plato and Aristotle on the Nature of Women', *Journal of the History of Philosophy* 21 (1983),
467–478

Snyder, J. M., 'Korinna's Glorious Songs of Heroes', *Eranos* 82 (1984), 1–10
The Woman and the Lyre: Women Writers in Classical Greece and Rome (Illinois, 1989)

Sourvinou-Inwood, C., 'Assumptions and the Creation of Meaning: Reading Sophocles' Antigone', *JHS*
109 (1989): 134–48

Spacks, P. M., *Gossip*, (New York, 1985)

Spaeth, B. S., *The Roman Goddess Ceres* (Austin TX, 1993)

Squire, M., *The Art of the Body: Antiquity and its Legacy* (London 2011)

Staden, H. von, 'Women, Dirt and Exotica in the Hippocratic Corpus', *Helios* 19 (1992), 7–30

Stanford University: *Mortal Women of the Trojan War—Briseis (Hippodameia)*, web.stanford.
edu/~plomio/briseis.html

Stannard, J., 'Marcellus of Bordeaux and the Beginnings of the Medieval Materia Medica', *Pharmacy in
History* 15 (1973), p. 48

Stanton, D. C., (ed) *Discourses of Sexuality: From Aristotle to Aids* (Ann Arbor TX, 1992)

Stauffer, D., 'Aristotle's Account of the Subjection of Women', *Journal of Politics* 70 (2008), 929–941

Stavrakakis, Y., 'Thessaloniki Brothel', *Archaeology Archive* 51 (1998) archive.archaeology.org/9805/
newsbriefs/brothel.html

Stehle, E., *Performance and Gender in Ancient Greece: Nondramatic Poetry in its Settings*. (Princeton,
1997)

Storey, I. C., 'Domestic Disharmony in Euripides' *Andromache*', *G&R* 36, (1989) 16–22.

Stratton, K. B., (ed) *Daughters of Hecate: Women and Magic in the Ancient World* (Oxford, 2014)
    Naming the Witch: Magic, Ideology and Stereotype in the Ancient World (Columbus OH, 2007)

Stromberg, A., *The Family in the Graeco-Roman World* (New York, 2011)

Suda on line: www.stoa.org/sol/

Sutton, R. F., 'Nuptial Eros: The Visual Discourse of Marriage in Classical Athens', *JWAG* 55-56 (1998)
    27–48

Swain, S., (ed) *Seeing the Face, Seeing the Soul: Polemon's Physiognomy from Classical Antiquity to
    Medieval Islam* (Oxford, 2007)

Swancutt, D. M., 'Still before Sexuality: 'Greek' Androgyny, the Roman Imperial Politics of Masculinity
    and the Roman Invention of the *tribas*', in *Mapping Gender in Ancient Religious Discourses*, 22ff

Swift, L. A., Sexual and familial distortion in Euripides': Phoenissae', *TAPA* 139, (2009) 53–87.

Syropoulos, S., 'An exemplary Oikos. Domestic Role-models in Euripides' *Alcestis*', *Eirene* 37 (2001) 5–18.
    Gender and the Social Function of Athenian Tragedy, (Oxford, 2003)
    'Women vs Women. The Denunciation of Female Sex by Female Characters in Drama', *Ágora. Estudos
    Clássicos em Debate* 14 (2012)

Tacaks, S., *Vestal Virgins, Sibyls, and Matrons* (Austin, 2008)

Taylor, C. C. W., 'The Role Of Women In Plato's Republic' in Kamtekar, R. (ed) *Virtue and Happiness:
    Essays in Honour of Julia Annas* (2012), special supplement to *Oxford Studies in Ancient Philosophy*

Taylor, J. E. Greece and Rome in *Jewish Women Philosophers of First-Century Alexandria* (Oxford, 2004)

Temkin, O., *Soranus' Gynecology* (Baltimore MD, 1956)

Tetlow, E. M., *Women, Crime and Punishment in Ancient Law and Society: Vol. 2: Ancient Greece* (1995)

Thorndike, L., *The Place of Magic in the Intellectual History of Europe* (New York, 1905)
    History of Magic and Experimental Science (Columbia OH, 1923)

Thornton, B. S., *Eros: The Myth of Ancient Greek Sexuality* (Boulder, CO 1997)

Toohey, P., 'Death and Burial in the Ancient World' in T*he Oxford Encyclopedia of Ancient Greece and
    Rome*, vol. 1, (Oxford, 2010), 364ff

Totelin, L., 'Sex and Vegetables in the Hippocratic Gynecological Treatises', *SHPBBS* 38 (2007), 531–540

Traill, A., *Women and the Comic Plot in Menander* (Cambridge, 2012)

Treggiari, S., 'Concubinae', *PBSR* 49 ((1981), 59-81

Tyrrell, W. B., *Amazons: A Study in Athenian Mythmaking* (Baltimore, 1989)

Ungaretti J. R., 'Pederasty, Heroism, and the Family in Classical Greece', *Journal of Homosexuality* 3
    (1978), 291–300

Valeva, (ed) *A Companion to Ancient Thrace* (Chichester, 2015)

Vanggard, T., *Phallos: A Symbol and Its History in the Male World* (New York, 1972)

van Hook, '*La Rue* The Exposure of Infants at Athens', *TAPA* 51 (1920) 134–45

Vivante, B., *Daughters of Gaia: Women in the Ancient Mediterranean World* (Norman OK, 2008)

Vout, C., *Sex on Show: Seeing the Erotic in Greece and Rome* (London, 2013)

Wagner-Hasel, S., *Women's Life in Oriental Seclusion? On the History and Use of a Topos* in Golden: *Sex
    and Difference in Ancient Greece and Rome* (2003)

Waithe, M. E., *A History of Women Philosophers: Ancient Women Philosophers Vol. 1 600 BC—AD 500*
    (Dordrecht, 1987)

Walcot, P., 'Plutarch on Sex', *G&R* 45 (1998), 166–187
    'On Widows and their Reputation in Antiquity', *SO* 66 (1991) 5–26

Walker, S., 'Women and Housing in Classical Greece: The Archaeological Evidence', in Cameron, A.,
    Images of Women in Antiquity, (1983) 81 ff

Walter, K., *The Secret Museum: Pornography in Modern Culture* (Berkeley, CA 1996)

Watson, P. A., Ancient Stepmothers, *Mnemosyne* 143 (1995)

West, M. L., 'Corinna', *CQ* 29 (1970), 277–287

Whitbeck, C., 'Theories of Sex Difference', in Gould (ed), *Women and Philosophy*, (New York, 1976),
    54–80

Whiteley, R., *Courtesans and Kings: Ancient Greek Perspectives on the Hetairai*, MA Diss, University of
    Calgary (2000)
    'Was Antigone Really A 'Bad' Woman? Christiane Sourvinou-Inwood's Reading of Sophocles'
    Antigone', www.moyak.com/papers/sophocles-antigone.html

Whittaker, T., 'Sex and the Sack of the City', *G&R* 56 (2009), 234–242

WHO *ICD: International Classification of Diseases* (10 version, Geneva, 2010)

Wider, K., 'Women Philosophers in the Ancient Greek World: Donning the Mantle', *Hypatia* 1 (1986)

Wiles, D., 'Marriage and Prostitution in Classical New Comedy', in Redmond, J., (ed), *Themes In Drama 11: Women in Theatre* (Cambridge, 1989) 31–48

Wilkinson L. P., 'Classical Approaches: I. Population and Family Planning', *Encounter* (1978) 50 (4), 22–32

Will, E. L., 'Women in Pompeii', *Archaeology* 32 (1979), 34–43

Williams, C. A., 'Greek Love at Rome', *CQ* 45 (1995), 517–38

'Sexual Themes in Greek and Latin Graffiti', in Hubbard (2014), 493–508

Roman Homosexuality: Ideologies of Masculinity in Classical Antiquity, (Oxford, 1999)

Winkler, J. J., *The Constraints of Desire: The Anthropology of Sex and Gender in Ancient Greece* (London, 1990)

'Laying Now the Law: The Oversight of Men's Sexual Behavior in Classical Athens', in Halperin, *Before Sexuality*, 171–209

Wohl, V., *Love Among the Ruins: the Erotics of Democracy in Classical Athens* (Princeton NJ, 2002)

Woman, N., *Abusive Mouths in Classical Athens* (Cambridge, 2008)

Wray, D., *Catullus and the Poetics of Roman Manhood* (Cambridge, 2001)

Wright, J., 'The White Man's Magic in Homer', *The Scientific Monthly* 9, (1919), 550–560

Yamagata, N., *Homeric Morality*, (Leiden, 1998)

Yarnall, J., *Transformations of Circe: The History of an Enchantress* (Chicago IL, 1994)

Younger, J. G., *Sex in the Ancient World from A-Z* (London 2005)

Zeitlin, F., 'The Dynamics of Misogyny: Myth and Mythmaking in the Oresteia', in Peradotto J., *Women in the Ancient World: The Arethusa Papers* (1984)

'Playing the Other: Theater, Theatricality and the Feminine in Greek Drama', *Representations* 11 (1985) 63–94.

'The Politics of Eros in the Danaid Trilogy of Aeschylus', in Hexter R. (ed) *Innovations of Antiquity*, New York, 203–52.

Index

Index of Women